To Maralyn:
Looki ...
To a ...
De.

"A writer remembers a Cold War–era childhood disoriented by the
impenetrable mystery of his parents' political lives . . . Pitcoff . . .
was only 11 years old when a pair of FBI agents visited his [New
York City] home in 1954, asking to speak to his father, Robert. His
parents, visibly rattled by the visit, made light of it. His mother,
Florence, insisted nonsensically that 'they happened to be in the
neighborhood and dropped by.' Far from the norm, this blend of
peculiarity and secretiveness was the hallmark of his youth. 'From a
child's point of view, I saw my parents' lives as a montage of unexpected scenes.' . . . This memoir, at its best, is reminiscent of the
literary work of French author Patrick Modiano, whose books
indefatigably investigate the underground in Paris during and after
World War II. Pitcoff was finally and dramatically able to discover
that his father led a cinematically eventful life . . . The author
unravels his stubbornly mysterious life with great skill and restraint
and paints a riveting tableau of a world made murky by 'complexity
and inherent ambiguities.' . . . A memoir overflowing with drama
that evocatively re-creates the atmosphere of peril and uncertainty
during the Cold War."

—*Kirkus Reviews*

COLD WAR SECRETS

Unscrambling the Certain Uncertainties
of Family Secrets

A Memoir by

PAUL PITCOFF

Momentum Ink Press

New York

Cold War Secrets: Unscrambling the Certain Uncertainties of Family Secrets
Copyright 2020 © Paul Pitcoff

All rights reserved. This book or any portion thereof may not be reproduced or used in any manner whatsoever without the express written permission of the author except for the use of brief quotations in a book review. For permissions visit PaulPitcoff.com.

Published in the United States by Momentum Ink Press, New York.

PUBLISHER'S CATALOGING IN PUBLICATION DATA
provided by Five Rainbows Cataloging Services

Names: Pitcoff, Paul, 1943– author.
Title: Cold War secrets : unscrambling the certain uncertainties of family secrets / Paul Pitcoff.
New York : Momentum Ink Press, 2020.
Identifiers: ISBN 978-0-9975239-6-6 (paperback) | ISBN 978-0-9975239-7-3 (ebook)
Subjects: LCSH: Children of spies—United States—Biography. | Greenwich Village
(New York, N.Y.)—Biography. | Cold War—Biography. | Communist Party of the United
States of America. | Espionage, Soviet—United States. | Family secrets. | BISAC:
BIOGRAPHY & AUTOBIOGRAPHY / Personal Memoirs. | TRUE CRIME / Espionage.
Classification: LCC UB271.R92 P58 2020 (print) | LCC UB271.R92 (ebook) |
DDC 327.12/092—dc23.

PaulPitcoff.com
MomentumInkPress.com

For information about special discounts available for bulk purchases, sales promotions,
fund-raising, and educational needs, contact the author at PaulPitcoff.com.

Book design by KSH Creative | KSHcreative.com

May 1943

First photo of author, few days old, bottom left, held by Grandma Mollie

Top row from left: Grandpa Jake, Uncle Howard about to be shipped overseas to war, *my missing father*, my mother, Uncle Milton before he left to fight in the Battle of the Bulge

I learned from Mollie, my grandmother,
that adults don't always mean what they say . . .

I learned from Florence and Robert, my parents,
that certainty has many hazards . . .

PROLOGUE

IT WAS A SUNNY SATURDAY MORNING and I was preparing to go to the park to play stickball. The doorbell rang. Any unexpected announcement of a visitor to the Pitcoff home triggered our dog Rollie to bark at his loudest and lunge at the door. More unsettling was my mother's double-barreled outburst of anxiety. I was fast to respond. Before the chime and Rollie silenced, my mother would go into her "state" and my father and I were left with the duty of guarding her from the intruder. "Whoever it is, I'm not home," she'd shriek as she headed for cover. "I'm not dressed and the house is a mess."

I didn't need to look to see that my mother was more than suitably dressed and the house was not a mess, but I knew that company was only acceptable if plans had been established weeks, if not months, ahead. She never wavered in her refusal to answer the doorbell, and my father, who continually worked at renovating our house, rarely heard it. Thus this essential responsibility defaulted to me.

Trying to preempt my mother's eruption of anxiety, I dashed to the door. Strangers, two men, stood in the hallway, erect as mannequins. They were duplicates of each other. They had crew cuts and wore well-fitting suits. I didn't know adults who looked or acted like these sour aliens. I felt helpless in their looming shadow, knowing I couldn't manufacture the respect they seemed to

1

demand. They asked if my father was home. They called me "junior" and "kid." None of my parents' friends patronized me like that. I stammered, "Well . . . , no one's at home." My voice trailed off as they walked around me into the hall. In unison they turned to face me and reached inside their jacket pockets to produce small leather ID folders, which they poked two nose lengths away in front of my eyes. I was not much of a reader, but the letters "FBI" stood out. My stomach seemed to drop out of my body.

"FBI, kid. We need to talk to Mr. Robert Pitcoff. Is he your father?"

Why would they want to see my dad? Was he in trouble? I tripped past them to the basement, where my father was working on running a new cold water line to replace the corroded galvanized pipes, and warned him of the presence of real G-men, not the ones in the movies. He tried to minimize my distress with a manufactured smile. We climbed the stairs in silence and I was dismissed after the men followed him into the living room. At least they didn't slap handcuffs on him or pull out their guns.

Stickball and time with friends held my attention the rest of the day. Family dinner was normal; my parents argued about the rationale of nuclear disarmament and marveled at Humphrey Bogart's portrayal in *The Caine Mutiny*. The next day I asked my mother, "Why did the FBI come here? Are we in trouble?"

"No, it's nothing to worry about," she said. She opened a fresh pack of Pall Malls and I helped her pick up the five cigarettes that fell to the floor. She lit one and added, "It's OK. They probably just like to talk."

"But why to Dad?" I asked.

She waved the smoke away from her face and appeared to be considering my question. Finally she found the answer: "Don't worry, they just happened to be in the neighborhood and dropped by."

Two different FBI agents must have been in the neighborhood more than a year later and they too dropped by. My father never discussed the FBI visits. Consciously and unconsciously my parents kept secret their past destructive mistakes. As I look back I see hints, in my early memories, of shadowy secrets that influenced my parents' lives. All young people have some difficulty forming a clear sense of who they are, but in my case, the oddities and contradictions of my parents' actions made the task unusually difficult. Their often bewildering behavior stymied all my attempts to get a hold on my own values, goals, and ideas—my identity. More evident was their absence of normal parental guidance, baffling behavior, and ingenious cover-ups for the questions I dared to ask. In this "don't ask, don't tell" environment, it would be up to me to get the essentials for preparing for adulthood.

CHAPTER ONE

Father and Mother several years before I was born

IT'S POSSIBLE THAT I WAS NOT PRIMARY in my parents' mind on
May 2, 1943, the day I was born. My mother and her sister Alice
were at the movies on Twenty-Third Street in New York City.
Slightly Dangerous, starring Lana Turner, was coming to a dramatic
end, when my mother complained of labor pains. Alice panicked.
She insisted my mother rush to the hospital. My mother's view was
she had paid for both films and there was still one more to see. They
stayed for the second feature despite my urgency to be born.

My father was working as an electrician, wiring Coolidge Air
Field, a US military airbase in Antigua. The war in Europe was
raging and the threat from U-boats in the Caribbean drove the
United States to build the base. He was working as a civilian
electrician on the runways. At forty-four, he was too old to be in the
armed forces.

Friends came to visit my mother at the hospital. At twenty-eight, her attention was on her budding career. Years later, with some contrition, she divulged that the day after I was born she put on fresh lipstick, pinned up her long dark brown hair, and powdered her face for visitors who came to the hospital to celebrate the publication of her first professional article in a social work journal.

My father didn't visit us in the hospital until late into the evening two days later. He could stay just ten minutes and didn't want to wake my mother, so he left her a scribbled note infused with guilt for not being there, along with one sentence mentioning how pleased he was to see me, before he caught the morning plane to return to Antigua. He was engulfed in trying to plan a way to support himself and now a family.

I've studied a particular family photo at many stages of my life. We're on the roof of my grandmother's East Thirty-First Street tenement building. I'm probably a week or so old. My grandmother sits in front of everyone and radiates delight as she holds me, her first grandchild, with confident tenderness. My grandfather stands directly behind us. He appears proud and pleased, but at the same time, distracted. In the same snapshot his sons, my uncles Howard and in uniform, Milton, work at displaying pride yet they seem preoccupied. Both will soon ship out to the war in Europe and fight in major battles. My aunt Alice is missing. So is my father.

My mother lurks in the shadows, farthest away from the camera. She looks distracted, perhaps bewildered or in shock. My grandmother's body language, coupled with my expression, suggests I would be in good hands if left with her. Is my mother having similar thoughts? From the time she was eight my mother had resolved to have a profession rather than work in my grandmother's store until she captured a husband. It was no easy path for a woman in the 1940s. When I was born, my mother was completing her master's degree in social work and had received a scholarship offer for a PhD, which she had to decline to take care of me. Having a child to take care of and being a housewife were resolutely ruled out of her career plans. My arrival crumpled her ambitions and caused my father to leave his secure job in Antigua. Perhaps my mother's seeming unease relates to all these sudden unknowns twirling in her head: whether my father will truly return, if she could handle an infant, and how her career plans will remain intact.

Eventually my father did return to New York, and my parents set up a one-bedroom apartment on Twenty-Sixth Street. It was next to the Third Avenue El, the last remaining aboveground subway in Manhattan. It is here we uncertainly played out the roles none of us expected or were qualified for: father, mother, and son.

Mollie and Jake's Five and Dime Store

From as early as I can remember until I was eight, on the mornings I wasn't going to daycare or school, my mother would announce, "Today I have to dump you at the store." The irony was that I loved being "dumped." As far as I was concerned she could work at her office without guilt if I could "work" at my grandmother's store. Even when young, I could sense my mother's anxiety in abandoning me to rush off to work. She was extremely rushed in the mornings, trying on various work outfits, pushing a spoon of cod liver oil into my mouth, hurrying me to eat my soggy corn-flakes or Cheerios, and trying to be friendly as if she was sending me off to somewhere unpleasant.

I found it strange that my mother didn't like the store as much as my grandmother and I enjoyed the action. I didn't yet know that the store had kept her mother so busy that she had no time to attend to my mother or fully protect her on the streets. Beginning in her teens my mother also felt that her responsibilities at the store created an impediment from opportunities outside the immigrant experience. These associations with the store prevented her from realizing how much I learned while in my favorite playland.

We would walk the four blocks, first under the Third Avenue El, for my mother to pick up a pack of Pall Malls, and then over to Second Avenue to the store. My parents and I differed on the aesthetics of our neighborhood. They saw the El as a depressing shadow that darkened Third Avenue, the noise of the trains and trolleys as a barrier for conversations, and the ubiquitous saloons as uncongenial for raising a child. My five-year-old mind tingled with excitement watching and listening to the clanging of the trolley bells, the rush of the trains, the workers huddled around coal-fired stoves in the landings beneath the train platforms, and the shouts and greetings and conversations that came from all directions. On Sundays I heard gospel music pump out of the Baptist church on the corner of Twenty-Sixth Street, our block, and Second Avenue. It roused my interest in becoming a Baptist, but my mother reminded me I was Jewish.

Haselkorn's Five and Dime was on the corner of Twenty-Ninth Street and Second Avenue. My grandfather started the store around 1910 and moved it to this location in the 1920s. My mother and her three siblings worked in the business before they had a chance to escape to various professions. The store was family. My grandmother, Mollie, came from Poland to the United States by herself when she was thirteen and lived with a distant cousin. By fourteen she was working in Jacob's store and by sixteen she became pregnant with my mother, the first of her four children. She quickly married Jacob, and the marriage worked well. When my mother was born, her mother was helping manage the store, so Mollie had little time for my mother. At six, my mother was made to work in the store and watch over her three younger siblings. My mother was expected to continue working in the store until she found a husband who could afford to allow her to stay home and bring up a family. By eight, my mother had a passion for a professional career and would do anything to get away from the store. During the Depression they barely held on to the business, though the bank repossessed their home in the Bronx. When Mollie was forty-seven and I was two, Jacob died and she had to manage the store on her own.

The store had two small display windows filled with a variety of items, like a tag sale. Small white cards leaning against toothpaste boxes, light bulbs, underwear, lamp shades, cooking pots, and other items for sale had prices, in cents, hand-painted in primary colors. If there were more than ten people in the store the aisles were clogged. The dark wood floor was smoothed and contoured by thousands of customers who had searched for items, bargained, and shuffled while engaged in conversations and storytelling.

Haselkorn's shoppers were mostly working-class and immigrants. Mollie knew them by their life stories and easily saw their similarities rather than their differences. Most everyone adored her. Before I was a year old, every customer and shop owner on the block knew me as "Mollie's grandson," a neighborhood title of esteem. At an early age, I thought the retailing business was no more than exchanging stories. The tales were often mesmerizing, and when my grandmother had time she would explain why Sophie's husband was yelling at her children, or that Mary had to work two jobs because her daughter was sick.

My grandmother was unguarded even when I questioned the source of her distractions. She had the capacity to make me feel very special, even though the most she could offer was to include me in her dynamic workday and, as with any influential mentor, answer a few of my questions with sensible explanations. The store offered a stable routine not found at home. I sensed controlling tensions in my parents' lives, but never could make any links to the source of their anxieties.

At six or seven, I felt a difference between my parents' fantastical stories intended to hide their secrets and my grandmother's straightforward approach to secrets. If she didn't want me overhearing, a conversation she was having with my mother or relative, she spoke Yiddish. If I asked a question that she didn't want to answer, she would tell me it was an adult matter rather than give me a ludicrous explanation. In contrast, my parents offered an answer to all my questions as if nothing was off limits, but often their reasoning didn't make sense of the peculiar things in our lives: an unknown nineteen-year-old brother dropping into my life from an airplane, an anniversary without a specific date, "Miss" rather than "Mrs.," tensions between them that had no discernible source. All together, these mysteries generated whiffs of suspicion about their truthfulness and nibbled at my confidence.

During the summers, until I was five, I spent every weekday with my grandmother. She took a daily midday break from the store to walk the three blocks back to her apartment. She prepared lunch for me and for Ann and Sam who were working back at the store. The summer heat in her one-bedroom apartment was oppressive. For relief she set me up on the fire escape with a large slice of cold honeydew melon. The juicy fruit was the best antidote for the extended heat waves. Directly across the street I watched men with sledgehammers and pry bars tear down a tenement. I sensed the danger and thought of how much fun it must be to wreck a building. A man with a sledgehammer and a well-placed blow could make a wall come tumbling down. Other men shoveled the debris into a chute made from the building's multicolored doors. The thunderous sounds of the bricks, plaster, wood, and glass on their way down to waiting trucks were punctuated by large explosions as the building's remains were blasted into the waiting dump trucks. I couldn't imagine any entertainment that could beat watching this activity from my privileged perch. Neither could I imagine any worker getting more satisfaction than from the complicated hard work to demolish a big building by hand.

Eventually my grandmother pulled me in from the fire escape. She took off her kitchen apron and packed a shopping bag with Sam and Ann's lunch. "Sam will be getting upset if we don't get back to the store," she said.

"But Grandma, aren't you the boss?"

"I couldn't run the store without Sam and Ann. We need each other." She let me push the button in the elevator and I counted the four floors till the door opened to somewhat cooler air.

"I don't like Sam. He never plays with me like Ann does," I said.

"Maybe he doesn't know how to play. He works so hard."

"But Ann works hard too, and she plays with me."

"She knows how to play. Maybe you can find a way to teach

Sam. What about trying to help him when he tests the light bulbs?"

"I'm afraid. He's so mean. He gets angry when I don't put out the toothpaste boxes the way he likes and he never smiles."

"You know, some people just don't carry things easily from their past. He means well and cares about everyone who works in the store and does everything to help customers get what they need. You just have to find a way to get along with him."

"What things from the past, Grandma?"

"Things happen that can change people. Make them act differently than you might expect. Sometimes you never know what those things are."

"Grandma, I like Ann much better. She knows how to have fun and laugh."

"Ann's just different. She's had some hard times too and now her husband is very sick, but she knows how to hunt for joy. Sam's not mean. He's just sad," she concluded.

Occasionally life with my grandmother would extend beyond our neighborhood. It couldn't get much better than a buying trip to downtown Manhattan. Instead of wearing her simple multicolored work dress, she put on heels, a hat, and a dress that appeared more fashionable. She projected a heightened authority only exhibited outside the neighborhood.

On one of those special outings we were in the midst of a summer downpour and my grandmother and I waited in the entranceway of the store. A cab driver saw her wave and stopped. I was never in a cab except with my grandmother. We headed to lower Broadway and spent at least an hour at several warehouses as my grandmother negotiated for merchandise. I became alarmed at the last warehouse when the owner screamed at her. I had never heard anyone yell at my grandmother, except my mother.

Sheldon, the owner, slammed a cover over a box of towels and pulled it away from my grandmother who had been feeling the texture of the contents. "Look, Mollie, if I give it to you at those prices my children will have no clothes," he barked.

My grandmother began to stack boxes of sheets on one end of a long counter next to a dozen large boxes of towels. "Sheldon, I can pay three eighty-five a dozen and only if you throw in four dozen sets of sheets for nine twenty-five. Otherwise I have to go back to Louie." She didn't seem bothered by Sheldon's children having no clothes. My grandmother picked up her raincoat, smiled at Sheldon, and spoke as if he was a family member. "I heard Arthur is going to City College. Ruthie and you have much to be proud of. When Arthur is a lawyer you won't have to work so hard and then you can give me better prices." She handed me my coat, turned to leave, and continued in her conversational tone, "If you get the stock to us Friday that will be fine. Tell Ruthie to come and look at our cookware. I'll give her wholesale prices."

As we left for the stairs Sheldon called out with a hint of resignation. "Mollie, at these prices Arthur is going to go to college without shoes. You'll get it all by Friday."

I was upset by this exchange. I knew my grandmother allowed customers to take merchandise when they couldn't pay, gave bonuses to her employees, and handled many family crises. So, I was confused about why she would leave Sheldon's children without clothes. In the cab going back to the store I asked, "Grandma, how can Sheldon's kids go to school without clothes? And Arthur isn't going to have shoes?"

She took off her clip-on earrings and put them and some papers into her pocketbook. She turned to me. "Don't worry, Sheldon's kids have clothes and Arthur will have shoes. You'll learn. Adults rarely mean what they say."

She must have seen the doubt on my face and continued, "Years ago, after your grandfather died, these wholesalers thought they could get away with selling to me at higher prices. They thought a woman would pay any price they asked. But now I get the same rates the large stores pay. It's kind of a game. And remember, our customers work hard and don't have much money so we have to get them prices they can afford." Although I didn't realize it at the time nor was it my grandmother's intention, I was learning through tagging along, watching, and listening to other people's experiences. Being "dumped" into the world of others provided me direction that was often overlooked at home.

I remember a Sunday when I was four. I already knew it was the only day of the week my mother would listen to my questions. "Mom, I want a brother or even a sister. My friends have them, why can't I?"

"We'll discuss it later." Pestering was the only available way of cracking her resistance and I kept it up till after dinner. Finally my mother had her speech prepared. "You were born because Dad and I loved each other very much. We want our love for you to be special and couldn't think of having another child." If I had been a lawyer then, I would have noted the phrase *another child*, but I was only in nursery school and it slipped right by me.

A few weeks later my father announced that he and I were going to watch an airplane land. I was thrilled since I had seen pictures of airplanes and some in the sky, but none close up. My father was wearing his best suit, a white shirt, a tie, and his favorite fedora. His blue eyes twinkled and his smile overran his face.

I sat in the front seat of his ten-year-old Buick. The generous placement of chrome on the fenders, dashboard, and steering wheel rattled to different rhythms depending upon our speed and the road conditions. Shafts of blue light and the distorted images of my father's hands and hat reflected off the inside chrome. The radio reception had been restored with a coat hanger my father fitted to replace the broken antenna. Gene Autry and my father sang "Home on the Range" and they both encouraged me to join in the chorus.

What joy to have my father completely to myself. I lost my craving for a sibling.

We turned into Floyd Bennett Airfield in Brooklyn and drove beside the grass adjacent to one of the runways. A silver-colored DC-3 landed and we trailed the plane until it stopped. Sailors in bright white uniforms poured down the ladder near the back of the plane. They waved their silly white sailor hats and some threw them into the air. Military parades were ever present close to the end of the Second World War, and I assumed this was such an occasion.

One sailor waved toward the Buick, and my father broke into his broadest grin and waved back. My father pointed toward the sailors: "Look. That's your brother."

Apparently my parents had reconsidered my request and instantly I had a new nineteen-year-old brother, George. He hugged my father and came around the car, pushed me to the middle of the front bench seat, and took my special seat next to the window. On the drive back I considered the idea that brothers came from airplanes. If that was the case I never wanted to go to another airport.

I was teased at nursery school and even laughed at by teachers when I explained this new notion of reproduction. Many years later my parents finally disclosed that my father, who was fifteen years older than my mother, had previously been married and had one son, my half-brother George. I would see him only once or twice over the next six years while he finished with the Navy, and then attended the University of Missouri on the GI Bill.

If my parents sent me into the world thinking brothers came from airplanes, how could they be trusted to give me the truth about anything else? It seemed odd, for example, that my mother called herself Miss Haselkorn instead of Mrs. Pitcoff. All the other mothers I knew used their "Mrs." title and their husband's last name. When I was around six I asked, "Why aren't you a Pitcoff like Dad and me?"

My mother lit a Pall Mall, took a few puffs, and answered, "Oh, I use Haselkorn because people knew me by that name before I got married." Even if her explanation was plausible, I was confused by why she referred to herself as a *Miss* rather than *Mrs.*

"When is your anniversary?"

She stubbed out her cigarette, which was only half smoked. "We don't celebrate it. But we think of it as around Memorial Day." *Think?* And why didn't they celebrate it?

Even aside from the nuts and bolts of reproduction there was murkiness about how I came into the lives of my parents. From the way my mother responded to the topic and my father avoided it, I sensed that our family was not well planned. I tried different ways to clear up this ambiguity. When I was around nine I asked my mother how she and my father met. As my mother told it, pursuit of building a better society gave birth to their romance. In 1931, when she was seventeen, my mother was a sales clerk at S. Klein's on Fourteenth Street. On a break, she crossed the avenue to Union Square, where she spotted my father trying to organize workers. "He was standing on a soapbox and I just fell in love," she said.

My mother's voice exuded excitement when she retold stories about her early dates with my father. He picked her up and drove to various buildings near the waterfront, often serenading her with "Ochi Chornyye" and other Russian songs he'd learned before he emigrated from Odessa in 1914 when he was fifteen years old.

When going to a movie or a diner he would park his jalopy under a streetlight if it was dark or with a view of the river if was still light out. *Wait here. I'll be back in half an hour. Read this book. You'll like it*, she recalled him saying. One night it was Chekhov, another Pushkin, and another Eugene Debs. One evening my mother shadowed him. She climbed a dimly lit stairway and followed the sounds of male voices arguing and laughing. She came to the entrance of a room packed with burly-looking men. They were house wreckers. In the thirties many New York City tenements were being demolished and it was mostly done by hand and with large wrecking balls swung from cranes. It was unregulated, dangerous, hard, and dirty work.

The smoky atmosphere didn't bother my mother. She was on her third pack of Pall Malls for the day. But the pervasive scent of alcohol made her edgy. She was the only woman in the room. The men wore colorless and frayed work clothes. My father wore his only suit, a broad colorful tie, and his fedora. She watched him make his way to the front of the room and stand on a chair to address the group. The men became silent and placed their bottles of beer on the floor. My father's speech focused on the importance of elevating the role of labor in a capitalist society and thus the need to organize into a union.

After his rousing speech my mother was charmed by how respectful the men were to her. One man put forward his hand. It was the size of a baseball mitt. "I'm honored to meet Bob's lady," he said. Her eyes sparkled as she repeated this introduction to me. She loved that title as much as her current one, casework supervisor at a social service agency aiding tuberculosis sufferers. These house wreckers amplified my mother's romantic feelings for my father. Without them I might never have been born.

―――――――

With her attention on her career and my father, combined with a lack of faith in her capability as a parent, my mother had little time to attend to all the needs of a young child. She tried her best to squeeze a few nuggets of time exclusively on me: a bedtime story, a spoonful of the noxious cod liver oil if she didn't forget, a hug when she got home in time to make dinner, but mostly she was preoccupied and drained from her work as a social worker, managing the home and supporting my father's efforts to start his own electrical business, which eventually failed. She visibly struggled to be a nurturing parent, but even at five I expected lengthy periods of detachment. I could never predict the duration of these periods, which could unexpectedly be interrupted with a bout of special consideration of my youthful experiences. I coveted these occasions, even though they often left me bewildered.

"We're going trick-or-treating." It was 5:30 and my mother had just gotten home from work. Her words were an unexpected indication that I would finally take part in Halloween for the first time. She seemed distracted as she cut two eyeholes in an old sheet she pulled off the floor of a closet. At five I knew that predicting the next moment with my parents was not something easily mastered, perhaps an unintended lesson for riding the uncertain waves of life itself. She threw the sheet over me and I worked at lining up the holes with my eyes.

By the time we hit the streets, the neighborhood was flooded with returning workers dashing off trolleys or bounding down the subway stairs to get home for dinners and their favorite radio shows. There were some grubby-looking men milling about a saloon. In those days the atmosphere of the Bowery easily reached beyond Twenty-Sixth Street. The saloons along Third Avenue, darkened by the El, were primarily for people with little money or hope. The noise and smell emerging from those sorrowful-looking taverns made me fearful of what might be found inside. There were no children about and only one ghost being towed by his mother, timidly beseeching tired workers coming home for the night. My friends boasted that they collected huge amounts of candy and money showing off their costumes to tenants in their apartment buildings. It seemed odd that we were going out on the street amongst strangers, when we had enough friendly neighbors in our own eight-story apartment building to satisfy the object of our mission.

I held out a bag for treats as we headed down the avenue. The bag was empty except for a nickel my mother gave me for good luck. We walked by a pitiful-looking man holding out a cup. "Got a nickel for coffee, sonny?" He looked toward our feet.

I jerked away from him. My mother asked what was the matter. "I don't want to get near those bums." I held my nose and looked up at my mother. "He smells. Aren't people supposed to give me nickels?"

My mother, who had been absorbed in thought, recoiled and gave the man an apologetic smile. She turned to me and repositioned the eyeholes in my sheet so I could clearly see her irritation. She accentuated each of her words. "They . . . are . . . not . . . bums. Never use that word. They are unfortunate people. They can't find jobs. They came back from the war and their jobs were gone. And they have other problems. Don't ever call them bums." She made me offer the nickel in my bag to the man. Reluctantly I dropped it into his cup.

"Don't you get yourself into any army, sonny," the man called out. He gave me a smile with darkened teeth. Halloween was losing its appeal.

My mother lit a cigarette and puffed rapidly. It was clear neither of us had the hang of trick-or-treating. She stamped out her half-finished cigarette and peered through a window of a saloon, as if searching for at least one reward to drop into my treat bag to end our sorry expedition. She turned to me and I could sense her disappointment and frustration. She took one more peek through the window, then took my hand and walked us to the entrance. "I'll wait here and you go into that saloon and try trick-or-treating. Maybe you'll have better luck without me."

I knew I shouldn't be in the Three Roses, but my mother sent me in and I wanted her to forget the "bum" muddle. I can't imagine what the regulars and the bartender thought when they saw a five-year-old ghost walk into their saloon. One man yelled at the bartender that his rotten whiskey was making him see ghosts. I could feel my eyes getting wider. The smells of alcohol, body odor, and sawdust made me gasp. The sounds of mostly men singing loudly off key and laughing hard enough to stumble into each other seemed more animal-like than human. I shuffled to the bar with caution as men and a few women careened around in jerky slow motion. This was a hundred times more frightening than the Hall of Mirrors at Coney Island. I had disappointed my mother by using the "bum" slur, so I forced myself not to flee. I approached the only woman sitting at the bar and hoped she didn't sense my panic. "Trick or treat?"

The woman looked down at me and shrieked to the others. "Quiet! We have a ghost in our midst." The conversations and laughter stopped. Instantly I was the focal point of attention. My little body tightened with alarm, but I couldn't get myself to run for my life. The boisterous woman looked down at me and, with a gentleness I didn't expect, placed her hand on my shoulder. I recognized the smile of an indulgent adult encouraging a child's performance. She looked around at the others at the bar and simply said, "Cough it up."

The bartender slammed a beer glass onto the bar and barked, "Sonny, get out of here before I call a cop." I backed up, but the overly happy woman tightened her hand around my shoulder and held me in place while her other hand hauled the bartender's head across the bar and gave him a long kiss. He struggled for air while other drinkers gave me pennies and nickels. Two of the men handed me cardboard coasters with a picture of three roses. A man whom others kept from falling over gave me a quarter and a hearty "God bless you, son." The bartender slipped out of the woman's hold, his face red with lipstick and embarrassment. He opened the cash register drawer, collected some coins, and begrudgingly dropped a nickel and several pennies into my hand. As I trotted backwards out of the Three Roses, others added their own "God bless you."

The cold night air was a relief from the saloon atmosphere, as was the familiar clanking of the trolley cars and rumble of an El train. I proudly showed my mother the collection of coins, especially the quarter, and the coasters she could use. She was thrilled. We'd hit the jackpot. She turned serious. "People who have been hit hard by life can be very generous."

I pulled off my sheet. My confused look triggered a conspiratorial smile and a slight tousle of my hair. "Next year we'll start at Three Roses," she said. If the ritual was measured by money the venture would have been deemed successful, yet when we returned to the apartment I crossed Halloween off my list of fun activities.

CHAPTER TWO

A PARTICULARLY GLOOMY GRAY DAY in 1947 stands out. My mother
didn't "dump" me at my grandmother's store nor did she take me to
daycare. Instead she stayed home with me. Our apartment was
filled with more than the usual haze of smoke from her cigarettes.
She tried on different outfits for herself and for me. During one of
her repetitive plunges into the closet I heard her muffled voice.
"We're going someplace special today. You'll have to pay attention."
At four I was well tuned into my mother's rising worry. This had an
upside, because she threw together a bowl of lukewarm cream of
wheat for me rather than soggy Cheerios and showed concern for
how I felt. She handed me a puzzle to work on but interrupted my
concentration by asking if a particular hat went well with one of her
dresses. "I don't have anything to wear. I should never have
returned the black-and-white polka dot to Klein's. Remember? You
said you liked it. Why did you let me return it?"

We skipped the elevator and ran down the three flights of
stairs. She didn't reveal our destination, the Little Red Schoolhouse
school, until we were on the Twenty-Third Street cross-town bus.
After transferring to the downtown bus, we finally arrived in front
of a small gray building, which I had expected to be red.

Before we entered Little Red, my mother unbuttoned my coat
and straightened my shirt, extinguished her half-smoked cigarette,

wiped my nose, lit another cigarette, and told me to relax. An especially attentive woman took us to an empty classroom and offered to play with me. She took my hand and led me to a small round table that was just the right height for a kid my age. "Would you like to do this puzzle or the one of the farmer?" I nodded toward the farmer puzzle. She spread the pieces on the table. Occasionally I looked up and saw my mother watching as she puffed on her cigarettes. When I finished, the friendly woman returned me to my mother and complimented us on my puzzle abilities.

My mother was flying high when we took the buses home. "I'm going to buy you an Oscar Brand record because you worked so hard on those puzzles." Most weekends I was hooked on listening to Oscar Brand on the radio. Even though I didn't understand the political undercurrents of many of his songs, I delighted in the sing-alongs and could easily imagine the stories flowing from the lyrics and his explanation of the songs' origins.

That night she explained to my father that I had done an excellent job and was sure I would be accepted. I turned to my father to learn more about what to expect at school. "Daddy, what was it like? What did you learn at school?" I asked.

"Well in Odessa, we shared desks that had inkwells for our pens. We practiced penmanship every day." His face turned from a serious look to one that was almost silly. "One time when the teacher wasn't looking, I dunked the long braid of the girl who sat in front of me into my inkwell. I wasn't allowed back at school for a week and everyone got angry with me." He seemed to enjoy my surprise.

"I wouldn't do that," I said.

"It wasn't so bad. Even the girl thought it was funny."

"Bob. What a story to tell." She gave my father a look that briefly erased his playful sparkle. Even at four, I was no longer fully baffled by these disconnected divergences in conversations. My father had now generated an even more expansive smile and my mother yielded to being charmed and turned back to me. "Anyway, there're no more inkwells in schools." She turned serious: "You're going to learn to read and do arithmetic and there is shop and art. It's going to be fun."

"Your mother knows a lot more about school. So listen to her." He paused to stare back at her. "But girls still have braids," he said, and winked.

I never fully learned why I was sent to private school. More than sixty years later I came across a paper my mother wrote for one of her graduate school classes in social work. "I would be totally worthless as a mother if I didn't have the stimulation from my work." I do remember her telling me that Celia, a work colleague, had suggested Little Red as a means of loosening the wedge of guilt lodged between my mother's desire for professional satisfaction and her sense of responsibility for me. The tuition was a significant expense (even if not proportionally as expensive as the tuitions of today). She paid it out of the $4,000 annual salary she was receiving as a result of a recent promotion to supervising social worker at Altro Health and Rehabilitation, an agency that provided services for tuberculosis victims and their families. At the time, my father was trying to start his own electrical business and his income was spotty. My assumption is that the decision to send me to Little Red was most likely a combination of wanting to see me compensated for their inattention as parents as well as to have an education that combined some of the features of each of theirs, formal and experiential.

There were few similarities in my parents' life experiences before they met, including their educations. My mother graduated public high school with honors, completed an undergraduate degree at Hunter, a public college, and went on scholarship to Columbia

University for her master's in social work. My father's formal education ended when he left Odessa at fifteen, yet he probably read more widely than most of their friends and my mother included, and was admired for his command of history, literature, politics, arts, and technology. This presented a dilemma for me. I preferred my father's unstructured, experiential approach to education and yet suspected that my mother's more conventional approach was what was called for. This duality surfaced in my own educational journey. On one hand I developed creative block-building skills at Little Red and later made films for my MFA, while on the other hand I survived standardized tests in public high school and mastered case law for my degree in law.

I doubt either parent was aware at the time of the Little Red Schoolhouse's political environment. Some teachers were Communist Party members or sympathizers. The majority of my classmates' parents were Communist Party supporters. The curriculum slanted toward Communist ideology, burnishing the values of Communist societies such as China and the Soviet Union. Yet my father was obsessively anti-Communist. At five I couldn't yet detect this bewildering contradiction nor do I believe that my parents were then aware of a dynamic that would soon come to complicate my school friendships, engender qualms about my father, and place me in uncomfortable situations when the inevitable subject of one's political inclination came up.

———

A few months after my unnerving saloon adventure I came down with the mumps and couldn't go to Little Red for a month. I wanted my mother to stay home with me and never return to work. After several days of attending to my needs she must have confided to Celia something like, *If I have to stay home one more day I'll go insane.* Celia came to the rescue and recommended a woman who had taken care of her daughter and might be available until I got better.

The next morning I woke up early, still fatigued and woozy from the mumps. The sun was making its brief visit to my room, intensifying the colors of the linoleum floor. It would be a good day for playing with my mother, but she said, "Paul, today I have to go back to work. It'll only be half a day. I've met a wonderful woman, Bernice, who's going to play with you and do everything you want." My mother invited Bernice to come into my room.

I had been betrayed. I knew this would be a defining moment and had to do something to keep my mother for myself. I pulled every toy, book, and record out of my bookshelf onto the floor. I tore apart my bed and used a dozen different phrases to convey my hatred for her. She tried to soothe me and at the same time reassure Bernice that I would calm down. For the first time, I acknowledged Bernice and screamed, "I'm not staying with her."

"Paul, Bernice likes to sing and wants to build blocks with you. You'll become good friends."

I wasn't listening. I would do anything to stop my mother's escape and I almost succeeded. "She's black. I don't like black." I hadn't a clue about racial issues.

My mother turned pale. I saw her raise her hand and swing toward me and stop just before she connected with my face. The ensuing silence rang as if I was under a clanging church bell. My mother's muscle control visibly faded. Her arm dropped lifeless to her side and she turned to Bernice. "I'm sorry. You don't have to stay. He's been very sick, but that doesn't excuse anything."

Bernice smiled at my mother, gently touched her arm, and said, "Go to work. We'll be OK. Don't worry." She put a record on the phonograph and smiled at me. Then gave my mother a slight nudge toward my door and said, "Why don't you call us in a few hours so Paul can hear your voice and you can see everything is OK."

Perhaps fifteen minutes passed while Bernice endured my crying, which transformed into a petulant withdrawal. Bernice calmly tried a few records until she hit on one of my favorite Oscar Brand songs. Detente transformed into alliance as Bernice and I played every one of my records. Then I built tall and intricate structures with my blocks, searched for treasures she hid around the apartment, and guessed whether it was an express or local El train that shook the apartment every few minutes.

The next morning couldn't come soon enough. When Bernice arrived, I pushed my mother out the door. Bernice liked soap operas and we took time away from our playing to sit by the radio and listen to *Stella Dallas*, *Just Plain Bill*, *Ma Perkins*, and a bunch of others. During the commercials Bernice asked me questions. "Why do you think Ma Perkins wants to hide those people who the bad guys from the Soviet Union are chasing?"

"I don't know. You think she feels sorry for them?" I liked Ma and thought she would always do the right thing, but wasn't sure why she was hiding people.

"Ma was saying something about how in America things are different than in Russia and the Russians won't let people come to our country. We'll find out more tomorrow," Bernice said. I struggled with untangling a marionette, which neither my father nor mother could fix. "What do you think Bill should tell the man whose wife wants to get a job at the factory working with all those men?" she asked.

Bernice took the marionette and made it workable and had it grab hold of my foot. I thought about her question. "He should tell her to stay home with her children."

Bernice laughed. "Well, let's see what happens." She paused as she considered a new thought. "Looks like you're doing pretty well on your own with your mother at work." She handed over the untangled marionette controls to me. It was as if I had been given a brand-new one. She continued, "You know your mother is doing good work. She's helping people who're in trouble, sort of like Ma Perkins and Bill help people. You should be proud."

After I recovered from the mumps, I went back to school. Every day Bernice was at school to pick me up. On the first day back, she and I skipped to the bus stop. Bernice was as excited as me. "Begin by telling me everything you did after you got to school. Did they miss you?" She listened and made sure I didn't forget anything, especially my conversations with classmates and teachers. After I told her about my day she said, "You should go on the radio. Your day is as interesting as Ma Perkins. Do you think your friend Ethan will forgive Elinore for spilling the red paint on his dungarees?"

My mother began going away to professional conferences. I missed her, but she called every afternoon after I got home from school. "I miss you," she'd say. "Hope you're having a good time. Did you make anything new in shop?"

My mother hid small gifts in the apartment for each day she was away. "Where is it today?" I asked. The ritual had been established.

"Today if you look inside the telephone table you'll find something you like." I couldn't wait to get off the phone to hunt for my surprise.

"Have a good evening. I love you. Got to hang up before they ask for another nickel," she said. Bernice and I rushed to open the telephone table and found a toy cowboy.

My desire to spend time with Bernice never diminished and I couldn't imagine her not in my life. When I was around eight and we moved into a house on Charles Street, Bernice got very sick. A few times each week my parents went to Harlem Hospital to visit. One day I sat in the waiting room while my parents took turns visiting her. The hospital wouldn't allow children to visit patients.

When I sat with my father I saw he had lost his sparkle and didn't talk much after his short visit with Bernice. When my mother sat with me, her liveliness seemed forced and she squeezed me. She said, "Bernice wants to see you. When she gets better she needs you to tell her what's happening with *Just Plain Bill* and *Stella*."

"And Ma Perkins too," I said. I saw tears in my mother's eyes and she had dumped ashes all over her dress. I felt ashamed I wasn't old enough to cheer everyone up, especially Bernice.

These trips to the hospital lasted a few months until one day my parents picked me up at the store. They were dressed up. Before we got home we stopped at an ice cream parlor and they ordered a vanilla ice cream soda for me, served in a glass that was held in a round metal frame with a handle. This was a big treat. My parents ordered nothing for themselves. My mother kissed me on my forehead. "Paul, you'll be very sad. Bernice died."

My friend was gone. I didn't cry. I knew nothing about grief. I pushed away my barely touched soda. Without Bernice, I felt as if I had been shoved onto a stage where I didn't yet belong. Years later I would remember Bernice as my second mentor, my grandmother being the first of many throughout my life. I had suddenly lost a partner for my continuing life dialogue.

———

The thought of someday becoming an adult often gripped my thoughts. I had all sorts of unanswered questions of how one became an adult and found myself repeatedly studying the small sample of adults I observed at my grandmother's store, at my friends' homes, and in the movies. Naturally I paid full attention to the behaviors of my parents, but soon developed a sense that they weren't showing me the most suitable way to be an adult.

From the time I could walk, Saturdays held out no other options than to go schlepping with my mother, since my father was at work and my grandmother's store was too busy on Saturdays for me to be dumped there. The routine began early in the morning. There were two closets in our family's one-bedroom apartment, both in my room. My parents slept in the living room, which adjoined a small dining alcove separated from a galley kitchen by a wooden screen. Most Saturdays, after I dressed, my mother rushed me out of my room in order to go through her closet. While I attacked my soppy Cheerios, she dashed in and out of the dining alcove wearing different combinations of dresses and hats.

"We're going to schlep across town today. I have to return a dress I bought last week, and want to look at some lamps uptown. We also need to get galoshes for you." I wasn't happy about schlepping because my mother took hours to try on dresses, but it did give me time with her and to learn how grown-ups behaved.

"I have a supervisors' conference on Tuesday and need something to wear. If we can get everything returned at Macy's and I find another dress, we'll have time for lunch at your favorite restaurant," my mother said that morning.

I had no favorite restaurant but was reminded that for children in tow by their mothers, Macy's had a restaurant decorated as a carousel. More important, Macy's, along with Gimbels and some other department stores, offered free surprises to children who behaved during shopping and lunch. The tin whistle or miniature set of jacks given to young schlepping companions had a disappointing half-life of no longer than the trip home and made me question the sacrifice of behaving. Yet these lunches broke up the monotony of going through hundreds of dresses, trying on dozens, and getting every salesperson's and shopper's opinion on the one to buy.

Thankfully, this Saturday we were not going to S. Klein's on Fourteenth Street. Klein's shoppers could easily trample a young child in their ferocious grab for bargains. After elbowing into the store the shoppers acted as if the last dress in the world lay on the counters or hung on the racks. It was my least favorite destination, while my mother seemed to enjoy the rough-and-tumble scramble to find and hold on to the best dress and bargains.

The key part of our Saturday campaign, the most daunting for me, was the return of a dress never used or worn just once. In those days it was a bit like confronting the Soviet bureaucracy. One stood on long lines in a dimly lit, windowless room. A few metal chairs piled with returned dresses, shoes, and other merchandise introduced the only colors into the room. A high gray metal counter conferred authority on a matronly looking woman who cross-examined the brave shoppers returning their purchases. I held on to the idea that my mother wasn't a criminal, though she and all the other women were treated like suspects in a major crime. The "return magistrate" barely paused as she threw questions at my mother. "Why are you returning this dress? Couldn't you tell it didn't fit when you tried it on?" The woman folded and unfolded the dress as if it had a contagious disease. "The label looks as if someone reattached it. Did you wear this to a party? How do we know you won't return the next dress?" She was a formidable match for my mother. "Wait while I call the fourth floor to see if this dress is even sold here. Don't leave." A security guard stood outside the room and I feared we would go to jail.

The questions had some merit in my mother's case even if the store employee's attitude was haughty. My mother's time was a precious commodity and sometimes she didn't want to go downtown to return a dress she bought at S. Klein's when the day's destination was Macy's. Earlier, on the crosstown bus, my mother had revealed her apprehension about whether or not the same dresses were sold at Macy's. The return magistrate waited on the phone to hear the answer from the fourth floor. She glared at my mother and tried forcing a confession from her by stretching over the counter, shaking her head at me, and loudly proclaiming, "Shame dragging your son into this." She finally got word from the fourth floor and slammed the phone with satisfaction. "Madam. We do not sell this style here." She shoved the dress back over the counter at my mother. At the same time, I tugged on my mother's arm to get her to leave the return room before we were arrested.

"Let me talk with your manager," my mother objected. "You should be selling this dress here. It's a style that's becoming. It just doesn't work for me." She held the dress closer to the magistrate. "Actually the style looks good on you. It would show off your great figure and the color goes well with your hair." The clerk was flustered, touched her hair, and reached for a phone to call her manager. My mother continued, "While you get your manager I'll leave the dress here, pick out the dress I want, and be back."

After trying on a dozen or more dresses my mother brought three of them back to the return magistrate. "OK, I'm going to take these three. All you need to do is deduct the price for the one I'm returning and I'll pay the difference." My mother's brazenness had the effect of demoting the return magistrate to ordinary returns clerk, who made the adjustment and blandly noted that Macy's could not accept returns from my mother again. I knew that the next week we would be returning at least two if not all of the dresses. I hoped we would be returning them at Macy's, not S. Klein's, and to a kinder magistrate.

On the way out of Macy's we stopped at the shoe department to select my new pair of galoshes. My mother told the clerk I would be growing quickly and requested a pair two or three sizes bigger than

I needed for this winter. My mother was convinced I would grow those two inches by the beginning of next winter.

"It will make it hard for your son to walk," the clerk warned. I easily slipped the new galoshes over my shoes. The clerk had my mother feel the space between the front of my shoe and the front of the galoshes. "Madam, the front will hang down and your son will trip walking down the street." This concerned me. The clerk seemed to know what he was talking about, but I made no protest because my old galoshes were so tight that I couldn't pull them over my shoes without the strength of at least two adults tugging and pushing at the same time.

"We'll take them. Leave them on his feet since it's snowing." On the down escalator, the galoshes were flopping and one got caught in the grate at the landing. I panicked as I was sucked toward the jaws of the escalator. I strained as hard as I could to rescue my foot. The escalator churned through the trapped two inches of my galosh, coughed, and thankfully released its grip. The front of my right galosh was gone, leaving edges as jagged as if it had been chewed by a tiger. It was easier to walk now, but I feared the damage would be discovered. My mother was ahead of me and hadn't noticed my entanglement with the escalator. If she discovered that her new purchase had been devoured I might be in trouble. I began to cry.

"What's the matter?" she said. I pointed to the serrated remains of the front portion of my right galosh and explained what happened. To gain sympathy I added how I had almost vanished into the bowels of the escalator. My crying was in vain. Neither the mangling of my new galosh nor my brush with death had the anticipated impact on my mother.

Our third trip to the tribunal for returns was no less gloomy or inhospitable. My mother had to drag me to the counter, where a different clerk waited for my mother's claim. "Look, we just bought these galoshes and there is something wrong with them." She pointed to my feet. "Look how the front has just fallen off."

The clerk requested to handle the evidence and made me take off my right galosh. He had us look carefully at the jagged edges. "You can see that these edges are caused by a tear of some sort, not a defect," he said.

"Impossible. He hasn't left the store. Macy's is responsible for defective merchandise." My mother's steadfast denial in the face of the truth left me bewildered.

"Madam, did your son get them caught in the escalator? They're awfully big and flop around." I moved behind my mother. The clerk must have been a kind of detective. He should have been working for the police.

"It's snowing outside. You want my son to get his feet wet and get sick? Frozen toes? This is Macy's. You shouldn't be selling defective merchandise. Maybe your escalators need adjusting. Let me speak to your supervisor."

"OK, OK, madam, here's a slip. Go back and get another pair. But get the right size this time so your son won't get killed."

On the bus home, when I asked my mother whether it was unfair to return a dress she hadn't bought at Macy's, or my galoshes, which I had destroyed, she said, "We buy a lot of clothes at Macy's and tell friends to go there too. When a store has a loyal customer they should give them special attention, like Grandma does in her store. That's a way to keep a customer coming back," she said.

"But you didn't tell the truth?"

"Not really. I never said I bought the dress at Macy's. And the galoshes shouldn't have been so easily destroyed on their own escalators. Sometimes you just have to help or insist on people doing the right things, even if it goes against the rules. If everyone just followed rules we wouldn't get anywhere."

My parents rarely discussed, made, or even followed rules. If there were family rules, they seemed to change for little clear reason, and thus I came to think of rules as mirages, which appeared and disappeared without any logic. At home there were few stated rules. Some nights I was told it was my bedtime and I had to go to sleep. Other nights my mother allowed me to stay up past my bedtime by three or four cigarettes. (Our domestic time-keeping was based not on minutes, but on the period it took to smoke an entire cigarette.) Occasionally I was told to finish my meal, but just as often when I was coughing from the bones left in a piece of fish my mother assured me was boneless, or a potato that was just on the warm side of raw, my parents didn't hold me to finishing dinner. I was told to take my vitamins, yet when a stash of two weeks' supply was found under my bed, my mother merely noted that I should try not to make a mess of my room.

My father's disavowal of standard procedure became most apparent when I was a bit older. Near the beginning of what I assumed would be a pleasant summer vacation from the city heat, my ten-year-old attention was captured by the sudden intensity on my father's face and frantic pumping of the brake pedal to no effect, as we gathered speed coming down a mountain road in rural New Hampshire. Our hydraulic brake line had rusted through, and only by swerving around slower cars and tugging on the emergency brake was he able to jockey us safely to level highway. My father felt confident that he could get us to the nearest garage with just the operation of the hand brake. It was a Sunday and we wouldn't find an open garage until we reached Augusta, Maine.

Coming off a bridge into Augusta, we waited until the intersection was clear to make a left turn across traffic. My father shifted into first gear and let out the clutch. Just as we got going my mother shouted, "Bob! The light is turning yellow!" Another car followed us through the turn. My father yanked on the emergency brake just in time to miss running into a police car, which had turned into our path. The cop made us stop and there was much confusion as to when the light changed, who had the right of way, and if the cop had jumped the light. From my mother's look, I could tell that the papers my father were handed were stirring her panic. The cop walked my father back to our car and told us we could pay the fine now or come to court on Monday.

My father announced we would spend the night in Augusta rather than drive through to the coast. We stayed in a tiny one-room cabin just outside of the city. My mother saw no charm in hauling water to wash, lighting kerosene lanterns for our source of light, and having her only son sleep on a narrow attached porch exposed to bears and other assorted country beasts. The cabin inspired my father for his court appearance. He wrote out his defense by candlelight and told stories about his hero, labor attorney Eugene Debs, who never wavered in his fight for the workingman.

"Dad. I saw it. The light was turning red."

"This is a country of laws and everyone has a right to defend themselves. You'll see tomorrow."

The courtroom's size dwarfed everyone forced to attend the legal proceedings. The walls were paneled with dark wood marred by age-old injuries. The light from two stately windows mocked the artificial illumination inside. The room had eight or more rows of benches, highly polished from the years of buffing by squirming defendants and their families. Nothing fun had taken place in this coliseum since it was first built, in the 1820s. Activity was limited to mopping perspiration from foreheads and necks and the defendants' ritualistic presentation of pleas before the judge's high dark bench. Officers in blue starched shirts accented by shiny belts, holsters, and guns stood on either side of the judge. We were seated in the third row and the judge's questions and orders were barely audible over the whispering of waiting defendants making comments about the judge's mood, the last fish they caught, and the nature of their crimes. All the defendants pleaded guilty and asked the judge for leniency. He reduced most everyone's fines. My mother urged my father to do the same.

"Your Honor I request that . . ." my father looked down at the summons and read the name, ". . . Officer Reed be called to the witness stand."

"Are you a lawyer?" the judge asked.

My father beamed. One of his few other heroes was Clarence Darrow. "No. But I think you'll find Officer Reed's testimony helpful."

Officer Reed seemed as confused as my mother and me. After hours of dispensing with a spectrum of cases this was the first witness the judge called to testify. Slowly, as if engaged in a group yawn, the defendants, spectators, and other police officers shifted their attention to my father and Officer Reed.

"Officer Reed. Does your police car have an automatic transmission?"

The officer flipped through his notebook. "Yes, but you went through a red light. I don't see what that has to do with my Powerglide transmission. I note that the other driver, a Mr. Giles, who went through the same red light just pleaded guilty."

"Nevertheless, just answer the question please." I had never heard my father use such formal language.

"Yes, it's automatic."

"Is it your practice to place the transmission in neutral when you stop at a red light? Isn't that police practice?" Automatic transmissions were not common at the time and many drivers felt it was necessary to idle in neutral.

"Look, what's important is that I had a green light and you almost hit me. You went through a red light. Just because you're from New York you can't break our laws."

"Officer Reed, I ask you again. Isn't it true that with automatics you place the transmission in neutral when at a red light? This is good police procedure, isn't it? And isn't it true that when you have to shift into your drive speed, you must look down? Isn't it possible you were not looking at the traffic lights and you might have anticipated the green rather than seen it?"

I moved closer to my mother. I feared the judge would have my father handcuffed and hauled out of court. Officer Reed was baffled as the judge took over the questioning about his shifting. The judge turned to my father. "Mr. Pitcoff, I don't know much about automatic transmissions, never drove one. You leave some doubt in my mind since I know our force is just getting used to the automatics. Therefore, your case is dismissed. Have a good vacation." He tapped his gavel and ordered the clerk to read the next case.

My mother beamed and squeezed me. I slid off the bench to run up to and hug my father and make an exit before the judge changed his mind. Officer Reed seemed dazed, still sitting in the witness chair, head down, writing something in his notebook.

But my father hadn't moved away from the judge's bench. I halted before reaching him. "Your Honor," he said, "I respectfully ask that you drop the guilty verdict on the previous defendant who was also stopped with me. His name is Mr. Giles."

"Mr. Pitcoff, the law doesn't work that way. Mr. Giles pleaded guilty. Leave it at that."

"Your Honor, he pleaded guilty before he understood all the

facts that we just learned. For the sake of justice, you must reverse your decision."

The judge hesitated, tightened his jaw, finally relented. "Mr. Giles. Your plea has been reversed and you do not have to pay the fine. Mr. Pitcoff, the best thing for this court, you, and your family is to return to New York before the end of the day."

"Your Honor, we look forward to our yearly vacation in Maine and hope you'll let us stay another week. It is also my hope that you add to the record that Officer Reed is one of the most courteous officers I have ever been stopped by and he reflects well on the city of Augusta and the great state of Maine."

"Stay in Maine if you like. But please don't go through any more red lights." The judge turned to his clerk to call the next case and my father reached out his hand to Officer Reed and the two of them walked out the front door together. When my mother and I caught up to my father, Officer Reed was telling him of some sights we should see on our way to the coast. My father had me shake Officer Reed's hand and then we went back to our car.

"Dad, why did you thank Officer Reed? We had to stay an extra day because of him."

"Paul, he was doing his job. It's the systems that made us stay, not the officer."

"Dad, I think he was right though."

"Maybe. But maybe we all made a mistake in what we saw. I talked with Mr. Giles and he swore the light was still yellow for us. The police aren't always right and it's good to make judges and the public realize that systems aren't always right either."

Watching my father play a leading role in a real-life courtroom drama had no precedent. What I witnessed was a man who appeared comfortable, confident, and familiar with a legal situation. Not anything I would have expected from him.

The recurring pattern of my parents' irreverence to obeying authority and standard orthodoxy was a model I didn't readily appreciate when I was a young boy. Neither of them spoke of this nor did they push me to either follow rules or not follow them. Yet they forever modeled that most situations had complexity and inherent ambiguities. When I was a young assistant professor, without a PhD, I informed my dean I wanted to be appointed the first chairman of the Department of Communications at Adelphi University. He said it wouldn't work without a PhD and until I was more experienced. I pushed back and became the founding chair, which I held for twenty years. I wonder if my own willingness to doubt taking traditional paths and submitting to authority had its roots in schlepping with my mother and watching my father take on the legal system of Augusta, Maine?

CHAPTER THREE

IT TOOK MANY EVENTS before I realized my parents had little awareness of dangers that could be perilous to a child: I almost drowned in my own bed when a rainstorm swept through a wall my father had never fully repaired. I was playing in construction debris from a cabin my father was building when a rusty 16-penny nail went through my sneaker and into my foot and gave me an infection. I fell down a flight of stairs and through a glass door that ripped apart my forearm, but there was no thought of taking me to a doctor to get stitches. I suffered frequent electric shocks because there were no electrical switch plates in our bathroom, even though my father was an electrician. And on and on.

It has always been a mystery to me whether my parents couldn't perceive risk or simply ignored it. Risk was the means they had used to achieve their goals. My mother had no role models for her dreams and her parents had little capacity to value or approve of her plans to build her life beyond marriage, family, and maybe the store. She broke societal norms when she decided she wanted a professional career, independence, and a life unfettered with the responsibilities of a man and children. To achieve her goals she had to ignore what others assumed were significant risks: not finding a man to support her, competing against men, placing her career on an equal footing with her man and her son, and speaking her mind without attention to normal decorum.

My father, for his part, emigrated from Odessa when he was fifteen. He landed in New York in 1914, lived in a tent in the outer Bronx, and had to find a way to be self-sufficient, initially as a Western Union telegram runner. In 1926 he joined the American Communist Party. I learned later he took significant risks in his covert espionage work for the Soviets. At the end of 1933 he turned against the American Communist Party, at considerable risk of reprisals from the Soviets.

Father at sixteen as Western Union runner a year after immigrating to the United States, and eleven years before joining the American Communist Party

Growing up I had no awareness of these courageous or perhaps carelessly considered life decisions. From my young vantage point I merely assumed that risk analysis was never a part of either parent's day-to-day strategy. For instance, my father's philosophy about his ten-year-old Buick was tough love. Only when it experienced severe pain and refused to move forward would he open the hood for emergency operations. In such crises, he would calmly and competently remove and clean a fouled spark plug, cool a vapor-locked gas line with a wet rag, adjust the carburetor, or use the lug wrench to give a threatening whack to some part that was not acting as required.

My first memory of a car trip was not as ordinary as I assumed at the time. I was three or four and looking out the passenger window of our used and abused six-year-old Buick, while we were going around a turn. My mother sat between my father and me. A clunk and then a clatter of scraping sounds were accompanied by a sudden gust of wind, which produced an animal-like scream near my ear. Before I figured out what had happened, I felt myself grasped by a terrible force. The feral scream and embrace were my mother's. Where there had been a door was open space.

My father pulled over to the curb and my mother squeezed so much comfort into me I found it hard to breathe. I was torn between the fear telegraphed through my mother and the great fun of the unfolding adventure. My father bounded from the car and walked down the road to retrieve our door. He grinned as he lugged it back and threw it into the back-seat compartment of the car.

My mother's comforting mode shifted to defiance. "Bob, we can't go anywhere without a door." He started the car and urged us to sit closer to him. My mother threatened him and called him names that weren't his.

My father became agitated. "Are you going to walk? Paul and I will meet you at home." The flyaway door experience was a fitting example of how even the simplest of their activities or least harmless of their surroundings were never without threat. For instance, elevators. Elisha Otis made elevators safe from falling, and I should have felt secure riding in one with my parents. However, visiting their friends Tommy, Mae, and their daughter Olive in the Bronx, we entered the elevator in their building. We were dressed up for the occasion and my father clutched his brand-new fedora at his side. My mother adjusted her dress with her right hand as she held a cigarette in her left. By the fifth floor we smelled smoke and waved it away from our faces. I began to cough and expected my father to push the red emergency button. By the sixth floor my father was vigorously shaking his hat to put out a small fire. By the eighth floor, when the doors opened, my father was sticking his finger through a singed hole in the front of his prized fedora that my mother had just scorched with her cigarette. He wore that hat for over a year as a reminder to my mother that her cigarettes could be instruments of destruction.

Even at home there was no assurance of safety. The Sunday night family meal heightened our fire preparedness. Sunday dinners were the one night a week we ate meat. When my mother was broiling the steak or lamb chops, the fat drippings inevitably caught fire. Flames leaped through the stove vents and sides of the bottom broiler drawer. Our alarm for action was my mother's panicked call, *Bob*! We each had our practiced responsibilities. My father rushed to smother the vents and spaces between the broiler door with wet towels. I ran to open the front door and windows to allow the smoke to escape. If we were unlucky, a Good Samaritan, seeing dark smoke escape from our house, rushed to the corner, pulled the handle on the red fire alarm box, and the fire department joined our Sunday festivities.

Small fires seemed to be a major occurrence in our home. With her career in full bloom my mother left the house early, but not before making attempts to fulfill her mothering role of preparing breakfast for me. Limp cereal or soupy eggs were her specialty and it made me feel guilty to drop them under the table for Rollie, our dog, to eat. One morning she was ahead of schedule and decided I should also have toast. I smelled smoke and ran to the kitchen. Orange flames leaped from the top and sides of the toaster. I turned the faucet on full blast and soaked a towel the way my father would do, but before I could smother the fire my mother held me back. "Not yet. I just put it in. It's probably not fully toasted." She said this with no more alarm than "Pass the milk for my coffee."

In 1949, my parents purchased a run-down brownstone on Charles Street. I considered leaving them the moment my father pushed open the rotten door to the basement. These living quarters smelled of death. The bottom landing, five feet below the sidewalk level, had been vacant for eight years after the previous owner died. There was no kitchen, just a burned-out hot plate in the similarly rotting addition to the back. The floor had more deceased bugs and rodents than the Museum of Natural History. My father tried opening windows to get air into the rooms, but the windows were painted shut. There were endless piles of moldy newspapers, a few broken chairs, and just one rusted iron lamp to illuminate the entire space. There were no doors and only one room for all of us to sleep in. The main and upper floors of the house were rented by the room, with a shared bathroom on each floor. The plan was that my father would renovate the house on his own at night and weekends while we lived in this mess. I overheard talk that I would help too.

In the winter the coal-fired boiler, which heated the entire house and the water, would burn out by midday, since it was unattended. My father assigned me the job of restarting it when I came home from school. I was not yet eight. My mother and I were in accord: it was too dangerous. I might burn the house down. My mother's rational appeal, punctuated with some screaming, did not persuade my father.

"You watch me do it and you'll get the hang of it," my father said. I followed him into the sub-basement. I was terrified. There was one light bulb barely outlining the earthen floor, which was dark black and layered with coal dust and small boulders. Large water bugs crawled everywhere; pipes and electrical wires hung down from a ceiling that was only five and a half feet high. My father cautioned me to be careful not to touch any wires. He opened the furnace, shoveled out the ash, placed some newspaper and wood inside, lit a match, and started the fire. While we watched the wood beginning to flame and turn red, he explained that I had to do this every day after school and make sure a rusted round meter—he hit it several times to get it to work—reached a certain position.

When the wood began to turn into coals he picked up a broad-bladed shovel with a wooden handle that offered splinters to its users. He used it to shovel coal from the pile near the furnace through a large iron door. "Just enough to cover the wood. Allow twenty minutes and then go down and fill the furnace. You'll have no problem."

I followed my father out of the basement wondering if I could ever have enough courage to descend into that dungeon on my own. Terror was eventually replaced by a sense of bravery. I endured numerous burns from touching the iron door until I got the hang of using gloves and pokers, and instead of fleeing the water bugs I gave them names. My sense of bravado extended to taking a perverse joy from luring my bravest friends into the hell that had become an acceptable realm for me. Slowly I was developing a sense that my chances of surviving childhood would greatly depend on how quickly I could develop my own risk-assessment skills. What at the time I came to accept as inattentiveness and a blasé attitude to risks was more likely a consequence of having survived more serious dangers that they kept secret.

CHAPTER FOUR

My parents craved intellectual give-and-take. There was no idea, opinion, or doubt held in reserve. Only until I could hold my own in a discussion, answer provocative questions, and refute their opinions did either parent find me of much interest. They debated everything from politics to their take on literature and films. Whether a book or an outing, everything had more than one meaning. They favored friends who would share and explore experiences beyond their own and whose curiosity seemed endless. The scenes that unfolded before me were somehow mixed together into a bewitching brew, which more than made up for my mother's singular lack of interest in cooking and my father's complete ineptitude in that area.

Early on, my mother's most enjoyable activity with me was a four-block walk to the public library to help me find books and pick up at least five or six books for herself. When she read to me or talked about books she practiced her professional character analysis skills. How Mike Mulligan *felt* when he couldn't get the steam shovel out of the excavation hole he'd dug was of far more importance than how he got there or what would happen next. How the Little Red Lighthouse contained its anger after the George Washington Bridge was built was of more concern than how the boats would now navigate the river.

My mother was stymied by small talk, which she termed "weather discussions," and seemed impatient when conversations weren't revealing, provocative, and scintillating (her word, which I assumed meant fast-paced, like playing Ping-Pong). We might be in the Museum of Modern Art and hear someone making a comment about how Jackson Pollock was changing the way we see. There was no "Excuse me, I overheard . . ." or "Why do you think . . ." She would turn to the stranger and act as if they were close acquaintances. "You must be kidding," she scoffed, and pointing to me, "My son can paint anything Pollock can."

The snared stranger would smile at me and then explain how looking at Pollock created sensations and feelings she had never experienced with realism. My mother would counter that she had always felt ashamed of never fully appreciating realism, but Pollock was bringing her back to the art scene. Other viewers joined in and soon my mother was anchoring a conversation about the impact of art on everyday life, exchanging phone numbers, and eventually admitting that Pollock had something I didn't.

My father had a more reserved approach, but like my mother he had no facility for small talk or customary beginnings. His curiosity about people elicited hundreds of fascinating stories from friends and strangers. He was forever repeating the opening line from the film *The Naked City*: "There are eight million stories in the naked city and this is just one." He reveled in the knowledge that everyone had a unique story and he sought to know each of the eight million.

I usually had two or three months' notice on the rare occasions my mother prepared for her own dinner parties. On one stormy Saturday my mother was preparing for a party she had planned two months earlier. During those months, she had devoted hours to calling invited guests to announce that the party was off and then calling back to proclaim it was reinstated as long as everyone understood that it would be nothing elaborate. In the final week leading up to the Saturday night splurge of conversation, my mother experimented with different menus for the party. On Monday the fish was overcooked, so she and my father agreed it would not be a good choice. On Tuesday she tried lamb chops, but there was an oven fire and my father suggested something less exciting, although she thought the lamb chops would be a good choice. On Wednesday she tried a stew and told us she had a big surprise for dessert. The stew might have been good, but was served so cold my father thought it might be the special dessert. After we muddled through the stew, my mother brought a large bowl to the table. It was filled with crumbs.

"What's this?" my father asked.

"Taste it. It's really good. And because it didn't stay together I didn't have to bother with icing," she said.

"Florence, what is it?"

"It's chocolate cake. I just couldn't get it to stay together, but we could serve it like this." She took a spoonful to demonstrate. It did taste a bit like chocolate cake, but I missed the icing and was embarrassed that my mother's cake couldn't stand on its own.

"If you serve that, I'm leaving. I'll buy a cake." My father began the combat over the pros and cons of atomized cake. I couldn't wait around for the conclusion and went to my room to work on a model airplane.

By Saturday my mother was frantic. Every pot got used and she must have cooked three different full meals. When she took breaks from cooking she tried on dresses and necklaces and ran up to the third floor to pull my father out of a crawl space, where he was doing some plumbing, to get his opinion. The few times she and I bumped into each other that day she told me in no uncertain terms to stay away from her.

When the doorbell rang, my mother yelled for my father to get it. "I'm not ready. Why are they so early? It's a disaster. Don't they know there's a storm? They should have stayed home."

"Florence, we told everyone to come at 7:00. It's ten after seven. Just put on your smile."

The party was a success. Within minutes my mother was laughing, provoking lively conversations by asking questions that made guests argue, and serving food that everyone liked. Her friends told her the stew was exotic and tasty. She beamed. After wine and crumbs, everyone agreed the dessert was a delightful new idea that only my mother could have baked up herself.

———————

I'm not sure what my parents thought of my friends, but I enjoyed theirs and liked doing things with them. Ray was in his late twenties and was a favorite for all of us. His friends were artists, writers, teachers, and photographers. He was slender, energetic, and filled with the electricity that captivates a child. He moved more like a cat than a man. In 1947, when I was four, he had a party to celebrate his photo essay of Coney Island recently published in *Life* magazine. It included a picture of him in the front car of Coney Island's famous Cyclone roller coaster, facing backward toward the riders, taking pictures of the faces contorted in terror and ecstasy. "Weren't you afraid you'd fall off?" I asked.

Wyn, another photographer, started to talk about technical things. "You should start using your Leica, Ray. That monster Speed Graphic is too bulky. It's good as a weapon, but not for taking candid shots, especially standing backwards on a roller coaster."

Ray handed me his large four-by-five Speed Graphic camera and I tried to lift it to my eye. It was heavy and I couldn't hold it still, but it felt great looking through the little viewfinder.

Meanwhile, Ray answered Wyn: "I know. But I had one chance and I needed the detail for the magazine."

"*Life* magazine! That's so thrilling," my mother said. I placed the camera down and looked at some photographs of Ray's and the magazines with his photos that were lying on a table. Most of the pictures were of women wearing different dresses. "I like your fashion work better," my mother said. "What's your next assignment? Any chance I can get a sample?"

Ray smiled at my mother and flicked his hand, showing it was impossible. "Florence, we've been over this before, you know—"

My mother wouldn't be deterred and interrupted. "At least let me know what the new spring styles will be?"

I listened to the banter, thinking of last summer when we were all at the beach at Coney Island. I had watched the last of Ray, his legs, disappear under the surf as he walked on his hands into the ocean.

Ray moved the party forward and called for drink orders. He poured liquids from colorful bottles, shaking them in metal containers filled with ice. Even though he worked fast he continued telling stories about his next assignment for *Life*. I enjoyed his show, which I thought was produced solely for my pleasure. Everyone stopped talking when Ray held up an empty glass in my direction. "Paul, what're you drinking tonight?" He paused while I shyly basked in the attention. Then with feigned casualness he suggested, "The usual, right?" I nodded and Ray began his dramatic concocting of my "usual"—Coca-Cola, milk, and chocolate syrup. He even shook it in the metal container for mixing adult drinks. I gobbled up the attention and drank my cocktail along with everyone else.

That concoction didn't remain my "usual." I continued to think of Ray and how he made people feel special no matter what their age or how they looked or acted. I was sure Ray was a child disguised in an adult's suit of clothes. I felt it would be fun to grow up to be an adult and photographer like him.

Mike and Leona were some of my parents' other favorites. Mike was a reporter for the *Herald Tribune* and told stories of smuggling himself behind the Iron Curtain and trying not to be caught. I imagined a large curtain somewhere on the other side of the Atlantic, but couldn't understand how it could be made of iron. After dinner, with everyone but me on a third or fourth glass of red wine, my mother shushed for silence. "Let's hear how Mike got behind the curtain," she said. The meal dishes hadn't been cleared and chocolate crumbs seeded most of the table.

"More important, how he got out," Leona said.

Everyone turned to Mike. He winked at me. "Last week I had to act like I was a businessman interested in buying cheap goods. The border guards knew I was lying, but I paid them off." I liked Mike's stories and thought how much fun it must be to pretend to be different people. "I had to crunch myself up in a crate for several hours while the truck took me back to our side of the border," Mike said. The only sound other than the story was from the red wine my father poured into empty glasses. Leona moved closer to Mike as he continued, "It was worth it, even though the paper cut my story."

My mother added to the drama of Mike's account by explaining to everyone that his job was too risky for him to marry Leona. His work sounded dangerous, but I couldn't understand why it would keep him from getting married.

Later that same evening, after dessert, the discussions got tense and my father and others shouted and argued about President Truman and other politicians. I wasn't sure why everyone hated Stalin, especially since he lived so far away. When it was clear that I didn't understand much, Mike stopped telling his stories and brought me into the conversation by explaining how a newspaper got made and what it was like to write.

Joe and his family were often at these gatherings when they were in the country. My father explained that Joe was a diplomat, but I didn't know what one did. I knew it was important because he always wore fine-looking suits. He worked for the State Department, which I didn't understand either. He argued that the Soviets were a bigger threat than most Americans realized and I sensed from the other adult reactions I should be afraid of Stalin too.

Visits to a friend named Vye were a special treat because of her playroom, which she and the other adults called her studio. I had a hard time understanding how an adult could spend her time just painting and wondered if it was because no one allowed her to paint when she was in school. Vye had a big party with lots of her friends, and even though everyone wanted to talk with her she grabbed my hand and took me through her apartment into her studio and told everyone to leave us alone. She showed me one of her paintings and explained how she mixed colors. "This looks easy, but try matching the red in my painting by mixing this red and a small amount of black and a tiny bit of that blue." She squeezed some colors from tubes and handed me a small butter knife and brush to mix the colors. I tried several times and never came close to matching the red. "There are hundreds, maybe even thousands, of reds, and it takes practice," she said.

One night we visited Bob and Celia, who lived next to Carnegie Hall. All their guests argued about the Cold War over the sounds, coming through a window, of someone practicing on a violin. Bob was an artist and his studio was part of his apartment. He had one of the first Polaroid cameras. "I want to try my new camera. It's the latest thing. Gives me a picture in two minutes." No toy could match that experience. He saw my delight and said something strange. "Let others argue about politics. You'll have more enjoy-ment being an artist and you can still talk politics." If I could take pictures all day, being an adult could be more fun than I had imagined.

Walking home or cleaning up after one of these parties I listened to and sometimes joined my parents' reinterpretation of what we had just witnessed. "Leona was quiet because she had had a fight with Mike about his refusal to get married." "Joe was particularly upset because his work at exposing the infiltration of Communists into Great Britain's labor movement was being ignored and he was being moved to a different country he didn't like as much." "Vye told more jokes than usual because she had sold a painting." "Ray was on edge because he was waiting to hear about a photo assignment." "Bob needs time away from people and he likes kids and that's why he took you away to take your picture."

From a child's point of view I saw my parents' lives as a montage of unexpected scenes. The dazzling mélange of my parents' friends—artists, writers, teachers, social workers—made envisaging a future career more perplexing. I aspired to be like all of them. No doubt this added to my sense of uncertainty of who I was or would become. And even after a lifetime of three or four major careers, I continue to feel the certainty of the uncertainty of identifying myself with just one walk of life.

Wyn, a commercial photographer, was the first in an influential line of my heretical mentors. He was married to my mother's sister, Alice, and rented a studio near the Metropolitan Museum of Art. He mostly photographed clothes and women posing in them, which made me think of the unpleasant Macy's return magistrate and schlepping with my mother, but the backdrops he created brightened my imagination. Wyn bought me my first camera, a Kodak Brownie Hawkeye. Sighting through a viewfinder, even on the cheapest of box cameras, stirred my passion. He talked with me about everything that fascinated him. He sought out my nine-year-old advice on the best ways to throw a top for the longest spin or my opinion on which baseball trading cards were the most valuable.

Wyn had only one conversational approach, which seemed entirely suited for my age as well as adults.

Every talk included his desire to be the first man to go to the moon. He studied science and science fiction books on the subject. It was the mid-'50s and few thought it was a practical journey, but not Wyn. He built a set in his studio that simulated the surface of the moon. He fabricated a spacesuit that looked more high-tech than the one eventually used by Neil Armstrong. He took self-portraits decked out in his futuristic spacesuit proudly exploring the moon's surface. Wyn was my first model of an adult transforming imagination and fantasy into reality.

I used my first roll of twelve Hawkeye pictures to photograph street-cleaning trucks filling up with water at the East River. My mother looked disappointed after thumbing through my first shots. "Paul, how could you waste the whole roll on garbage trucks?"

"Mom, they're water trucks."

That weekend Wyn came by. "These are remarkable," he said about my snaps. "Where did you shoot them? I can feel that guy struggling with the valve. You weren't afraid to get close and hold the—"

My mother interrupted, seeming sheepish. "I told him they were a waste of money."

"Florence, you're nuts. These are striking. The photos make you feel as if you know these guys. You have to give Paul space for a darkroom, this week." He turned to me. "Your mother is impossible. She's top-notch at her work and everyone admires her, but don't expect her to know anything about photography . . ." he gave my mother a look of reproach, ". . . or many other things." He nodded at me. "Just don't listen to her."

My mother beamed. "You really think so?" She took a long, joyful sip of her coffee. "Hear that, Paul? I don't need to play the mother role much longer."

Wyn took me to a Brooklyn Dodgers' game when I was ten. "The Dodgers have a class to them that the Yankees never will have," he said, as we entered Ebbets Field.

"What does class mean?" I asked.

"It's the most important thing to have," Wyn responded.

"Is it the way they bat?"

"No." He pointed to the Dodgers who were on the field. "That team knows how to play ball. They're artists, and no one understands the game better than they do."

"But they lose all the time." I wasn't about to abandon my Yankees.

"They're not just losers. Anyone can lose. They love the game so much that they have fun. That's class. Being an artist and having fun. Take your Mickey Mantle; he's neurotic. He can't have fun." Wyn whistled to an ice cream hawker and had two pops passed along the aisle for us.

"What's neurotic?" I asked.

"Look at your mother. She's always in a state, even though everyone thinks she's so sharp. She constantly worries about something bad coming from something good. She's anxious all the time. She's a little . . . no, a good deal neurotic."

"Is neurotic bad, like a disease?" I asked.

"No, no. It can be good too. Makes you see things in unusual ways. A little of it will make you a good photographer." At last, someone was explaining how to construct an identity.

During the seventh-inning stretch, he told me about a party he and my aunt Alice had for a potential client. "At the end of dinner, I pulled out a garbage can and tossed all the dishes into it."

"You mean until you washed them?"

"No! The dishes shattered. You should have been there; it really caught their attention. I told them we never have time to do dishes. That really impressed them."

"But how can you afford that?" I was so enthralled with this outlandish story that I hadn't kept ahead of my melting pop and my hands turned slimy with warm chocolate.

Wyn laughed, but was interrupted by the roar of the crowd. Jackie Robinson had just stolen second base and the fans jumped out of their seats. I had to stand on mine just in time to see Jackie dust off his pants. "See? These fans don't care if the bums lose or not; they come to have fun and see Robinson do what everyone knew he would."

The crowd sat down and Wyn continued. "We had just bought a new set to replace all our cracked and missing dishes. Using the old ones saved us the work of having to wash them. Plus my clients would never forget that dinner." Wyn seemed more daring than my ten-year-old friends.

Wyn hadn't reached thirty when he died. I was eleven. I didn't realize that he knew he would have a short life, having contracted rheumatic fever when he was a child. My mother explained that I wasn't old enough to fully understand his death. She was correct. For years I imagined seeing him on the street and actually ran up to men who looked like him, only to be devastated when they turned into strangers.

Years later I named my son Winton, which was Wyn's given name. After my son was born I learned that Wyn was named after a car, the Winton Six, the first car to cross the United States. I have a photograph of my son, at age two and a half, standing next to the gleaming red Winton Six in the Smithsonian. The photo reminds me of Wyn's dream of going to the moon, just as the Winton brothers dreamed of crossing the country by car before the two coasts were connected by roads. For Wyn, there was no bright line separating fantasy from reality.

I had no time to become bored nor did I ever want to retreat from the adults. When their conversation sounded like a foreign language, I watched how they laughed or moved their bodies to emphasize parts of their stories. Even the silences, when a story-teller paused to light his pipe or pour some wine, held my attention. I was mesmerized by the variety of the life experiences of my parents' friends and found myself fantasizing about trying out different identities for myself when I grew up. My own work later in life, as a documentary filmmaker, looking for stories of how people navigate their particular challenges, must have had its roots in witnessing the layers of conversations of my parents and their friends.

By the time I was seven I sensed my parents found comfort in the world of uncertainties, and inevitably steered toward turbulence. Communism and money were fundamental ideologies, incendiaries for tumult. My father's feverish denouncement of Communism and Soviet totalitarianism, and my mother's tendency to mediate

Photo of the three of us taken by Wyn

between liberal and conservative ideologies, produced tsunamis of family discord. Issues around money produced equally intense, combustible eruptions, spawning a level of resistance and inflexibility that could be terrifying. At times I felt as if some hidden force was stealing my parents from me.

I could only imagine that months if not years of disputes had gone into hammering out the details of who would be responsible for paying particular expenses. As with most treaties and laws, language goes only so far. When the three of us ate out at a restaurant the meal concluded with clashes over categorizing the meal as food or entertainment. If I was lucky I had finished my meal and was no longer in danger of choking from fright as my parents applied their brinkmanship.

In 1949 we moved into our house on Charles Street. Our apartment had no kitchen. It took my father eight months, working nights and weekends, to build one. We were forced to eat out or rely on a hot plate. We washed dishes in the bathroom sink. Most nights we went to Mother Sally's, a local restaurant three stores down from a popular strip club. I usually had fried chicken surrounded with French fries, all held together in an oil-soaked napkin. To add appeal, Sally cradled the dish in a shiny red plastic basket grimy with multiple coats of oil. At the end of the meal the waitress dropped the bill in front of my father. My anxiety level shot toward the redline as the often-repeated battle erupted.

With a purposeful shove my father passed the bill to my mother. He extinguished his cigarette with an exaggerated flourish and reached for his jacket. "Florence, you take this."

My mother checked to make sure we weren't "gypped" a nickel for the second glass of milk that wasn't delivered and then slid the now oil-stained check back in front of my father's face. "Bob, this is your responsibility."

My father slid the bill under my mother's coffee cup, stood up and positioned his fedora. "No, Florence, this is yours. It's food."

My mother faked a laugh. "Ha! Don't be ridiculous. If we eat out, it's entertainment."

My father pointed to an uncleared dessert plate. "Florence, that's food." They never departed from the script. I could recite the words of their dialogue before they were spoken. Was eating out food or entertainment? One might think they were modeling a Talmudic discourse or preparing me for legal education, but at seven I feared that no one would pay the bill and we might be arrested or made to wash dishes.

I learned that as long as I was to be dependent upon my parents, it was necessary to figure out their allocation of financial responsibilities. If I needed money for food it came from my mother. However, if I needed clothes or entertainment, funding came from my father. I eventually learned that my mother covered educational expenses. When I needed money for a book I was never sure whether it was entertainment or education.

———

At nine I was fascinated by electricity, especially knowing that my father was a union electrician, now that his business had failed. Sticking a plug into an outlet made a light bulb turn on or a radio play. Nothing seemed as mysterious or powerful as the force from an electrical outlet. Bragging about my father's work as an electrician seemed natural. Dedicating his days to tangling with electricity seemed as dangerous and exciting as being a lion tamer; and everyone relied on electricity more than being protected against lions. My admiration for my dad's work increased as I grew older and was magnified after I worked one summer as an electrician.

One afternoon my curiosity compelled me to wiggle a butter knife into the slot of an outlet. For several brief milliseconds I held on to the knife while my body shuddered, threatening to split into thousands of pieces. I let go, but the knife remained inserted. I was alive, but feared that my stupidity would reveal itself. The knife looked harmless, but it had to be retrieved for its intended purpose. As much as I feared being found doing something unsafe, nothing could make me touch it.

A few hours later my father entered my room. "Do you want to watch *Action in the Afternoon* with me?" I loved watching this Western with my father, but first the knife. I contrived a surprised expression and pointed. "Look, Dad. There's a butter knife sticking out of the outlet."

My father's face tightened, yet he couldn't hold back a pinch of a smile. "You know that could kill you. You were the path of least resistance for all that current wanting to return to the ground." He went to retrieve his electrical pliers.

I had no idea what he was talking about. My father returned with his heavy electrical pliers, its handles wrapped in black electrical tape. He rescued the knife with the pliers and handed it to me. "Better use is for butter."

He never boasted about his work nor seemed particularly interested in discussing it. I watched him do electrical work while renovating our house on Charles Street and building one on Long Island fifteen years later, when I actually helped. If I wanted time with him I had to offer my assistance as his apprentice. I felt a sense of achievement from the work, even when snaking wires or connecting outlets meant missing a ball game with friends. When I was twelve and wanted to gain his admiration and develop my sense of power, I wired my bedroom to turn lights and the radio off from my bed. I never realized how much working as an electrician disappointed him. He had so many things to talk about, from science to politics, from the challenges in renovating our home to books, that I let slide the complete void in the mention of his work. My mother explained that he had initially wanted to work in radio electronics, which was in its infancy, but a prejudice against Jews barred his entry. Resentment was an emotion I never witnessed from my father, but it was evident that he would rather fix our radios or TV than do electrical work around the house.

Mostly my father kept his work life and personal history to himself. On rare occasions, he would light up and reveal a fragment of experience from his past. These moments made me aware that he had a far different life experience than what I witnessed at home. I wanted to write a story about my father as the most interesting man I knew even though I began to realize that I would never crack open half of his secrets. My sense of connection to him heightened on those rare moments when he would share his stories. Yet with each occurrence, I became increasingly aware of how little I knew about him and thus increasingly confused about my own identity.

As he handed me the released butter knife a new chapter was revealed. "You should've seen our ship. It was the worst freighter in the Atlantic. We spent most of our time bailing with hand pumps and fixing the one electric pump." He broke into a broad smile thinking about his ship.

"But it floated, so it couldn't have been that bad."

"Even the Germans thought it worthless. During the First World War a German U-boat surfaced near us." Until then, I never suspected my father had faced such peril. "Our captain ordered me to man the freighter's only three-inch gun. We saw the German crew laughing at my frantic attempts to uncover the gun and get a shell into the breach. They waved at the captain and me and pointed at our ship in a manner that was clearly mocking. They made it clear our ship wasn't worth a torpedo." I couldn't wait to tell my friends this story.

"Did you ever shoot the gun?"

"Luckily no. If I had, the gun would have blown up in my face. That was one mistake I didn't make, but . . . there were times I wasn't as lucky." His face lost its vibrancy and he picked up some tools and headed for his latest project, replacing old pipes in our house. I was left feeling uneasy about whether or not I wanted to learn about the times his luck ran out.

———————

"It tore me to pieces when Dad had to apply for welfare." We were finishing lunch and my mother had a rare moment to answer my nine-year-old question of why she went into social work. I had assumed that my parents' concern for those struggling to survive grew from their sense of altruism and witnessing hardships others had experienced. An intimate experience with desperation hadn't occurred to me, until this moment. Despite their fears of not making ends meet, we always had food, a vacation trip in the summer, a private school for me, and a double-bill movie on most Friday evenings.

"Dad and I had to go to California for Dad to look for work. We drove in Dad's jalopy until it fell apart in Chicago. We jumped on a trolley and took it to the outskirts of the city and then hitched the rest of the way to California." My mother held out an apple for me, but hesitated before handing it over. I sensed she was distracted and gently freed it from her hand. "It was 1938 and the Depression was pounding millions of families. We had days with no food or money. For weeks Dad spent every day looking for work. There was nothing. I walked two miles every day to a part-time job as a waitress. We couldn't afford a bus. Dad and I walked over four miles to the welfare office. They treated him as if he was a criminal trying to steal money." My mother stubbed her cigarette out in an ashtray, hard enough to make the table rock.

Parents before going to California sometime in mid-1930s

I nibbled my apple closer to the core than usual. My mother must have noticed panic tighten my nine-year-old face. "It's OK now, but back then I feared he had lost his spirit. I didn't see how he could ever recover. It was at that moment I decided to become a social worker. No one deserved to be treated that way. I would treat people better." My parents felt systems and circumstances were the forces that pushed people into dependency, not weak effort. Rather than avoid a person begging for money, my parents offered spare change and stopped for short conversations. I cringed in recalling my mother's flare-up at me while I was trick-or-treating and referred to a homeless person as a "bum." Now it was evident that her harsh scolding derived from personal experience as well as general sympathy. My mother tried soothing my gust of worry with her muscled smile. Once again I was faced with the knowledge that my parents weren't all I thought them to be.

Home was no harbor of tranquility. Whether discussing nuclear disarmament or if a baked potato had been cooked thoroughly, my parents found infinite points for contention. While doing my best to grow up, I found myself rattled by the range of issues that ignited skirmishes between them.

My mother's work pressures left little time for meal preparation. To her they were burdensome interruptions. Assessing the kind of care her clients and caseworkers needed seemed more important than running the house. When baked potatoes were on the menu, whether on a Monday or a Thursday or any workday evening, the back-and-forth exchange was identical.

"Florence, the potato isn't cooked. Take it back and cook it more." My father's accusation was thrown at my mother as if she had committed a felony.

My mother, having shortly arrived home from work, had to do it all, which included checking to see that I was alive and attending to the general responsibilities of the house. Well-cooked dinners were not high on her to-do list, but she was not to be intimidated. "It's cooked. It's fine. See!" She grabbed my father's fork. He flinched as she riveted his attention with her backswing, which brought it hazardously close to his face. On the down stroke she mashed the baked potato with all her force. Under several *gs* of pressure the heavy mahogany dining table rocked, the floor squeaked, and the stubbornly undercooked potato cracked into a few solid blocks. A jackhammer would have been more effective. "See, you can even mash it."

As my father considered the potato chunks on his plate, my mother counterattacked with provocations such as, "Why can't your Ike act like a reasonable man? If they don't stop atomic testing the world is going to blow itself up. Eisenhower was a general. He should know better."

My father's composure unraveled. "Florence, you don't know what you're talking about. I think he's the only sane one who wants to stop testing, but he's fighting for reciprocal actions and verification from the Soviets. Khrushchev was Stalin's boy and they don't value human life. I've been there." Did he mean he came from Russia or something else?

"But our friends see this differently. Tommy and Celia and everyone at work say if we show the world we don't want war—"

Often at this point my father slammed a heavily crusted torn piece of French bread onto the table. "You're talking like a Communist, Florence. If we lose our advantage, Stalin will dictate conditions to the world. We'll end up slaves to that totalitarian regime. You think returning a dress at Macy's is hard?" His face turned red and he spluttered. "The Soviets are barbaric. Our lives would be meaningless if they had their way."

While trying to find a soft spot in my potato, I sided with my father's position on the baking time, but the A-bomb matter was different. I had friends whose parents were leaving the city because of fear of the bomb. I hated the bomb. Thus by ten, I supported banning the bomb. My mediation attempts only expanded their antipathy, and I feared that Communism would precipitate my parents' divorce.

We watched the Andersons in *Father Knows Best*. It was curious that we all agreed that they were an ideal family, but we couldn't pull it off for ourselves. I craved the serenity of the Andersons' home. A well-cooked potato and no mention of Communism might be an ideal way to live. How about a mere sigh to indicate disagreement rather than hollering and provocative threats with forks? At school we were learning about peace movements, but selfishly my priority was for peace at home.

If my father wasn't home by 4:30, one of our more alarming family rituals began. My mother would disappear behind the floor-to-ceiling curtains of the front window to watch the street for my father's return. This unusual act touched off a sense of looming threat to my family's security. "Mom, are you OK?" I knew she wasn't and her fear activated my own doubts about whether he'd come home.

The curtains muffled the anxiety in her voice. "I don't know. I'm worried about Dad. He should be home by now." An hour passed and she remained peering out through the dark window. Moments before her anxiety ignited into a meltdown, she turned to me for reassurance and we assessed all the possible accidents and misfortunes he might have encountered. In her face I could see she wasn't fully thinking of me, but was off in some distant thought or place.

I tried to lure her away from the window. "Why don't we watch TV?"

Her stylish dress was disheveled, her hair wandered out of its bun, and her face lacked its usual dark color. My panic began to eclipse hers and we reversed roles. She tried to comfort me. "If . . . rather, when he gets home, we'll celebrate," she said.

My fears were fueled by my mother not receiving an *I'm a bit late tonight* phone call. On *Father Knows Best*, they used the phone to tell each other of changes in their plans. Why not in my home? Even more than the potato conflict I wondered why my parents continued a tradition that caused such tension. Why couldn't she stay calm through his lateness and why couldn't he simply call? What was offstage in their lives that I was unaware of?

Our roles reversed again as her agitation exceeded mine. I reclaimed responsibility for remaining calm. "Maybe he just has to work late," I said. This was inevitably the explanation, but past experience never became part of the ritual.

My mother jumped on my response. "Paul, you're so smart. Why didn't I think of that?" If I played the adult I might pull my

mother back from her despair and then we could return to hopefulness about my father's return home.

Eventually my father came home. They agreed that the work
emergency made it too difficult to call. My mother's emotions
exploded into tears and hugs all around. The ritual was finally
exhausted. Our family returned to its normal activities, awaiting the
next crisis.

———————

When I was growing up, the three of us referred to an event in
1950 as the iconic exhibit of my mother's tendency toward hysterics.
Our family was spending two weeks in the Catskills on summer
vacation. "Florence," my father said. "Paul and I are going to hike
up the mountain, and take a look around the abandoned hotel."

She seemed content to remain as far away from nature as
possible and close to her books. "How long will you be?" she asked.

"One or two hours," my father replied.

We left my mother in the lobby of a hotel at the base of the
mountain, where she could read and get a cup of coffee while we
trekked up the steep dirt path to the top of Mount Overlook in
Woodstock, New York. It was a cool day with an intense blue sky.
Our purpose was to explore the abandoned Mount Overlook Hotel
and to climb a fire tower to see seven states. My seven-year-old
enthusiasm helped me endure the steep climb. The supplies for
building the hotel had been taken up by donkey or mule and the
guests had to take horse carts and later four-wheel-drive jeeps to
ascend the two and a half miles. The remains of the hotel and the
surrounding vegetation had begun to merge, creating an eerie sense
that we were looking into a past moment of time. Most of the
fixtures were missing, the plaster had washed away, and the floor-
ing was rotten or missing. The adventure of walking through a

grand abandoned building quickened my imagination. Most important, I had my father to myself. He was engrossed in explaining how hard it was to build the hotel and how magnificent it must have been to stay in a room with such a far-reaching view of the Catskill Mountains and valleys. We pretended to be guests checking in where we thought the main lobby once existed.

We spent what must have been over an hour going up the mountain and two hours walking through the hotel and climbing the fire tower where a ranger pointed out the direction of the seven states. I was impressed, but disappointed that I couldn't see the state boundaries. Another hour and fifteen minutes was needed to descend the trail. Our moods sparkled as we exchanged delights in what we saw.

"Paul, you're an expert hiker. You probably did over five miles today." My pride expanded and I picked up my pace.

When we were in sight of the hotel where we had left my mother, I saw two state police cars parked across the front entrance. I followed behind my father, feeling my heart race. We entered the lobby and saw a small crowd of police, hotel employees, and a priest administering to a woman who was the center of attention. As my mother later explained through tears of relief, someone had told her there were bears on the mountain and since we were gone more than an hour, she called the police to come rescue her son and husband. When they explained it was normal to take many hours for the hike, she threatened the police with having our deaths on their conscience. The police called for backup and a priest was sent. My mother, the woman at the center of all the attention, had a visceral distrust of Catholic clergy and yet, as she later related, she liked the priest and tried to convince him to become a rabbi.

My father, shaken by the fuss, seemed embarrassed. Later in the car he vented. "Florence, why can't we go for a hike without having the entire federal government called out?"

"Bob, it was only the state police."

My parents, who had an abundant capacity for irony and mining humor from dramas, retold the Mount Overlook story as a parody of how my mother's hysterics could expand into the need for state troopers and a priest. The humor did not keep me from wondering why my mother, who was so respected as a supervisor at work and competently handled a wide range of challenges at home, could fall apart when my father and I were late by a few hours. Yes, someone told her about bears, but the priest and cops persisted with rational explanations for our lateness. The scene played in my mind over and over again as I grew older.

As many of these sorts of events played out it became disturbingly apparent that I could never survive in the serenity of the Anderson family. Turmoil had become my familiar zone. What might not seem tranquil events, such as disrupting an ordinary elevator ride by torching my father's new fedora, the conclusion of a perfect day's hike with the call for police and a backup priest, or returning dresses purchased at Klein's—all became expected and my normal. As I grew older I began to think that anything that represented the stability of the Anderson family was strange and unsettling.

CHAPTER FIVE

THE LITTLE RED SCHOOL HOUSE sounds like a name chosen to describe the political leanings of the parents, teachers, and even my more precocious classmates. To us, the name was merely an echo of the little red school houses we read about in children's books, and in fact the name's origin was that innocent. "Little Red" prided itself with being the first New York City school to put some of John Dewey's progressive ideas into practice, building curriculums around experiential learning where students were active in their education. Whether studying slavery in America, learning about the culture and needs of peasants in China or India, or celebrating the Supreme Court desegregation decision of 1954, all lessons were accompanied by singing spirituals or folk songs, learning peasant dances, and coming closer together in a belief that we could play a role in righting wrongs.

It was at nine that I began to realize that my father's politics set me off from my schoolmates. One early fall day before the 1952 national election, I came home from a rally for and a speech by Adlai Stevenson in Washington Square Park. I interrupted my father, who was reading the *New York Times*, and my mother, who was reading a social work journal. Seeing a person up close who could become president of the country was thrilling. I wanted to

seem like their adult friends. After I explained how impressed I was
with Stevenson, I added that my friends told me he wanted peace
and Eisenhower would go to war with Russia. My father's face
turned dark red and I sensed his attempt to control his emotions.
My mother interjected only one word along with a stern look at
him: "Bob!" I looked for some sign of what I had done wrong. All I
could think of was that maybe I came back from the park too late,
although my father never had been concerned before.

"Eisenhower had to deal with the Soviets during the war. We
need him. The Soviet Communists will run all over Stevenson." I
had no idea what my father was talking about other than he would
be voting for a general.

My mother relaxed and reassured me. "How nice that you saw a
candidate running for president. He's a smart man and no wonder
you were impressed."

The school drew parents who wanted alternatives to the rote
educational methods they had experienced in public schools. The
horrors of the war had chilled their optimism and they wanted their
children to be able to challenge the thinking of the establishment.
Many believed the Soviets had been far ahead of the United States
in seeing the dangers of fascism and defeating Hitler. They had
lived through the economic disruption of the Depression and come
to see capitalism as corrosive to promoting equality of opportunities, especially for workers and minorities. There was no tolerance
for our national policies that heightened the Cold War.

Some of the teachers were at Little Red because of New York
State's Feinberg Law, which required public school teachers and city
workers to pledge their allegiance to the United States. This denial
of the right to free speech, parts of which dated back to 1917, had
been reinforced during the McCarthy period. It barred anyone from
teaching in public schools who did not take this oath, and many of
the Little Red teachers had refused to do so. This heightened the

sense that at Little Red, we had political views that diverged from the general public's.

Stalin died when I was ten years old, in 1953. Some of my classmates turned to discussions about what this would mean for our lives. I didn't engage in those discussions, most likely out of ignorance of the Communist movement and even more likely because of a conscious and unconscious desire to stay away from any subject that ignited my father's pain and irritation about Communism. I sidestepped labels and presumed we were all on the same side of finding ways to end oppression of any kind.

Communism was a third rail at home. One chilly March day my friends and I were hanging out in the park after school. Everyone was talking about the news of Stalin's death. I wasn't as sophisticated in politics as my friends and didn't know if Stalin was a good guy or a bad one. I came home thinking that my father could straighten me out. "My friends were sad about Stalin's death. They're worried that the revolution will also end and communism will die. Do you think they're right?"

My father was on the floor connecting a newly purchased used stove to the gas line. He gave the stove a harsh shove and unhinged himself to a standing position. "Stalin's a butcher." He stopped, as if some invisible force had struck him. I knew he didn't mean butcher in a common sense, and was a bit frightened by the growing explosion of his words. "Your friends don't know what they're talking about. They get this propaganda from their parents. Their parents were duped." He kicked a large Stillson wrench across the floor, which dented the stove.

I knew I had triggered something awful, but wasn't clear what. I was angry with myself for not knowing much about Stalin, other than he was the leader of the Soviet Union and looked like an ordinary guy with a bushy mustache. I had never heard the word "duped" and assumed it meant something bad. I unwittingly poured oil on a blazing fire. "My friends want peace and they think Communism will be fairer for everyone."

My father picked up the wrench and banged it against the stove for no reason. I tried to bury the conversation I had started. "Sorry, can I help you with the plumbing? Get any tools for you?"

My father placed his messy, pipe-joint-compound-covered hand on my shoulder. "Communism is an illusion. Stalin was evil. I know what I'm talking about. Someday you'll understand." Clearly my father's attitude toward Communism was at the polar opposite to my school environment. I understood Communism as little as I understood electricity and stayed away from both. I was too young to discern differences between Soviet distortion of the philosophy and those who believed in the idealistic values of Socialism and communal economics. My ever-present fear was that discovery of my father's abhorrence of Communism might get me emotionally electrocuted at school. No one ever said or suggested that I would ever be excluded or shamed, but I was still afraid.

If one ignored the shadow of shame over my father's political beliefs and the fact that I wasn't reading, writing, or doing numbers at grade level, Little Red fit many important needs. It gave me the freedom to skirt around formal educational goals and independently explore wider horizons. During a woodworking period I accidentally chiseled through the bottom of a boat I was building. My boat and pride were destined to sink. Leo, our woodworking teacher, calmly waded into my ten-year-old tearing and explained his outlook. "If you want to be good at something you need to make lots of mistakes. That's how you learn. There's nothing you can't fix. And in fixing you'll learn even better skills." He showed me how to mix a concoction of artificial wood. Together we made a mold out of scotch tape, poured the fluid in it, waited a day for it to set, and painted the boat. Only Leo and I ever knew of the mistake.

My pride and the boat floated again and precipitated a life-long pursuit of woodworking and mistake-making in every realm.

Charity Bailey, Little Red's music teacher, played the recorder to settle us down, and also used music to make us laugh, cry, or want to dance. To understand how others lived, she had us move to African and Caribbean rhythms. Charity was music. She carried a box of instruments everywhere she went and invited anyone in her path to select one to play. Within minutes of sweeping into our classroom she had us shaking marimbas, beating Haitian drums, clanging symbols and triangles, playing recorders, and strumming instruments that had weird names and unusual sounds. With just a few suggestions from Charity, we produced music, at least to our ears and her delight.

The parents at Little Red played an important role in our education. There were two Pauls in our class. Paul Epstein was called Eppy and I was called Pitty. Eppy's father, a doctor, took us to a children's hospital ward. Talking with children in iron lungs was scary and made us aware of the battles some kids faced merely to breathe. Working in hospitals with children seemed tempting, but I was afraid of the needles and the smell of antiseptics. Greg's father was a biologist and he took us to his lab to dissect a frog. I would have gladly passed out if I only knew how. Kate was my closest friend. As both of us had grown up in one-child homes, we became as close as brother and sister, until the age of nine when we decided to get married and the class organized a mock wedding for us. At the last minute the wedding was called off by the teacher because of the boys' unwillingness to rehearse, which resulted in too much conflict between the boys and girls. More far-reaching than a cancelled wedding was the fact that Kate's mother was a film editor and took us to watch her edit a film on a Moviola, a big green machine that could play picture and sound backward and forward.

Years later I worked on the same type of Moviola for editing my own films.

I don't think I was ever aware during my time at Little Red that I was a recipient of a progressive education, but I knew it was a place that offered me opportunities to grow up and experiment with a wide range of activities in an effort to discover my particular passions. Making and developing friendships was a fundamental art form in this environment. I had known most everyone in my class of twenty to twenty-five students since I was five. In such a small group we had the time to fall in and out of friendships and to repair them and to watch each other grow up. Other than my effort to keep secret my father's extreme anti-Communism, I felt safe.

Offsetting the safety at school were reminders that we were in the Cold War with Russia. It was in the air, the news, at school, discussions at the diner, and always at home. The execution of Julius and Ethel Rosenberg, parents of small children, was a striking reminder of the nonsensical nature of politics and produced great fear. The overwhelming injustice of this propaganda act was a rare area of political harmony at home. I heard the word "brinkmanship" for the first time when I went to see Adlai Stevenson talk. It sounded like a game of chicken, but with far more devastating results for the world. Coincidentally it gave me a new term to describe the escalating tensions at home. My father was making more provocative threats—such as "I'm leaving for good"—but none materialized into an action. Except once.

One day my father was on top of a four-story scaffold he had built to reshingle the back of the house. The scaffold was made of previously used lumber. Its palette of fading paint colors and the muddled way it was fastened together made it resemble an abstract art sculpture more than a construction platform. It winced and whined in response to every blow of my father's hammer.

My mother pleaded, "Bob, get off the scaffold. You'll kill yourself." I trusted my father's competence, but seeing him occasionally clutch for an open window or the fire escape as the scaffold moaned and wobbled compelled me to adopt my mother's alarm. He had made himself a perch, and no other human in his right mind could get to him.

"Leave me alone. I have to fix the leak." This was the leak that had almost drowned me while I slept in my own bed during a torrential rainstorm. He continued his shingling as the scaffold teetered away from the wall.

Ten minutes later my mother accompanied two police officers into the backyard. "Get my husband down from the scaffold. It's unsafe." The officers assessed the situation and evidenced slight amusement. My mother shook the scaffold to demonstrate its precariousness. My father grabbed for the wall as the oscillations amplified.

"You crazy, lady?" One of the officers pulled my mother's hand off the scaffold. "You'll kill him."

"You must do something. Get up and pull him down." My mother waited for them to do something. My father kept hammering. One officer closed his notebook, wished my father a good day, and retreated, along with his partner.

A few days later my father was still seething over the "scaffold scene." My mother remained furious at the risks he had taken. From what I could understand, my father's position was that his independence had been threatened; my mother's position was fear of abandonment due to his death. I used the rift to gain an ally in my campaign to play ball on a Jewish holiday. My mother tried to prevent this, but we were not observant and thus her prohibition seemed hypocritical. I turned to my father. He told me to ignore my mother and go to the park.

What followed was a battle armed with accusations of each other's human failings. My father ordered me to put on my jacket and we left the house. The door didn't slam as hard as he expected and he opened it again to make sure the house shook when he slammed it. We got into the car and drove downtown. Giving up a parking space highlighted the seriousness of the situation. I was upset and feared I had caused the final separation. "Dad, Dad, where are we going? What are we doing?" I couldn't control my tears.

My father turned to me with a comforting smile. "We're running away from home."

I was terrified. I wasn't even sure what it meant to run away from home. Would I ever see my mother again? What about my room? Where would we live?

My father drove onto the Staten Island Ferry. We climbed up to the deck and watched the downtown skyline recede. He pointed out the Woolworth skyscraper and then the Empire State. "A few years ago I helped wire the mast on top of the Empire State Building." I felt sympathy for my father, imagining him climbing out alone on the tallest spot in New York City. He faced challenges I would never have the courage to match.

Being on the water lessened the tension. When we drove off the ferry onto Staten Island, my father turned the car around and drove back onto the ferry. I was confused. My apprehension reemerged. "Dad, where are we going?"

"Guess we got to get home. It's getting late and we don't want to worry Mom."

When we arrived home my parents readily resumed their normal bickering. We sat down for dinner to an undercooked potato, burnt chicken, and politics.

The turmoil at home was slightly offset by reminders that there were even bigger issues such as the real Cold War between the

Soviets and us. And McCarthy had made everyone edgy, but I reassured myself that the outside world had no impact on us. It wasn't as if the FBI was at our doorstep.

———————

My parents' bizarre behavior added to my lack of confidence: my mother's falling into a "state" when my father seemed in danger or was unexpectedly late, the hole in my father's history, my parents' lack of an anniversary date, a brother who came from an airplane, the physical hazards they invited into our lives, my father's fanatical anti-Communism—all made their roles as parents questionable and bewildering. Even more frustrating was their singular inability to offer prescriptions for how to move my life forward.

Both parents were fully occupied in their lives. My father's strenuous workday ended at four, and he barely had energy to read the *New York Times*, discuss or argue the news at dinner, and work about an hour on the house renovation before going to sleep around nine. My mother returned home around 5:30, threw something together for dinner, and then did writing for work. After we got a TV she would watch Channel 10 while working, which was a combination of the picture from Channel 9 and sound from Channel 11. It seemed not to bother her.

Even on weekends their work occupied most of their time, and if I needed adult connections I would have to attach myself to a friend's father who might take us to play softball or fly our model airplanes. At times my mother would suddenly jump into my life with a special outing or a sit-down conversation, but there was never a discernible pattern to when these interests in my life would occur. The same with my father, who might get interested in some project for school and let me use his workbench and tools in the cellar. If I wanted closer contact it occurred when I helped my father on weekends renovating the house, or on school holidays when I hung out at my mother's work office. There I was well attended to by the social workers she supervised and Ann, the switchboard operator who was the focal point for the entire office and taught me to operate the switchboard and erase Dictaphone cylinders so they could be reused for new recordings of case notes.

Evenings, I occupied myself by learning the craft of building model airplanes, mostly from doing it myself along with some instruction from a salesperson at Polk's hobby store, forty blocks uptown, which I walked to many weekends. Afternoons and weekends I played stoopball in Washington Square Park. This separateness from my parents left me not fully knowing what was expected of me. I learned from them mostly through observation rather than parental advice. I knew their lives seemed interesting, but what about my life? The what and how to grow up seemed elusive.

My father's bountiful curiosity, ability to see things (other than Communism) from unanticipated perspectives, and hunger for knowledge made him seem smart. He relished reading books: history, science, biographies, twentieth-century American literature, and all periods of Russian literature were his favorites. He had no trace of a Russian accent and rarely did I hear him speak the language except when he felt something needed more emphasis. Then he stood erect and recited lines from Pushkin or other Russian poets with passionate inflections, as if I understood the language and the meaning.

I wanted to but couldn't follow my father's example. Schoolwork eluded me. Rather than do homework I spent hours gluing and pinning together model airplanes, covering their wings with dope-soaked paper, and attaching and adjusting their pint-sized gasoline engines and fuel tanks. Rarely could I impress a teacher with my writing, spelling, or command of an academic subject. I ventured into discussions only if the topic included stories. The history of slavery captured my sense of justice as well as drama because of Harriet Tubman. The stories of her shepherding slaves to freedom in Canada were inspiring models of heroism. I doubted I could achieve her level of courage, but what she accomplished in spite of the fact she didn't know how to read or spell made me feel there were pathways around my deficiencies.

My parents were divided about my academic headway, as they were about most everything. My mother encouraged me and claimed that every effort on my part was a major breakthrough and achievement. If I received low grades or poor comments, she gushed praise and emphasized that the classwork was particularly arduous or the teacher exceedingly demanding. My father was a bit more skeptical and suggested that I work harder. At the time, my mother's assessment was preferable, yet I wanted to find ways to assure my father that I was a worthy student.

Once in a while, perhaps three or four times, my father succumbed and offered advice. The anomaly of these occasions made me pay particular attention. But the guidance appeared peculiar when I discussed it with friends who were receiving confident life and career prescriptions from their fathers.

My father usually arrived home from work around four-thirty in the afternoon. His routine was to pour himself a shot of bourbon, relax by turning on WQXR, a classical radio station, and settle into our brown-and-white-striped love seat to read the *New York Times*. One afternoon I decided to impress him with my schoolwork and get some help. With purposeful casualness, I broke into his reading and told him we were discussing Communism in our sixth-grade class. "Mr. Sarlin devoted four weeks to China and explained how Communism would make the peasants better off."

My father folded his paper, a sign that he was fully engaged in our conversation. He probed my teacher's analysis. "Does that make sense to you?" he asked.

"Yes."

My father looked into my eyes. It didn't make much sense to me, but I aspired for his recognition of my worth as a student. He remained silent. He placed his reading glasses on the shelf next to his chair and switched off the lamp. I studied his movements looking for signs of his reaction. He straightened up and shifted to the edge of the love seat. His attention was more than I had anticipated.

"Don't trust your teachers." My father looked at me without switching on the light or picking up the newspaper. I had no response. A triumphant portion of a Tchaikovsky symphony squeaking through our tinny radio filled the silence. Why would my parents stretch their income to send me to Little Red School House, a private school, and advise that I shouldn't trust my teachers? My father did nothing to further define his baffling advice. He switched on the lamp and resumed reading the *New York Times*.

Don't trust your teachers reverberated in me like a stuck record echoing the same five notes over and over again. What was received as irony in my eleven-year-old mind, *don't trust your teachers* evolved as a touchstone for my wariness of authority in later life.

———

One evening, I heard something different in my parents' argument. It had none of the familiar themes of money, politics, or food preparation. My father's tone was locked in certainty. "They kill people in hospitals."

"You're spitting up blood. Bob, you're bleeding inside. You must have the operation." My mother had passed her redline of hysteria and matched my father's firmness with an overdose of insistence. "You'll die if you don't do it."

In the next room, I was drenched in fear. I wanted desperately to believe this was just a normal skirmish, but talk of blood and dying disabled me. I needed comfort and yet my most cherished rescuers were otherwise absorbed. The distinctly different tones in their voices heightened my sense of foreboding. I avoided their path or contact until a half hour later when we all sat down for a silent dinner. No dramatic spinning of the lazy Susan, no forced mashing of undercooked potatoes, and not even talk about the demagogue McCarthy or duped Communists. I kept my own movements to a minimum and ate very little. I had learned to not trespass into my parents' citadel of secret lives. This was yet another secret being played out in front of me.

Three weeks later my mother arrived home after I had come home from school and with mannered calm explained that my father would be in the hospital for a week or more. She held my hand and assured me there was nothing to worry about. The control of her words suggested otherwise. Every evening, she would visit him at the hospital while I was at home with either my grandmother or my uncle. After five days, I was told my father had an operation and he would be home in a week and he would love to hear my voice on the telephone, although he wouldn't be able to talk to me. I was scared and made various inventories of things I missed most about him: his bountiful energy and sense of childish humor, playing chess, feeling good about helping him with renovating the house, his offbeat answers to my questions, his curiosity about everything, the joy of going to the movies with him and hearing his take on what he would have done in such situations, singing cowboy songs together, and his loving hugs.

When he returned home his voice had become more gravelly and occasionally I couldn't understand a word. He told me he would miss most not being able to sing cowboy songs together. Apparently he had a polyp on a vocal cord. No one ever dared talk cancer in those days and we slowly resumed our lives as if my father had just had a bad cold, although I never remembered him ever being sick for a day.

A year or so later I heard him talk about his operation with some friends around the dinner table. "They operated for nine hours. I think I almost died. You know, in between talking about what they're doing, they talk about baseball. Strange, I didn't feel much but could hear sometimes. At one point the surgeon asked someone if this guy is still alive." My dad said this with a sense of sharing just another interesting experience, without any drama about how close he came to dying.

"You would have if you hadn't . . . You were so stubborn. Dr. Finkelstein saved your life." My mother turned pale. Their friends were speechless and somber.

"I think your Dr. Finkelstein was more worried about the Yankees than me." He laughed and poured himself more of his cheap Beaujolais.

CHAPTER SIX

WHEN I WAS TEN I was keenly aware that many citizens were fearful of "commies." This panic seeped into my daily consciousness, as it did for most citizens. New York City installed yellow FALLOUT SHELTER signs on buildings to guide people to "safe" hiding places. School children learned to scrunch under their wooden desks to practice protecting themselves from nuclear bombs, but not at Little Red. They made a policy decision to opt out of preparing us for a nuclear annihilation. I felt cheated of the fun as well as from the security of knowing just what to do in a nuclear attack. On the other hand, even at ten I thought it was odd that anything could save us from a nuclear bomb dropped on Times Square.

I couldn't decide whether to be afraid or brave. The impending threat of nuclear war, dramatized in newsreels showing A-bomb tests, made the topic a weekly conversation in school and at home. I was aware of the growing urgency and skepticism about the way our government was protecting us, but remained ignorant of the issues. Television changed that.

One afternoon in 1953, my father brought home our first television set. It was really half a television set since it had no chassis. All the tubes and wires were exposed and I was told not to go near the side or back of the set. It had no knobs and we were to change channels by squeezing pliers over the channel shaft and twisting. My father built a TV cabinet, probably to protect my mother and me from electrocution and to camouflage the electronic monstrosity. We devoted part of our dinners to watching the news and then turned off the TV to argue about what we had just seen and heard. One of the cabinet's design flaws was that the heavy door that hid it hinged up instead of to the side. Having no catch was a critical defect. If you didn't hold the door at the same time you were switching channels with the pliers, the shudder from the channel shaft would make the cabinet vibrate, causing the door to drop down and wallop you on the head. The combination of the terror of electrocution and fear of being knocked unconscious triggered our hesitancy before determining whether to watch the ever-present test patterns and early TV shows.

The McCarthy hearings in April of 1954 changed my interest in television. At school I began to hear his name from friends and teachers. Was he a baseball player? Maybe he played for a team outside of New York? I was beginning to get a sense that he wasn't such a great guy. At school, I pretended to know who he was, which deepened my shame. An opportunity to discover who he really was without the humiliation of revealing my ignorance came when a friend told me his show was to be broadcast on TV. I raced home after school, turned on the set, and waited for it to warm up. The cloudy gray images of the smoke-filled hearing room appeared fuzzy, with little contrast. The lack of visual clarity added to my confusion about what was happening. Harsh authoritarian voices crackled with repetitive questioning and bellicose finger pointing.

Eventually I came to understand that McCarthy was a senator and not a baseball player. On TV, McCarthy seemed pathetic, dull, and dreary. I was sure he was going to have a heart attack the way he bellowed and scolded about Communists taking over the world and lurking in every corner of our lives. Many of my friends told me they thought their parents were Communists and that we had to help the Soviet Union and China demonstrate the benefits of Communism. My parents also had friends who supported Communism and were appalled at what they termed "McCarthyism." All these Communists seemed as normal and likable as anyone else. Maybe they talked more and joked more than other adults, but nothing to be fearful of. Why then was McCarthy claiming they were evil enemies? I asked my father if he could explain McCarthy and the hearings.

He told me to sit down. "Communism is evil. It deceives people into believing that a government can take care of them. Instead the system enslaves workers." Shadows emerged on my father's face. He hissed, "McCarthy is the worst kind of demagogue. The worst. Every day he converts more people to Communism than Stalin ever duped." In an effort to turn his lamp off, he knocked into the shade, and the lamp crashed to the floor.

My tepid inquiry was awakening my father's rage. I stopped and switched the topic to Allie Reynolds, our favorite Yankee pitcher.

Author at right, amidst political discussion

My parents continued shattering my yearning for normalcy in unpredictable ways. The first FBI visit to our home, in 1954, was, from my eleven-year-old perspective, a normal pattern of the bewildering events in the Pitcoff family. My mother's explanation that *they just happened to be in the neighborhood* was an effort to sustain a sense that we were an average family. My father wasn't led off in handcuffs nor did the agents draw their guns, but neverthe- less this "visit" and the next one two years later were disturbing evidence that much was being covered up by my parents. As I grew older my view of these visits most likely migrated to the denial section of my mind. With time the echo of my mother's nonsensical explanation began to emerge as a warning to stay away from my parents' clandestine life. I was left wondering if the visits were encouraged by my father or were forced upon him.

My eleven-year-old classmates discussed McCarthy with a sophistication that escaped me. I pretended to mourn Adlai Stevenson's loss to Dwight Eisenhower, but feared banishment from my friends if I slipped and disclosed that my father "liked Ike." At home I tried again. "What's wrong with being a Communist?" After all, my father was a Russian and I assumed that Communists came from there. And my mother told me he had been a union organizer, and I now knew that Communists were for the workers.

"They aren't bad people, just *duped*," my father fumed. I wasn't sure if that was a fancy word for dopes, but he spewed the word with such force that I sensed it was worse. What would I do when someone asked me about his political beliefs? Why couldn't I have a normal communist father instead of a Republican one?

My friends at school seemed to be making definitive plans for their future. My friend Eppy was on a path to follow his father and become a doctor; Kathy, the born organizer in the class, was des- tined to be a lawyer; Ethan, my best friend, studied hard to do something in science or math. All my friends had strong tastes for what they liked and disliked and all seemed to favor socialism if not communism. For me, each day was like spinning a board game dial, never knowing what I would pursue from day to day, let alone for my life. I didn't want politics to be the defining characteristic, yet I was surrounded by it, and the ever-present threat of nuclear war had descended into our daily conversations at school and home. I heard the term "blacklisted," but never understood its meaning until a classmate told me some of our teachers had been blacklisted, resulting in the loss of their jobs in public schools. They made it sound like a badge of courage. At school my friends dared me to jump into the world of politics, but I could only manage dipping in a toe, for fear of demonstrating my political ignorance and disgracing myself if my father's beliefs were disclosed.

This reluctance was tested when events pressed me into my first political action at eleven years old. Up until the sixth grade there were no restrictions on girls and boys playing sports together. Kathy and other girls played softball with the boys and everyone accepted that she was better at it than most of the boys. Lou, our playground teacher, decided we could begin playing touch football at the neighborhood playground. The concrete field was barren and pockmarked with murky puddles of water. As we walked the half block from school to the playing area, we chose up sides for our touch football game, including Kathy.

I struggled to appreciate the joy of touch football. At the start of each play the ball was tossed to Lou. Everyone ran toward the far fence, our goal, trying to get free for a pass. Lou threw a pass to whoever was free or to whoever hadn't been in a play for a long time. The snap of his pass caused the entire defense to descend on the intended receiver to deflect the football or to wallop him or her as hard as possible. I prayed that no pass would be thrown my way. My strategy was to entangle myself with a defender, making it plain that I wasn't free for a pass. If I failed and was unlucky enough to be clear, Lou would blaze a bullet pass at me before I could retreat. On such occasions I froze with fear until the football bounced off my chest, causing me to stagger or fall backward. I knew I would live, but instinctively I inspected myself for spurting blood and cracked ribs. My physical wounds lasted only minutes, but my humiliation endured.

The third week of touch football season, Lou told us that Kathy couldn't play. The rumor was that it had something to do with the differences between girls' and boys' bodies. The boys and even the girls, who were smart enough not to play this barbaric game, declared their outrage. No one had heard of feminism, but we believed that girls should be treated equally, and if they wanted to be pummeled in football they should be allowed that thrill! The school resisted our attempt to make all activities, including sports, coed. We were so enraged that I suspect we saw none of the obvious irony that this policy was made within a context of supporting equal rights as a principal political philosophy of the school.

The unfairness of prohibiting one of our best athletes to play just because she was a girl festered until someone suggested we protest. None of us would play touch football until Kathy could join our game. Instead we'd go to the dreary urban concrete playground and stand around with nothing to do except chant, "Keep girls in the game." Secretly I enjoyed the protest more than playing touch football.

During breaks in our chanting, Steve got all fired up. "Communists treat women equally with men. My father was . . . well, he knew someone who was a member and they said that in the Soviet Union they let women do the same jobs as men." My father felt women worked harder than men, admired my grandmother for running a store, and enjoyed arguing fully with women as much as men, a sign of respect. He admired my mother's friends who worked at different jobs. So why was he not a communist?

"Yeah, having a general for president shows the world we're *colonialists*," Judy added. From her tone, I concluded that colonialists were bad. I pulled my hat down and tried to cover my ears. Did they know my father's vote got Ike elected? Ike looked like a nice old man, much friendlier than Stalin. Why wasn't he a good president? He didn't seem threatening. Didn't he end the Korean War?

"My parents say FBI agents or people who snitch for them are watching everyone," Arthur said.

"You know, I even heard they may be watching us at school. To get information about our parents," Michael added.

"Why?" I asked, trying to move the conversation to ordinary things. "Do they think any of our parents are bank robbers?" The flow of conversation stopped. One of the boys threw the idle football hard at my stomach. For a change, and a thrill, I caught it.

"You kidding? They look for commies, not bank robbers. It's a good thing your parents aren't commies," Arthur teased.

How did they know my father wasn't a commie? I felt electric pulses pinging through my spine. Did their knowledge doom my future with my class friends?

"Paul's mother is a social worker. That's the same thing. She's probably a commie and he just doesn't know it. My mother told me it's best we don't know anything, then we can't get anyone in trouble," Sarah explained. I didn't understand where this discussion was going and felt uncomfortable with not knowing what my friends knew. I pulled back from the group and lobbed the football to Ethan and ran away from the conversation to get a pass. If I wasn't a communist, what was I?

After we got through the baked potato conversation one evening, my mother explained that she and Celia were going to a lecture celebrating and explaining the Supreme Court's *Brown v. Board of Education* desegregation decision. Crumbs splattered everywhere as my father ripped off a large portion from the long loaf of French bread. "Florence, you of all people should know you can't force people just by laws to do what they don't want to do. If you force it, you make it worse. You have to show them better ways. People have to be secure to change."

My mother brushed the crumbs back toward my father, some landing on his lap. "Bob, you of all people should know how unfair this is. Everyone deserves equal education. I can't imagine what it's like to live in the South under those conditions."

My father swiped the remaining crumbs back toward my mother. I pulled my legs to the side of my chair in preparation to flee when the argument escalated beyond my emotional tolerance. "This is the way the Soviets recruit. They get the Communists to hold rallies and lectures, and good people get duped by their propaganda. I'm not saying you or Celia will be swayed or even that this lecture is all propaganda, but—"

"You're being absurd." My mother's volume rose. Rollie, our dog, had heard this fight a hundred times. He stretched on his four legs, yawned, and curled back in his favorite corner of the dining room. "You think I can be duped?" My mother concluded with a furious spin of the lazy Susan causing the butter to fall onto my plate and salt granules to highlight our dark mahogany table.

My father slammed down his bread and picked up his *New York Times*. Rarely were there more than fifteen seconds of silence at dinner, but no one talked for the remaining five minutes of the meal. I longed for lifting my burden of concealing my father's political beliefs from my friends.

After dinner my father went to work on running a new electric line to the fourth floor and I was left in tears. My primitive abhorrence of Communism was not its meaning, which I didn't understand, but rather my father's reaction to it. If the word was mentioned in his presence or even a suspected connection to the term whiffed into my father's mind, his blood vessels expanded, his face turned red, his body tensed, and his movements went from gentle to robotic. He became unhinged and the father I adored left his body.

"Did something happen to you in school today?" My mother tried comforting me.

"How come Dad doesn't belong to the Communist Party or do anything to help Negroes?" From the corner, Rollie must have sensed my mother's mounting irritation and scooted under the table.

"That's not true," she bristled. "Did you know Dad worked in a West Virginia coal mine?" New revelations didn't seem to have the same surprise anymore. My mother was steamed, just like when I used the word "bum." She continued, "On his first day at the mine he became friendly with a Negro man who had been hired for a cleaning job. Dad offered to bunk with him since they were both new. Angry men approached them with a noose and told Dad he would be lynched along with his new pal if they shared the same cabin." Rollie emerged from under the table, tail wagging as my mother's irritation subsided while recalling the story.

"What did he do?"

"They were lynching Negroes, and sometimes even white friends of Negroes. Dad told the men to go to hell and if they touched his friend they would have to deal with him. You know how Dad gets when he's maddened."

I did know. When it came to rage about Communists my father went from zero to sixty in two seconds. "But how come they didn't lynch his friend?" I asked.

"The men knew there was no way Dad would give up bunking with his new friend and they also were afraid of Dad's fury. So they left them alone."

Shame around my father's politics was converted to pride at learning of his courage. Yet his malignant anti-Communism puzzled me, since he projected values that weren't that much different from what I heard from Communists I knew about.

One day my father and I passed Jackie Robinson on the street. They made eye contact, but my father let him pass by with just a nod. "Paul, did you see his face, the pain in it? He's the best second baseman ever, but struggles every day of his life."

"But we cheer him, even us Yankee fans." I was bewildered by why such a famous person could have the pain my father detected.

"You probably don't remember this, but there was a guy who walked into the Automat and was attacked just because he was a Negro," he said.

He was wrong. I never forgot that horrifying incident. It was the first time I saw adults punch a man. My father took me to a Horn and Hardart cafeteria in midtown for lunch when I was five. I fancied the automatic dispensers with their white porcelain knobs. I hunted for a sandwich behind the glass doors, shoved in a few nickels, and turned the knob to lift the small window door to get the tuna fish sandwich I liked. The action and sounds of so many people dropping their nickels into the dispensers created a sense that we were in an amusement park.

"Break it up! Break it up!" I heard men yelling.

"Fight!" another man hollered. Tables scraped against the floor like fingernails on a blackboard. Glasses shattered. People leaned around each other and poked their heads out to see what was happening. "Break it up!" Two tables were upset and chairs had been shoved away to clear an area. Two men in suits were punching and shoving a third man who was wearing a tie and white shirt. My father pulled me away as one of "the suits" punched the "white shirt" in the nose and he stumbled toward our table. My father and another man pulled the fighters apart. The man who had been punched scared me because he was holding blood-soaked napkins against his nose. He tried to pick up his sandwich from the floor as other men told him to leave. "Best not to have coloreds at lunch-time," somebody jeered.

My father handed fresh napkins to the bleeding man and pulled back a third chair from our table. He said, "Finish your lunch with us." The man seemed hesitant, but my father took his cellophane-wrapped sandwich and placed it on our table. "Forget them." He gave me a nickel and asked me to get coffee for the man. I jumped up, my mind on the ornate wall dispenser that spurted out just the right amount of coffee after you dropped a nickel in a slot.

When I returned to the table the man had stopped bleeding. He thanked my father and me for the coffee, but then continued to eat in silence. After several minutes my father asked if he had heard about the Dodgers' latest win. The bleeding man smiled and talked about Pee Wee Reese for a while. My panic eased with the talk of Pee Wee, who played shortstop for the Dodgers, but in my head I heard the ominous echo of the angry men yelling about coloreds. I tried to avoid looking at the darkly soiled napkins on the floor. I had fallen through the cracks into an adult horror story and wanted fresh air.

Sure, I remembered the experience even though I had only been five. I had been transfixed seeing that man's expression, exhibiting no more life than the hollow falseness of an undressed store mannequin. Jackie Robinson was no longer in sight. My father seemed pleased that I remembered the incident at the Automat. "Mr. Robinson is a brave man. He's a hero."

"But someone said he's a Communist," I ventured.

My father laughed out loud. "Who knows or cares if he can steal home and beat out bunts? He's a man, a baseball player, and can't be bullied. He's doing more than any of those demagogues in Washington." Maybe if Communists stuck to baseball my father wouldn't get so upset.

———————————

"Do we have anyone in our family who was blacklisted?" I asked my mother. It was a plea to help me fit in at school and an attempt to understand what the label meant.

"Howard," my mother said. She took two long puffs on her Pall Mall and mashed it into an empty tuna can. Howard was my mother's youngest brother and he was in that first photograph on the roof of my grandmother's tenement. Growing up, I loved being dumped with Howard almost as much as with my grandmother. Luckily my parents couldn't afford babysitters and Howard, back from the war in Europe, seemed genuinely happy to help my parents the few times they went out on their own. The first half hour with Howard was a ritual of funny faces, throwing me up in the air, and testing my mental powers with simple arithmetic problems. When Howard's routine was completed he talked to me as if I was a contemporary, without the slightest hint of child talk. Even though I was four or five he took me to movies on Forty-Second Street when the theatres were grand and the movies first-run. Taking me home way beyond my bedtime, Howard replayed the movie's story and we traded our emotional reactions to different parts of the plot.

During the war Howard served in Europe. Ninety percent of the men he trained with were killed. The war was over before he was shipped to the Pacific. Once back in the United States, he entered the University of Iowa to study physics under the GI Bill. His curiosity led him to specialize in nuclear physics. At the time, the only jobs in that field were working for the government, and his first job was to sample and measure radiation during the atomic bomb testing in Nevada. "You know how casual Howard is about everything?" my mother continued. Once, Howard and I headed for his car parked on Charles Street. He had stayed over while my mother was away at a conference and offered to drive me to school.

I relished having more time with my favorite uncle. When we reached his car, he opened the driver's-side door and we were consumed with the odor of stale alcohol. I jumped backwards when I sensed movement in the back seat. Howard reached in and gently shook the shoulder of a man sleeping in his car. "Sir, sir, you have to wake up now. I need the car." Before I could bolt Howard turned to me. "He probably had nowhere else to sleep. Lucky for him I forgot to lock the car."

Howard believed a car should take care of itself. The shifting arm on the steering column of his old Dodge was broken and rather than fix it, he handed it to his wife, Ann, after he released the clutch to shift into the highest gear. One particular day, Howard was driving Ann, my mother, and me across the George Washington Bridge. He struggled with the steering wheel, which finally came off its post. He stopped the car in the middle of the bridge, blocking two lanes of traffic, and handed the steering wheel to Ann while he assessed his predicament.

My mother yelled, "Your car is unsafe." She said this loud enough for the residents on both sides of the Hudson to hear. She tried to open the door for us to get out onto the roadway of the bridge, but a motorcycle cop blocked her exit. "Lady, you can't just stop and go for a walk on the bridge." He turned to Howard. "You gotta get this heap out of here."

Horns blared and traffic had come to a halt. Howard had no intention of upsetting the cop any further. He retrieved the steering wheel from his wife and handed it to the police officer. "Here, you can drive the car off the bridge for me so we can get traffic moving."

The cop noticed me in the back seat and took off his sunglasses. "Sonny, this is a very bad lesson for you, very bad. Hope when you grow up you'll check your vehicle before driving." He was tough-looking and I assumed he would take us to jail. Then I detected a trickle of a smile coming across his face. "Hey sonny, don't worry."

The cop got Howard out of the car and together they pushed. The cop kicked the front tire to steer the car to the side of the bridge and told us to wait while he radioed for a tow truck.

When Howard's work in Nevada was done the Army had him return to New Jersey. Rather than wait for a lengthy military transport, my uncle decided to pack the radiation measurements, bureaucratically labeled "secret documents," in his personal trunk so they could be available immediately for analysis when he returned to his New Jersey military facility. With the McCarthy hysteria bleeding into daily life and now focused on the Army, this unauthorized transport of secrets was reported, and Howard was formally accused of being a security risk and a Communist. A comprehensive army investigation uncovered the fact that when Howard was nine years old he had a two-week stint as a paperboy selling *The Daily Worker*, a Communist newspaper. A military hearing was convened. Howard's commander came to his defense, but this was insufficient to resist the fears cultivated by McCarthy. Howard lost his job and was blacklisted from working for the government. He would never be able to pursue the career he loved and trained for because of the McCarthy witch hunts.

Learning how the government had crushed Howard's passion for nuclear physics scared me. My father was on Howard's side and abhorred McCarthy. A father who hated Communism and McCarthy at the same time confused me. How could anyone's identity have such inconsistency?

At school, I continued working on my own identity. Despite my father's rage about Communism I was more than adapting to the strong left-wing environment of Little Red. I shared the values of equality and peace, although I felt prickly with the "ism" stuff. Getting to and from school was a different matter. That environment was far more threatening. I was never knifed or shot, but street gangs threatened me with switchblades, and incidents of shootings with zip guns in my neighborhood were reported. *West Side Story* was a reality on many of the neighborhood streets, but without the music. I couldn't fight or run fast enough. My prime defense was plotting circuitous routes to my destinations, avoiding the Charles Street Gang, which held territory on part of my block and the next, the Thompson Street Gang, and even the Carmine Street Gang, one block from school.

If I miscalculated and found myself ambushed, I spewed illogical and confusing rationales for why beating me up would detract from the gang's macho prestige. This honing of my argumentative defensive skills had only sporadic effectiveness. The gangs somehow suspected I was a loyal Little Red commie and anti-American, cause enough for punching me into standard patriotic allegiances as well as liberating any material possession that represented my flirting with capitalism. These neighborhood toughs never realized that their form of re-education strengthened my sense that Little Red was where I fit in, despite my tension over being "outed" if my father's reactionary political beliefs were discovered. The alternative of going to school with the neighborhood street kids seemed too alarming to consider.

However, offstage, my parents were plotting a dramatically different plan, one that would jolt if not derail the progress of my personality formation. While I was mulling over the meaning of the FBI visits, my parents decided to transfer me to a public school, rather than send me to the junior and senior high school that continued Little Red's methods, Elizabeth Irwin (usually known as E.I.). I was halfway through the final year at Little Red when my parents informed me of their decision. My father explained that public school would expose me to a more egalitarian world while my mother sprinkled guilt related to the financial strain on our family. With my mother framing the FBI visits as nothing to be concerned with, it never occurred to me that there might be a connection with the decision to extract me for Little Red.

My immediate and primary issue was safety. The only "safe" public school for an overprotected private school student was Public School 3, an honors junior high school where students did three grade years of work in two and then entered high school in their sophomore year. But one had to pass an entrance test. At Little Red, I easily slid by without aptitude for regular schoolwork. There were few if any tests. If we had a spelling bee, no one wanted me on their team because I couldn't spell or, for that matter, read at any level consistent with my classmates. I liked math, but my calculations were sloppy. My report cards were filled with superlatives about my woodworking skills and *getting along with others*, peppered with gentle reminders that there was room to improve my academic talents.

My entrance exam for PS 3 was a notable failure. I had never seen a multiple-choice question and couldn't understand how there could be merely one correct answer for any question. My mind froze through the vocabulary, reading, and even math units. I had yet to hear of Kafka, but I was in his world. The final section did me in. I was confronted for the first time with adages or metaphors. Each word had meaning but together they were a foreign language. Never having seen a black kettle, I didn't get why a pot would call it black. Why would anyone, including a bird, get up early to eat a worm?

My parents faced a dilemma. They could send me to a regular public junior high, but even they feared for my physical survival. The other option was to keep me enrolled in the *expensive, Communist* Elizabeth Irwin. Fortunately the three of us agreed that my life was worth saving, but my confidence about ever entering the unprotected world beyond the Little Red/Elizabeth Irwin setting crumbled. My reprieve was issued with a firm warning that it was limited to two years and then I would leave E.I., no matter what.

"It will be fine, you'll go to Stuyvesant." This proposition verified my mother's state of denial. Stuyvesant was a competitive public high school that was safer than most other public city high schools. But it too required an entrance exam and I had just provided incontrovertible evidence that I was not qualified for passing such exams.

Meanwhile, to prepare me for the harsher turf of public high school, whether Stuyvesant or the local school, my parents jumped on the opportunity to sign me up for the Boy Scouts, at the rank of Tenderfoot. This made little sense since the troop consisted mostly of boys from E.I.

Before our troop was officially certified our fathers had a contentious meeting. Most of the E.I. fathers believed the Boy Scout uniforms represented fascism while others, including my father, felt they were just uniforms. They crafted a settlement that allowed us to be Boy Scouts or fascists from the waist up, by wearing the official uniform, but to be proletariat kids from the waist down, by wearing ordinary dungarees. This central policy group added a final clause that prohibited the official Boy Scout scarf. Each patrol would purchase fabric and sew distinctive scarves. If King Solomon had only chaired our fathers' meeting, we could have avoided the fate that followed.

The scoutmaster was a young teacher, and for reasons I didn't understand, selected me as one of the patrol leaders. I balked at this momentous responsibility that required me to design our patrol scarves, become skilled in igniting campfires through excessive rubbing of sticks, and assign responsibility for bringing food for our first camping adventure.

On a beautiful spring morning, after a night of torrential rain, my father walked with me to the IRT subway station to meet up with the fourteen other boys in our troop. We were divided into two patrols. We wore our freshly washed and ironed official Boy Scout shirts and our own dungarees. Our patrol scarves were a patchwork quilt of fabrics with bold colors, tacky illustrations of license plates, cowboys, and cartoon figures that gave our troop a renegade look. Seeing our scarves in sunlight made a few of the Scouts reconsider our sense of fashion and one or two were wise enough to lose their scarves on the subway.

It took us over two hours by subway and bus before we paraded into Ten Mile River, the official Boy Scout camping grounds in New Jersey. The bright sun illuminated our compromise uniforms. The breeze showed off the loud multiple colors of our scarves. Other troops were busy doing Boy Scout things, such as sharpening large sheath knives on boulders, testing knot-making abilities by tying smaller Scouts to trees, and mostly playing mumblety-peg, a game popular in the 1950s, especially amongst the juvenile delinquents in the city. The game was simple. A player threw a switchblade or long jackknife as close as possible to his own foot. The bravest player who successfully spun his knife into the dirt nearest to his own foot was the winner. The evident danger was offset by the fact that if one impaled his own foot he was automatically recognized as absolute winner.

My terror over whether I would be prodded into joining this sport was overshadowed when the warier Scouts detected our dissident uniforms. "Where're your pants?" "Look at the lost Cub Scouts." "Hey, they're afraid to wear their skirts." "This is going to be big fun." Then a few of the mumblety-peg players began throwing switchblades at our feet. Mike and Bob were shoved into the mud.

"Get yourself the right uniform," one envious Boy Scout said, as he held up Bob's mud-splattered scarf.

"Hey, are you making fun of us?" another veteran Scout said, while he grabbed the scarf and put it over his head and pretended to be a girl. "Hey, these guys are from Greenwich Village. Thought the Boy Scouts didn't allow fairies."

Our missing official pants mattered. Secretly, I no longer wanted anything connected with uniforms. But there was no time to contemplate my look. Seeing fright in our eyes, our scoutmaster moved us to the outer perimeter of the campgrounds and diverted our attention to practicing proper axe handling. He emphasized safety, a concept rarely given a second thought in my own home. First, we made sure no one was in the range of our swing and then he showed us how to place our feet to prevent hacking off our ankles. I was given first try, and had the satisfaction of hitting the log and seeing yellow pine chunks shoot into the air.

Bob was given the next chance. After he took a couple of swings with satisfaction—whack—we heard something smack into a pine tree, ricochet, and quickly decelerate as it landed, blunt edge first on Phil's foot. The axe head had bolted loose from its handle with Bob's last swing. Phil picked up the axe head and Bob turned the handle in his hand to figure out what had happened. We were dazed by our near-death experience. Our scoutmaster showed no signs of concern and smiled when he took the axe handle from Phil and told us that this reminded him, and should help us remember, that we must inspect the tightness of the axe head before we chop. It seemed that the Boy Scouts followed my father's theory about experiential learning.

If our patrol's survival depended upon our ability to start a fire with a flint and steel or rub sticks together, we would perish. So I had broken several Boy Scout codes and secretly cached multiple books of matches, which we used to start our fire. The other patrol was impressed with how quickly we got our fire going and our scoutmaster suggested this was due to my superior leadership skills. It had not yet been revealed that under my management, every member of our patrol had brought bacon rather than the full assortment of menu items we had carefully allocated as each patrol member's responsibility. The only one who followed instructions, unfortunately or not, was responsible for just dessert and filled his knapsack with Oreos.

Before we mastered how to cook the bacon on a wood fire, our only food for dinner, someone knocked over the pan, drenching my hand in hot greasy fat. I was in excruciating pain. When I quit cursing and dried my eyes, our scoutmaster observed that this was an opportunity to practice first aid. Everyone took out their manuals and my patrol members took turns dousing my wound with butter and bandaging and unbandaging my hand.

Few of us slept that night. For six months we had practiced outdoor camping tasks in the warm, comfortable setting of the basement floor of our synagogue. We had all visited the Hayden Planetarium many times, but sleeping under real stars unprotected by bricks and concrete exaggerated our frailty. The stars were bright and closer than we ever saw in the city and the air seemed different, almost threatening in its sweetness. The sounds of nocturnal animals and bugs had to compete with the sounds of my patrol's uneasiness.

"Paul, what's that?" Bob whispered.

"Paul, you think it's a bear?" Carl inched closer to me.

"Naw. No bears so close to the city. Must be those mumblety-peg guys. Right, Paul?" Artie tried in an authoritative voice that lost its assurance, as his voice moved up an octave.

I tried to act calm and confident like a lieutenant I saw in a war movie, but everyone's fears magnified my own. Bob complained that his stomach ached and I was feeling a giant vise squeezing mine, most likely from the poorly cooked bacon with more than a dash of Oreo cookies. Our first shakedown experience as Boy Scouts shattered any faith in my survival.

Without warning, the trees and ground brightened and the sky turned a muted gray. The stars returned to their abodes. "What do you think is happening? It's not even six." Bob looked frozen and was huddled under an army-navy surplus poncho.

Artie hopped up and down, his Boy Scout shirt torn and black from handling coals. "Paul, you got to build a fire quick or we'll freeze to death."

The combination of sleep deprivation and cold made everyone move in slow motion, hands in pockets to keep warm, aimlessly kicking what was left of firewood, pots, and uneaten bacon strips. By now, the sky was brightening to a deep blue dotted with puffy white clouds moving without purpose. The blue, the clouds, even the warming sun just aggravated the pain in my hand. With my good hand, I lightly massaged what felt like a fatal gunshot wound to the stomach.

Our campfires would never be reignited by our troop. Shortly before 8:00 a.m. three cars pulled up. One was my father's. Apparently, our scoutmaster smelled defeat and called for an orderly retreat. The three fathers looked over the scene. Eppy's father, who was a doctor, asked to look at my hand. He examined me and informed my father that I had first-degree burns and almost second-degree. He asked how I felt. I flinched from the pain when he re-dressed my wound. I told him the highlights of my stomachache. He asked what I had been eating, and poked around my abdomen, and suggested to my father that I might be suffering from ptomaine poisoning. He urged that all of us get home and go to bed. He found three other boys with similar symptoms.

Nightmares of scouting filled my next two days of sleep and painful non-sleep. Relief only came when I decided that I must resign my commission as patrol leader and quit the Scouts. Clearly my identity didn't reside in being a hardy outdoors guy in the midst of seasoned Boy Scouts. "Mom, I don't want to be a patrol leader. I'm not going back."

"Why? You're such a good patrol leader. People look up to you."

"Mom, they poisoned me."

"You'll get over that. With all the responsibility of being a leader you're most likely having an anxiety attack."

My mother had labeled my ailment: anxiety. Whether it was having a car door flying off, having a visit from the FBI, fighting about Communism, this diagnosis seemed the same. But at least I didn't need to be hospitalized, and although my mother seemed to force the words, she assured me it wasn't fatal. I would survive.

Author in the front row of pairs of actors in school play at E.I., *Wise Men of Helm*

The plans to transfer me from E.I. to the academically demanding Stuyvesant public high school were on track and I found myself taking another baffling entrance exam accompanied by my now constant partner anxiety. The stakes were high. If I failed, it would be the local public high school for me, where I wouldn't survive.

It happened. My mother speculated that I must have failed at a high level and my father added that it wasn't the end of the world. There was no family interest in my date with destiny. My mother discovered that the local high school, an all-boys vocational school, had a small honors program for college-bound students. "This will be perfect. Not as much pressure. A small group of students planning on going to college," she cheered. I remained suspicious. "The honors program is very small so the teachers can work closely with you. I made an appointment for you to observe, next Tuesday." My mother focused on the education while I fretted about being beaten up by desperadoes with switchblades, zip guns, and brass knuckles.

I arrived early at the school to find my way to the honors program. A side street that ran in front of the school was blocked off to car traffic. The sounds of laughter, shouting, and singing floated up the street, creating a carnival atmosphere amidst the gloomy gray tenements. This impression dissolved as the percussive sounds of fists hitting bodies, bodies hitting pavement, and bones and street garbage hitting unsuspecting parked cars echoed through the otherwise empty street. I moved tentatively toward the groups of fighters, chasers, back jumpers, and crooners. The collective activity, while not choreographed, had a rhythm and energy that was mesmerizing as well as alarming.

My attention zoomed in on one pack of aged adolescents ripping off car aerials. Their discussion was spirited and their opinions well researched as to whether Chevys or Fords were best suited for the .22 caliber bullets used for their zip guns. Two "hoods" were punching and choking each other in front of the closed school doors. The guy on the bottom had his shirt torn off and blood oozed from his nose. As he gagged, three others jumped on his assailant. Another four guys jumped on the three rescuers and I lost track of who was on which side of the original fighters.

Sharp clanking sounds pulled my attention to the "style" section of the mob. Three guys took turns using the door mirror of a late-model two-toned Ford to preen their ducktail hairdos. They paid little attention to another group of pitchers who were using the same car doors as targets. Rather than chucking baseballs they hurled glass soda bottles to resolve who could make the biggest dent in the sheet metal. A hair guy scooted away when a bottle ricocheted off the front door handle.

The swarm of aging teens wore white T-shirts with their sleeves rolled up around their shoulders and cigarette packs. They sported two-inch-wide black leather Garrison belts to accentuate their tight dungarees. These belts were the current rage as weapons for thrashing opponents in gang fights. Although the sun had yet to hit this urban canyon, most everyone wore dark sunglasses. As I looked for anyone who might come to my rescue if needed, I noted a complete absence of commonplace urban activity. The ruffians commanded the street.

"He's got a knife. Get the fucken cops," someone yelled from under the steps of a tenement. The police never came. No head poked out a window in any of the tenements facing the street. This was the blackboard jungle without the blackboards.

A swift wave of silence rippled across the factions. A middle-aged woman emerged from nowhere. She wore a white blouse, dark skirt, and carried a large pocketbook. For five or ten seconds, activities ceased. The only sound was the clack and scraping of her high heels hitting the pavement. A tight path opened for this bold or reckless woman as she proceeded up the steps to the school.

"Hey, need some loving after class?" I couldn't see the charmer who called out this remark. Cackling and taunting broke the momentary silence. "You know what I got here?" A youth moving out of her way grabbed his crotch.

A third accomplice tried charm and edged closer to her and said, "Let me take you away from this depraved world. You can be my special teach. Just you and me."

I was stunned by the woman's bravery. She stopped and reached into her bag. The thugs nearest her began to back away. I expected her to pull out a notebook to write down names for a report to the principal. The woman slowly raised her hand out of her pocketbook and the guys couldn't move out of each other's way fast enough to escape.

Calmly, she took careful aim. Panicked shouts erupted from the mob of hooligans: "Look out, she's got her gun." Instinctively I moved backward. She straightened her arm and aimed the gun. It was green rather than gray. She pointed it at Charmer. He held his hands up to cover his face and struggled to backpedal, but two "friends" held him in place. He flailed his arms, legs, and head in a pitiful attempt to free himself. The woman pulled the trigger. Her aim was good. A strong stream of amber-colored liquid squirted from her water pistol, splashing Charmer's shirt and hair. His two restrainers released their hold with parting remarks. "Phew. You smell like a broad. Fairy!"

A tall guy noted my shock. "Hey, it's cheap perfume, not piss. Now Frankie has to go through school smelling like a broad." He laughed as I tried to comprehend what it would be like attending this school every day of my life, most likely a short one.

"Hey, you." I snapped my attention to a throng of a dozen or more toughs. I pretended not to hear and tried to shuffle away. But the group had me surrounded. They began their interrogation. "Yeah, you. What're you looking at? Where's your mother?"

I didn't think they were really interested in where my mother was and tried to change the subject. "Any of you know where I go for the honors program?"

"What's that? Do we look like honors students?"

"Well, I'm supposed to—"

"You kidding or something? Last two honor students had dreadful accidents. You know what I mean?" I took the longest pause I dared, to calculate how fast I could run to the busy avenue.

The leader of this orientation squad presented me with an opinion that cried out for repudiation. "Your mother is so ugly your father goes to bed with a blindfold."

From years of being confronted by gangs near home, I knew that if I refrained from responding, the taunts would escalate and I would be dishonored and beaten up. If I took a swing, I would be thrashed. I formed my saddest look while the group sneered. "You must be wrong. My mother died two years ago."

My adversaries were caught off balance and exchanged looks in an attempt to regroup. I had unintentionally hit their vulnerable spot, their love for mothers. But I had only a momentary reprieve until one ruffian ripped off one of my buttons. "No one wears buttons here. You got me?"

Another "welcome" pushed me hard. The coins in my pockets gouged into my thigh when I hit the pavement. I dug deep into my pocket and clawed for every nickel, penny, quarter, and dime. All attention was on my front pocket as I pulled out my fist. I heard the unmistakable and ominous sound of two switchblades snap out of their handles. Before their knives got used, I scattered all my change far enough away so I could flee while they dived for the money. I ran home faster than any bus or subway.

My destiny seemed clear. I managed to calm myself in the few hours before my parents came home. When they arrived I was pretending to read *From Here to Eternity*. They seemed genuinely interested in learning about my experience visiting the honors program. If I admitted my panic I feared they would be disillusioned. I tried staying in their comfort zone while somehow persuading them not to send me to that school. I knew my face was pallid with fear when I conjured up a cliché that might motivate them to rescue me. "You know the work is not very useful and no one seems to read books."

"You'll get used to it. There're lots of ways to learn. I'm glad it went well. We're proud of you." My mother improvised a look of calm and turned to her business of lighting another Pall Mall. "Now you won't be anxious over the summer. You'll know what to expect." Was she that clueless about how ill-equipped I was to defend myself against the city's toughest assortment of juveniles at my neighborhood school or just trying to appease her own anxiety?

CHAPTER SEVEN

"We're going to take Route 66 to the Grand Canyon." My mother's announcement drained my anxieties about the fate waiting for me in the blackboard jungle. In spite of the fact that we would be travelling beyond her comfort zone of Manhattan and the Bronx, my mother beamed. "I'll buy you five rolls of color film to take pictures of our trip." This surprise was way beyond any non-birthday expenditure I could remember.

The enthusiasm and focus on the trip was airing our home of its normal tensions. There was little talk about Communism and my mother hadn't had a single "state" since announcing the trip. Perhaps her sessions with dozens of New York City psychiatrists had finally stifled some of her usual anxiety. It would be more than twenty years before I discovered the actual explanations for this burst of joyfulness and the catalyst for our epic family journey.

We crossed the George Washington Bridge and any thoughts of leaving E.I., or even facing certain death at the new school, dropped into the Hudson. My father and I adjusted our vent windows to offset the paralyzing heat. From the back seat my mother narrated the change of scenery as we made progress west and south through Pennsylvania. Around midday we limped off the road for what my father assumed was another vapor lock blockage in the gas line.

This time his efforts to revive our ten-year-old Ford failed. He slammed the hood and declared big trouble.

Something felt strange. The heat and the mortally wounded Ford should have roused the usual family tensions. Instead, the only disruptions in the atmosphere were the mooing of curious cows and a rattling metal barn roof. My mother opened a book about new theories in psychoanalysis. My father pointed to a large boulder across the road with an arrow and painted black lettering: *Auto-Fix apprx. 1 M.*

"We're in great luck," my father exclaimed. He hiked off in the direction of the arrow. A half hour later he returned as a passenger in a beat-up woody station wagon missing its windshield and left fender. "Clarence is going to push us to his garage." Clarence nodded and swung his wagon behind the Ford to push.

Spicy odors of oil and gasoline monopolized the atmosphere of the garage. An assortment of running boards and solid tires smothered hope that our 1948 Ford had a chance in a garage more suitable for 1930s cars. Clarence unscrewed the spark plugs one at a time and held his large finger over the holes while my father cranked the engine. After each of the eight cylinders were evaluated by touch, Clarence asked my father what it was like to live in New York City. They discussed the distinctions between rural and city life. Clarence's austere demeanor loosened up into a smile after my father remarked on the spiritual serenity of country living.

"What do you do in the middle of nowhere?" my mother interjected.

Clarence scanned my mother as if she was from another planet. He ducked his head under the Ford's hood. "You ever hear of Lincoln Steffens? He wrote *The Shame of the Cities*? Seems like nothing has changed much since he exposed your Boss Tweed. Can't trust people living on top of each other in a city." He pulled back and wiped his hands with a greasy rag, smiled enough to expose white teeth, and nodded at me. "Guess he's too young to be corrupted."

"This is our vacation. You've got to do something." My mother released an unextinguished cigarette and lit another.

Clarence ground it out with his boot. "Don't know. You got a number two cylinder with no pressure and number five is weak. Got to take the head off. See what's what." Clarence kicked my mother's cigarette out the door.

"Bob, we can't stay in the middle of nowhere." Her voice fractured.

Clarence turned to my father. "If you and your son here help, we might get this done by morning." He checked my mother and continued, "Flo has a rooming house up the road. Three and a half bucks gets you a clean room and breakfast."

Clarence honed in on my eyes. "Collect every wrench you lay your hands on and your father and I will do the heavy stuff."

A few hours and more than a half dozen stories later, Clarence and my father had lifted the engine head off and went to work fixing the stuck valves. My father beamed after he started the engine and it roared its old standard tune. Clarence's talent and self-confidence tagged him as a hero. Secretly I hoped our Ford would break down again so we could meet another character like Clarence.

Three days later we were passing through Arkansas when hunger trimmed our conversation. "Stop, Bob. All those parked cars must be a sign of something good to eat." We parked next to horses absorbed in swatting flies, hitched near the entrance of a restaurant called Lilia's Home Cooking.

Inside a hostess explained that service was family style and sat us down at a long table with four other families. Conversations halted after my mother asked the group whether we were in the Ozarks. A woman who introduced herself as Emma clarified that indeed we were in the heart of the Ozarks and we should feel at home.

"You seem so happy, but living in such wilderness must be hard," my mother probed.

Emma threw her head back laughing, as did others at the table. "Do we look wild?" A few tables away people were square dancing. A man stood on a table calling out different square dance steps.

"As a matter of fact this does seem kind of wild. You can't eat like this every day. And why so many horses?" No one seemed bothered by my mother's absence of reserve.

"Wild? I've read about you city people. You're the wild ones." Emma impulsively got up and hauled my parents over to the square dancers. She coaxed a dancing couple to give up their place in the square for my parents. After do-si-doing with the wrong person, and confusing everyone by messing up allemande left and right commands, my parents ultimately got the hang of it and almost caught pace with the rapid square dance calls.

Emma returned to the table and sat down next to me. "Guess you'll be staying here. Hope you won't miss the city."

Parked among the horses, the Ford seemed eager to get going after lunch. I was impatient to get to full speed to find some relief from the heat through all the open windows and hood vent. My mother leaned over the front seat to shout over the road noises coming through the open windows. "I don't know, Bob, I thought people in the Ozarks would be less sophisticated."

Discussion ceased as my father swung out into the oncoming lane to pass a slower car. Chrome rattling, the Ford nonetheless seemed to be dozing rather than accelerating. The back seat was a void of silence, highlighting the suspense of whether we would make it before the oncoming truck slammed into us. My father downshifted into second and the Ford woke up. We passed the slower car and swung back into our lane just as the swoosh of air from the truck rocked our car.

My father hadn't lost the thread of conversation. "Florence, they work hard like anyone else. It's a hard life, but it doesn't mean they don't read. The Russian peasants treasured Gorky's books."

As they talked, I began to grasp that one of my parents' great strengths was connecting with people, especially those with a touch of the maverick in them. My mother's directness and undisguised anxiety was taken as an invitation to others to similarly be open and direct. My father's curiosity and ability to disregard any hint of social hierarchy made people feel safe and want to relate to him.

In the Arizona desert my father parked the Ford, now adorned with new decals from the Ozarks, Amarillo, Albuquerque, and Santa Fe, in front of a small one-window cinder-block building with TRADING POST in faded yellow lettering over the missing door. The roof's overhang was the only shade offered for miles. A man sat under its protection on an ancient chair. Other than in the movies, he was the first man I had ever seen with hair in a braid. My mother went into the trading post to hunt for something authentic to buy. My father dragged over a forsaken car seat and sat down next to the man. They began to talk. I followed my mother into the building as she examined rugs and pottery. The relative coolness of the store was refreshing, but the darkness made everything appear dingy. I wandered back outside.

My father introduced his new companion: "This is Nastas, but everyone calls him Nat. He says he can't remember a day without seeing the sun. Imagine that?"

Nat turned to me and nodded. "Your father's right. I'm sixty-one. Never seen a day without sun. Reckon you can't say that."

My mother had relaxed during the trip. She allowed her long dark hair to hang loose rather than be pinned up in its usual bun. She wore casual slacks and a comfortable shirt. Her skin as well as mine was naturally dark, more so because it was August. During the summer months in New York, people occasionally spoke Spanish to us, assuming we were from Puerto Rico. She came out of the store looking for someone to give her prices. Nat told her to wait for his wife who would be back in ten minutes or maybe two hours, he couldn't remember which.

A dust-streaked Chevy station wagon pulled off the highway and skidded to a stop. The wagon had decals splattered over the back windows of more states and attractions than I could count. A middle-aged couple emerged from the car and cloud of dust they had created by their impulsive stop. The woman's whisper could be heard for miles into the desert. "A real Indian! Get her picture, honey." She pointed at my mother.

"Honey," wearing a brand-new cowboy hat, approached my mother and took a coin from his pocket. "How about you let me take a picture of Joanie and you and I'll give you a quarter." My mother looked confused and stepped backward. He added, "You're the first Indian we've met."

My mother's face froze. She looked mortified. Before she had a chance to regain her dignity my father got up and took the quarter from Honey. "Sure she will," he said and turned toward my mother. "Florence, why don't you stand at the entrance and you two stand on either side and I'll take the picture."

My mother complied. Honey and his wife got their picture of their "Indian," and my father gained a quarter. Nat simply watched and waited to resume his conversation with my father about where to go in the Petrified Forest.

Finally, we headed off for the Grand Canyon. "Bob. Why did you take that man's quarter? You made them think I was still in retail. I worked my whole life to get out of Mom's store and—"

My father laughed mischievously as my mother feigned ridicule. "Florence, they liked your looks and we made a quarter. Everyone's happy. Well, except for Nat. He can't figure us out. People offer him and his wife money to take their picture every day, but he won't let them."

"Why, if he can make money?" I asked.

"Something about taking away their soul. Some kind of power that pictures have that we don't understand," he said.

"I'd go crazy living here, but you sure hit it off with Nat. Bet the Party would never bother to recruit in this wilderness," my mother said.

I waited for the escalation of political arguments, but out here we seemed to have escaped the political vortex back east. I assumed our next family bonding experience would happen soon, although I didn't anticipate I would be nudged to do it on my own.

For the next hundred miles to the canyon my father made frequent stops to pay his respects to the desert before we climbed higher into the forests. "This is God's country." The stretches of red and brown running to the horizon made his eyes twinkle, broadened his smile, and caused long and loving embraces of my mother and me. My mother took more time to see details in the landscapes and had dropped down to two packs of Pall Malls instead of her habitual three. What had changed my parents? Had someone slipped them a mickey? No mention of Communists and still no hints of panic?

After we arrived at Grand Canyon National Park we walked toward the edge. The land opened up to a sky that radiated a cobalt blue. For the first minute or so I felt something was wrong. The canyon was missing. There was nothing. Gradually the hidden reality appeared; I was looking into a universe of open space consisting of mesas and rocks horizontally striped with bands of different shades of red, muted by distance and atmosphere in this unique world. My father stood still. Uncharacteristically, my mother and father had lost the capacity to produce a single word. They held each other close.

The next morning after breakfast we walked to the mule corral where tourists were getting ready to ride to the bottom of the canyon. My mother asked the wrangler if I could go to the bottom on one of his donkeys. "They're mules, ma'am, not donkeys. Cross between a horse and a donkey, much smarter. Got one mule left for tomorrow. Her name's Chocolate."

He led Chocolate up to my mother. She touched the mule's wet snout. I had never seen my mother touch an animal before. Chocolate nodded and my mother made sure we noticed her bravery. Even though the ride would cost more than a day's worth of lodging, my mother reserved Chocolate for me.

"You'll have the adventure of a lifetime and it will give Dad and me time to ourselves," she said. More than my bar mitzvah or the Boy Scouts, this journey into the depths of the planet would serve as my first of many significant coming-of-age rituals.

I was up early the next morning and went to watch the wranglers saddle the mules. A cowboy approached eleven of us who were scheduled for the trip. Floyd was the epitome of every western hero: a robust body, sheathed in a worn red-and-blue western shirt, chaps, cowboy hat with multiple high-water marks of sweat splattered with a few jagged holes. "Whatever happens just hold on to the saddle horn. You won't fall over the side. Mules never fall." Floyd checked my saddle and looked me straight in the eyes. "Partner, I need you. You ride last to make sure everyone keeps going. You handle that?"

My heart leapt to outer space. Could I handle that? A real cowboy, relying on me to help! Maybe he would ask me to ride herd with him.

Eleven greenhorns and Floyd descended into the canyon. The narrow trail gave our mules only one or two extra feet of wiggle room. Alarming and frequent slides of loose rocks made us urge our mules to hug the wall of the canyon.

Since I was Floyd's partner I took it upon myself to reassure the riders near me. "Everything will be OK. Just hold on to your saddle horns." I wanted the other tourists to believe I was a cowboy and not a fourteen-year-old New Yorker. I tried to be commanding and nonchalant. "Stretch out your water till we get to the bottom where we can refill our canteens." At the bottom we had a view of the Colorado River. It was dark reddish brown unlike the murky gray of the Hudson. Its thundering sound vibrated through the rock.

After we ate lunch and prepared to return to the rim of the canyon, one of the mules refused to get up from its rest. No matter what Floyd did, the ornery mule would not get to her feet. Her rider, a middle-aged woman from Boston, was panicked at the thought she might be left at the bottom of the canyon. Floyd didn't hesitate.

"Paul, I need you again." Was he going to leave me behind instead of the woman? He checked my saddle while I speculated on my chances of surviving the night by myself. "Paul, between you and this young woman there isn't more weight than an average fat man. You have a passenger." The woman looked at me and became even more unnerved than before. Now she as well as the mule wouldn't get up.

Floyd tried one more time to coax the reluctant mule onto his feet. He looked at the woman firmly planted on the ground. He spoke to himself, but wanted me to learn too. "Women. Got their own minds." The mule caught the insult instead of the woman and got up. We were back on the trail headed out of this revealing crack in the earth's makeup. In their own ways, Floyd and Chocolate opened up an awareness of my talent for learning while untethered from my parents. I was ready for the unexpected and unplanned new adventures.

As we made our return to New York City, somewhere in Kansas my father requested that I plot a detour to Niagara Falls. "Bob, we've already driven over three thousand miles. Niagara is such a cliché!" My mother puzzled over my father's impulsive change in plans as well as the additional costs. I knew Niagara was a waterfall, but didn't know what a cliché was. My mother explained that people went there on their honeymoon, but she felt it was kind of stupid to go where everyone else did.

"Where did you go on your honeymoon?" I asked. My father lightened his foot on the accelerator and allowed a '46 Olds to pass us on the two-lane highway. "Oh, we didn't need one. Our celebration was you," my mother said. "It's kind of silly, a honeymoon. Did you think Kansas would be so flat?"

My father accelerated and passed the same Olds that had just passed us.

Somewhere in the Rockies, parents unusually happy on trip across country

CHAPTER EIGHT

BACK FROM NIAGARA FALLS after our cross-country trip, I envisaged Charmer and the rest of the gang at my new high school planning my demise. I considered filling a water pistol with my mother's perfume, but my pistol leaked and such a scent leaching from my dungaree pocket would magnify my presence in the blackboard jungle.

Before the trip to the Grand Canyon, I had developed a crush on Nadine during three weeks at a YMHA camp. I felt compelled to explain why we couldn't get serious; I didn't expect to live past the start of school in September. This had the unintended effect of making her more interested in me. I was her first neurotic friend. The last hours before my first day at the new school were spent calling Nadine and other friends to say final goodbyes. At 4:36 p.m. the phone rang just as I was to dial Ethan to pass on my photography equipment, which would have no use for me after my body was found by the police with a switchblade in my back.

"Has the phone been off the hook all afternoon?" My mother's tone didn't relate to my impending demise, and thus I was disoriented by her next words. "Tomorrow you're starting at Brooklyn Tech." Brooklyn Tech, a leading New York City vocational high school, couldn't possibly be as much of a threat to my life as the neighborhood vocational one; it was an eleventh-hour reprieve. "I didn't like the feel of your new school and talked with the principal at Tech. I also spoke to the principal at Stuyvesant and you'll transfer there in January. I arranged everything. All you have to do is get an 85 average your first semester at Tech."

Thinking of the plight of the principals at Stuyvesant and Brooklyn Tech, I chuckled. Doubtless they had never met anyone like my mother. For her, systems were to be worked. I was the only student who ever transferred into Stuyvesant in the middle of the year, not to mention without passing their entrance exam. Apparently she had strong-armed the Brooklyn Tech principal to accept my failing Stuyvesant score and bullied the Stuyvesant principal to uproot all their admission rules. Their alternative was to spend more time with my mother.

The pattern was clear. My mother was a 911 mother. She could and would take on her role of parent just in time to prevent the most obvious of catastrophes, but with normal challenges and need for advice I was on my own, dumped into situations where I could learn from different mentors.

My first day at Tech was formidable. I had transferred from a school with a population of 150 boys and girls to one with 6,000 adolescent boys. On my first day a tsunami of hormone-charged boys herded me into a gigantic elevator, huge enough to fit fighter planes or efficiently spread 6,000 students over twelve floors in twenty minutes. I was literally in the midst of the masses, with a little education sprinkled on the side.

I surprised myself by surviving to the end of the first semester. I had transferred from a world of care and concern for my individuality to one that displayed no interest in whether I could outlast the bureaucratic and student forces assembled to mute my identity. Yet the mixture of pattern-making shop and mechanical drawing classes, which I thrived in, softened the challenge of the leftover academic classes. I accepted my sudden fall into anonymity, took what I needed and forgot the rest. I squeaked by with an 85 average and coped with the seemingly irrational structure and discipline required to control an army of juvenile boys.

The remaining barrier to my transferring to Stuyvesant was passing a gym test, which included climbing a twenty-foot rope to the ceiling of the gymnasium. Throughout the semester I could never lift myself more than two feet from the floor before weak muscles and fear let loose. Others were strong enough to claw up the rope without using their feet, and stronger boys could even keep their legs at a 90-degree angle to their body, while they effortlessly climbed. Even with all four limbs I was useless in this bizarre rite of passage. The gym teacher warned me that I would not pass gym until I could reach the ceiling.

My close associate, anxiety, kept me up the night before the final ordeal. If things went as feared, I might get up four feet, fall to the floor in a pool of blood, shame, and ridicule. My transfer to Stuyvesant would be quashed, and my mother would be let down. They might let me continue at Tech, but without climbing the rope I would never graduate. While not as rough as the vocational school hoodlums, these boys had no sympathy for weakness and I would be forever a target of their bullying. Valium was still five years from public consumption, I didn't smoke, and so I resorted to panic. After throwing up, I decided calm resignation and disclosure were my only route forward. At breakfast I prepared my mother for my upcoming failure as gently as I could, knowing I was crushing her dream of my transfer to Stuyvesant. Revealing my imminent failure didn't keep either of us from shoveling down our burnt toast.

Instead of rushing off to work, my mother took another sip of her coffee. "Sounds dangerous, but it can't really be twenty feet. I'm sure if they see you're in danger they won't force you. It's just their way of making every boy try."

"Mom, I've been trying all semester. It's impossible. I keep slipping. And if I ever reached the top I would be so scared I would just let go and smash to the floor." I felt the shadow of shame fall over me. Disclosing fear to my mother felt like waving a white flag of surrender. I could no longer hold on to my pride in marshaling enough self-confidence to get through the first semester of an indifferent world.

"Should I write a note?" I winced at noting the highest level of anxiety and alarm in her voice.

"You don't understand, everyone will be watching and hoping I fail. If you sent a note to the teacher it would just make it worse for me. What about I just stay home and be sick? In fact, I am sick."

"Look, if you can do this you'll go to Stuyvesant. I'm sure they wouldn't allow this if it wasn't safe." My mother's words seemed to have no recognition of how tough the world was for non-combative boys. She lit a second cigarette before she had finished her first. "Call me when you get home. Maybe they'll let you do another long jump instead." I had passed my long jump, but that's because I entered a check in the gym teacher's book when he had been distracted by an errant baseball, which hit his head.

My heartbeat overshadowed the clanking sounds of the subway wheels. I dreaded the ridicule awaiting me as my classmates took joy in the comedy of watching me hang frantically six inches off the ground, unable to climb further. I couldn't remember any experience at Little Red or E.I. where fear was used to motivate action or achievement. On the streets fear only led to flight.

Yet fear had its day. With effort and adrenaline, I inched up the twenty feet and then yelled like hell for the teacher, who wasn't paying any attention, to record my accomplishment in his book.

"OK, Pitcoff. You looked like a crippled cat, certainly not human. Pass."

I slid down the twenty feet, hands and legs burning and parts of my skin ripping off, and landed on the floor so fast I felt my head sink through my body as if it too had hit the floor. Although dazed, I managed to produce a touch of swagger through the rest of the day despite seared hands and legs. After school I found the nearest phone booth, which seemed to shine with glory and triumph, and called my mother with the good news.

"See, you over exaggerated the problem. I'm sure the rope was only a few feet, not twenty. It just seemed that way in your mind."

"Mom, it was twenty. Ask anyone."

"I have a client coming in. Thanks for letting me know. I'll call the principal at Stuyvesant to tell him you're on your way."

Brooklyn Tech hadn't defeated me. So transferring to Stuyvesant, considered one of the most academically competitive public schools in New York City, seemed almost commonplace, like changing trains. I was now seasoned in handling public school bureaucracy, filling out endless forms, standing on lines, and being treated merely as an object. Stuyvesant was markedly smaller than Brooklyn Tech, but nevertheless 2,000 boys continued to be a threatening departure from the close-knit family at Little Red and E.I. As much as I desired to fit in, I couldn't. The ferocious academic competition was ever-present and intensified my feelings of inferiority. The lack of girls cut off a primary area of interest and strengthened a sense that I was trapped in a rotten artificial situation. My mind was continually on escape, but I had no strategy or allies. Survival was my most conscious goal.

My parents' fantasy that Stuyvesant was the place for my superior intellect propelled them to suggest I work harder and hang out with the high-achieving students. My complaints about the rote recitations were parried with equally rote responses to do my best. They were disappointed in my inability to get into the academic groove, yet they were not harsh. Perhaps they feared the large, bureaucratic, and indifferent atmosphere might be more than I could handle. More probably, their work and lives demanded most of their energy and left them little time to act on any of their concerns. Without acknowledging it, we all understood I had to make it on my own. Perhaps to no one's surprise but my own, I ended my first year in public school on my feet.

When my parents wearied of using hollow clichés to prod me to perform better at school, I felt reprieved but also assumed they had lost all interest in me. So I was surprised when, near the end of the semester, my mother suggested a new tack to straighten out my life. "Paul, maybe you should consider a different camp this summer." My mother broached the subject while she dictated a list of groceries for me to pick up. Her limited efforts to improve my academic competitiveness had failed, and she was no doubt searching for parental action that might lead to success.

"Mom, I'm not sure I want to go to camp. I'll get the groceries when I come back from the park." It was an unusually warm day for February and I knew my friends would be playing basketball.

"Fine, as long as you get home by five. Here's a quarter and two bucks. There should be change," she said. "You have to go to camp for three weeks and I want you to consider one a friend of mine runs."

I opened the door to leave but stopped. "Mom, it's going to be more than three dollars and I don't have any money. Give me four bucks and I'll get change. I'm not trying another camp or going back to the Y camp. What would any of your friends know about running a camp?" Begrudgingly my mother found enough loose change in her pocketbook to add up to $3.35.

My mother greeted me when I arrived home just around five with, "You have my change?"

"Mom, you short-changed me again. We owe Frankie 35 cents." I loathed this pattern around money.

"Hurley sounds like a good camp, but it isn't easy to get into. We'll need to go for an interview this week. The camp isn't any more expensive than the Y camp," she added.

My best friend Ethan and I had spent two years at a Y camp and were looking forward to relief from what seemed more like a penal camp for wayward teenagers. After the last summer, one of my friends revealed to his parents that our counselor felt that preparing us for adulthood necessitated recounting his sexual exploits, including the use of whipped cream and watching ball games while "doing it." After checking with me that this was true, (although she avoided asking for more details about the whipped cream), my mother listened to my protests about the Y camp. Ethan and I hoped we could talk our parents into a better camp with more activities, perhaps horseback riding, tennis, and a decent ball field. No one had ever heard of Hurley and equating it with the Y camp, in terms of expense, made me suspicious it would turn out the same or worse. My mother called Ethan's parents and encouraged them to consider Camp Hurley too. My mother charged into this challenge, seeing it as an opportunity to utilize her persuasive abilities and *pull*. I was not consoled by my mother's enthusiasm, but Ethan's willingness to investigate the possibility of a better camp made me agree to the interview.

On Tuesday after school my mother, Ethan, and I entered a narrow and worn office building on the corner of Fourteenth Street and Union Square. It took several minutes for the elevator operator to lift us to the eighth floor. The corridor was dimly lit by the glow of bubbled frosted glass panels in massive dark wooden doors. My mother tapped her knuckles on the door that read *Murray Ortof, Director, Camp Hurley*. Nothing happened—an inauspicious beginning to the five years that would give shape to my adult life. She tapped louder. An irritated shout penetrated the door. "Florence, you expect me to open the damn door for you?" Ethan and I cringed.

My mother opened the door and we followed her into the office. A musty dank smell of wood and old papers aroused my instinct for retreat. Seated behind a beat-up wooden desk was a man with black hair, cut long for the time, and combed back in the style of a movie star or street hood. He wore a white shirt with tie and was highlighted by a large window facing Union Square. Murray projected elegance that was readily distinguished from most adults. In no way did he look like a camp director. I couldn't picture him in the country or directing hordes of kids.

My mother sat across the desk from Murray and began reminiscing about old times and social work. Ethan and I took chairs at the side of the desk. "Remember when he was two?" Murray pointed to me. "You told the professor you'd miss the next class for his birthday." I wasn't sure what this had to do with camp.

"Certainly do. You embarrassed me." My mother's face brightened. "But we're not here about that."

"All I did was tell the professor it was a big event for both of us," Murray said.

My mother searched for her professional voice. "You put your arm around me and acted like we were married and all to just get out of a class."

Their conversation came to an abrupt halt when Murray turned his attention to Ethan and me. "Look, Florence, these look like nice boys. They need a nice camp. Put them in Welmet, Buck's Rock, or . . ." Murray listed a number of upscale camps. Murray believed that mixing campers from different social, economic, racial, and physically challenged backgrounds provided a better experience for everyone and leveled stigmas associated with camps exclusively for a particular group. However, this approach limited the openings for middle-class kids.

Ethan and I reflexively pulled back as Murray turned toward us. He questioned us as if he were a lawyer attempting to depose a witness. "What do you boys want to do next summer? What are your favorite activities?"

Ethan responded, "Well, we want to work on our tennis, and would like to learn how to ride horses."

"We're also interested in social things with girls," I added.

"And a decent ball field," Ethan stressed.

Murray leaned back in relief, turned to my mother, and pointed at his two star witnesses. "See, Florence, they want horses, tennis, and dance lessons. Hurley's not for them." He turned to us. "There are no horses, no tennis courts. You hit a grounder on our ball field and it goes all over the place depending upon which rock it hits. You wouldn't be in a cabin. You'd sleep on a tent platform. There would be other kids there who would think this is heaven, but you two wouldn't be happy."

Murray held his hands palms up in a pleading gesture. "Paul, do me a favor. Don't come to Hurley. You know your mother. If you come to Hurley, you'll write home and complain to her. She'll call me and drive me crazy. I have a camp to run and I can't be devoting time to tranquilizing your mother." My mother smiled. Perhaps she was pleased that Murray remembered her nature.

Murray continued, "If you come I won't let your mother call you and I'll intercept all of your letters to each other. Her neurosis could close the camp. Get out of here and go to some other camp and keep her off my back." It was clear we were not wanted and there was nothing appealing about the camp. Ethan and I looked at each other and then at my mother for a sign it was time to leave.

"OK, business is over. Now we can relax." Murray pulled open a desk drawer and placed a bottle of whiskey and some paper cups on his desk. He poured a drink for my mother. She raised no protest. In the same motion Murray continued to pour three more cups, one for himself and one each for Ethan and me. He placed the cups in front of us.

Ethan and I looked at each other in bewilderment. A suspicion began to emerge that perhaps Murray was unstable. Clearly this wasn't a standard interview. We might look older, but Murray knew we were applying to be campers. He had to know we were fourteen. It was odd that my mother ignored her role as a parent. Couldn't she see we were being perverted by his debauchery? I sat motionless with a foolish grin, waiting for some hint on how to proceed.

Murray interrupted the back-and-forth soundless communication between Ethan and me. "You boys don't drink?" He paused to let our discomfort sink in. "Oh, I get it. You don't drink in front of your mother." He seemed honestly offended that we didn't pick up our cups.

My mother paid no attention to Murray's sidebar with us and took a sip from her cup. "Look, Murray, Paul and Ethan must be in the same bunk. You need to assure them of that."

Murray locked eyes with me and used silence to seed my embarrassment. Before I could fully grasp his incredulity, he spoke. "Are you two fairies or something? Why do you have to be together?" He turned to my mother. "Florence, you of all people should know the dangers of codependence. These boys have to learn to make other friends and not be heavily reliant on each other. Look that up in one of your journals. Surely they can live three weeks in separate bunks."

My mother's history with Murray made it doubtful he could oppose her doggedness. "It's all settled," my mother declared after we left Murray's office. Murray, and my mother's relationship with

Murray, topped my assumptions of a camp interview. Why would my mother sit idly by while an unhinged man struggled to intoxicate my best friend and me? And more importantly, why would she hand me over to this crazy man?

All this happened during the tense two-week period of the first round of preparations for my Regents exams, New York State's method for evaluating each student's proficiency in major subjects. I pondered these questions as I waded through the mob of 2,000 students massed outside Stuyvesant High School. Few of the students knew me well enough to engage in conversation. Phil was an exception. He worked in a drugstore and sold mild uppers to "help us study." He was a brilliant writer and had an altered view of the world. Instead of handing in a physics journal that demonstrated the leverage calculations for an experiment in our physics class, he turned in a short story about a boy whose life was over-leveraged.

Most of the boys exchanged predictions about what topics would be covered on upcoming exams. Others, smart enough to pass their subjects yet not inclined to battle their way to the right side of the bell curve, talked about how getting laid helped with their sports. A much smaller caucus of students, considered the "toughs," occupied an isolated slice of the closed-off street. These guys played cards and one flashed open his leather jacket to show off a zip gun he was refining in shop class. They threatened any outsider who wandered into their domain.

I made a wide circle around the toughs and walked through the other groups on my way to homeroom. I sat there waiting for the first bell to ring. It occurred to me that I was in the midst of an alienation experiment. I was surprised how much it didn't hurt. Rather, I congratulated myself on my adaptive skills. During my first fifteen years I had adjusted to my parents' inconsistencies, learned to harmonize with the culture of my Little Red classmates, developed friendships with Communists despite my father's reactionary diatribes, and was now holding my own in public high school. Yet I wasn't exactly comfortable as I crossed days off my calendar like a prisoner anticipating his release date. I wanted to fit in, but knew I couldn't, and would always feel alienated. Yet I didn't seem to stand out from the crowd as much as I felt. My anxiety focused on passing courses, but no longer on whether I could survive the loss of the protective environment of Little Red. My thoughts focused on Regents exams, getting through the day, trying to block out the fact that my mother was set on sending me to a camp run by a crazy man. At this moment there was no way I could envision that Hurley might possibly be a comprehensive antidote to my persistent feelings of alienation.

In the morning after the bell rang, everyone automatically got up to pledge allegiance to the flag. I sidestepped the words "under God" as a tribute to Little Red, where we learned to resist the merging of religion and state. Another bell rang and we grabbed our books and headed for our various first-period classes. I shuffled into the English classroom along with twenty-five other freshmen. Dr. Bronson (we assumed his PhD was self-anointed) wore a threadbare sport coat with the pocket linings showing through the fabric. His white shirt was rusted around a collar that hung loosely around his emaciated neck. He didn't permit anyone to speak in class unless called upon. Student questions were prohibited as a waste of his time. His system for outlining had more than a half dozen levels of indentations. Only a quarter of the class mastered the format, despite being quizzed on it every Friday.

Dr. Bronson handed back assignments and stopped at my desk. "Ditcoff," he said. This new surname could be credited to my indecipherable penmanship. At the start of the semester students filled out small Delaney cards, which were used to enter attendance and test scores that were placed in the teacher's binder with slots representing the seating chart. Once assigned a seat, it became permanent. Dr. Bronson deciphered my "P" as a "D" and refused to accept my apology or recognize that my name was Pitcoff. The benefit from my illegibility was my first opportunity to sit near and converse with boys whose last names began with letters near the beginning of the alphabet. He continued, "You can't spell, you're not following the outline structure, your handwriting is indecipherable, and you will fail my class, which is a good indicator for failure throughout your life."

I thanked him for his feedback and returned to staring out the window. In twenty-three minutes the bell would ring and I would have to take my algebra test. Murray popped into my thoughts. He was wacky. Yet the thought of twenty-three minutes more with Dr. Bronson had me more panicked than three weeks at Murray's camp. The minute hand pulsated and leaned backward as if in a struggle with some invisible force holding it in suspended animation. I held my breath till it finally snapped forward, twenty-two minutes till the class ended. I was wasting Dr. Bronson's time.

I squeaked through the state Regents exams and was off to Camp Hurley, in the Catskill Mountains about a hundred miles north of the scorching city. The first thing I noticed was that Murray no longer wore his stunning suit. He dressed in dungarees and a blue work shirt no different from Dennis's, the camp's head truck driver. They both created a riptide that pulled people toward them. At fifteen, I was increasingly apprehensive about losing the freedom associated with youth, but I also wanted what I assumed were the benefits of the adult world. I would have a double life, not unlike the spies my father and I watched on the TV series, *I Led Three Lives*. From the moment Dennis and Murray greeted campers coming off the bus I saw them as my models for how to keep a child's perspective cloaked in adult maturity. I would learn from them.

Murray greeting campers at Camp Hurley

The focal point for the camp was a circle of flimsy green benches under tall pines that lay between the mess and rec halls. The shade and its location invited idle campers and counselors to sit, talk, read, write postcards, or just relax. To make up for the limited camp facilities, Murray sent campers on day hikes and overnight trips. A Dodge farm truck had been modified for these adventures by bolting two long wooden benches to the back plat-form—just enough seating for eighteen campers, their counselors, and camping equipment. To get in or out of the rear platform the wooden sides were removed and used as ladders. When it rained, a large tarp was rolled over metal hoops over the truck, which made it resemble an army transport.

All attention focused on the red truck as it lumbered into the campgrounds, spreading dust and sounds of campers singing the last refrain of "Which Side Are You On," or some other labor folk song. Dennis, one of the camp's luminaries, would emerge from the driver's cab, often with a camper or counselor who rode shotgun and needed individual time with him. He had a keen interest in everyone's life story and injected hopefulness into anyone within sight. He had faith that any challenge could be overcome. He was black and came from an exceptionally poor, racially segregated, dangerous neighborhood in Washington, D.C., and had witnessed close to the worst that anyone had to endure. He was thirty-something, and his muscular build combined with a determined stride contrasted starkly with the tenderness evident when he affectionately patted someone's shoulder. Dennis showed a mischievous gaze that transformed into the kindest smile when he listened to someone struggling to resolve some issue or just complain.

This day, Carl, an eleven-year-old camper, slid down from the cab. His face was streaked with dust and tears. His conversation with Dennis continued across the heated hood of the truck. "Yeah, your foster mother fools everyone. At least she doesn't fool you," Dennis said. They walked to the back of the truck and Dennis asked for help unhooking the gates. Carl attempted to imitate Dennis's moves, but no one could fully duplicate Dennis's physical strength and dexterity. Dennis continued, "Carl, they'll move you to another home and it will probably get worse. I know. But look, you're here now, having fun, aren't you?" Dennis spoke in a serious tone and at the same time offered his wry smile while casually dislodging one of the truck's back gates that defied Carl's efforts.

Campers in the truck tossed bedrolls, ponchos, and other camping equipment to Carl, who was lining them up near the truck. "Hey Carl, everyone's talking about how you were the only one who could get the campfire going with all that wet wood. Where did you learn that?" a camper asked.

Carl looked up at the camper. "Just know. That's all." His facial muscles relaxed enough to crack some of the caked dust on his face. Dennis caught a tossed bedroll and instead of piling it up, fired it back up into the truck.

"Hey! What're you doing?" a camper huffed as he reflexively caught the force of Dennis's toss.

Dennis ignored the diversion to continue, "Carl, you know how to do things. You know what? You're going to get out of foster care someday. And you know what? You can do things. So you're going to be OK . . . OK, you hear me? Listen, I'm hot and bothered. Why don't you and me get something to drink and let these guys do all the work?" Carl followed Dennis into the mess hall to get lemonade.

Most of the camp's supervisors were social workers and some of the counselors planned to go into that field or psychology. Everyone valued Dennis's perceptions and he was often a first choice for a camper who needed to talk things out. The next year, when I was taking off in a romantic relationship with a counselor a few years older than me, I sought Dennis's advice. Dennis said, "Who cares what anyone thinks about your age?" advice I'd heard from others, but coming from him, it sunk in. Was Dennis a truck driver or a social worker? I quickly learned he couldn't be confined to a single identity. He was a man cut loose from normal boundaries, as were many of the adults at Hurley. In this community I might unearth my uncertain identity.

The austere country setting of the camp seemed to foster close relationships. Rustic—not planned rustic, but merely limited-funds rustic—was the camp's look. The youngest children were assigned bunks with scarcely enough electricity to power a few aging 40-watt light bulbs, insufficient to illuminate the darkened wooden floors, the army surplus beds, and the campers' trunks used as dressers. There was no glass in the windows to protect from the occasional cold nights or blowing rain, and no screens. The only artwork was the bunk's work wheel, which indicated each camper's rotating responsibilities: sweep the floors, clean the bathroom, scout the outside for any litter, mop the worn floors with a disinfectant, bring trash to the main area, serve and clean up at meals, collect the campers' mail, or the most coveted assignment, *day off*.

Teen campers, I among them, slept in more primitive bunks or tents on wooden platforms. Flashlights were the sole source of light and there was no running water other than rain. There were approximately fifty teen campers living in three bunks and three tents, served by a gray cinder-block building with a few toilets and showers. Six cold-water faucets were directed into a single concrete trough sink, sitting on an open concrete slab. Washing up was a communal coed activity, a marked departure from the quarantined girls at the Y camp or the all-boys Stuyvesant High School. Here, girls were everywhere and I had no idea how to prepare for my first experience of sleeping in the woods with them.

As with most new broadening experiences I had come to realize I would have to learn through doing. Instinctively, I knew that neither parent would be of much help in preparing me for fifteen-year-old girls at a coed sleepaway camp. My mother relied too much on theoretical knowledge, which seemed of little relevance in the area of girls. My father was the ultimate autodidact and was reluctant to offer any normal advice. Rather than seeking advice from experts, he bundled his experiences, failures, and readings to acquire new skills and knowledge. I had already suffered from his wacky advice about girls when I was thirteen, when I was drowning in apprehension when my first hormonal stirrings thrust me into arranging my first date. In spite of his bizarre advice not to trust my teachers, I was desperate. Just the act of asking a girl to go to Palisades Amusement Park, across the river in New Jersey, made my Boy Scout camping trip—my first official anxiety attack—seem like a picnic. I had no other alternative but to seek advice. "Dad, what should I do on a date? Do I pick her up? Do I take her for a meal after we get back?"

He squeezed out just one piece of advice. "Let the girl pay her own way." He seemed so certain, I felt shame for having saved enough from seven weeks of allowances to pay for the girl for the long trip there and the many rides. Was his advice because she was a girl or because her father was a nationally known defender of Communists? Should I not trust girls any more than my teachers?

The hour-and-a-half subway and bus trip to a destination I didn't even want to go to felt like a run-up to a nightmare. I knew I should like amusement parks, and this one was supposed to be the grandest, but on the one previous class trip there my friend Arthur vomited over me while high on the Ferris wheel, my classmates noticed my cowardly act of disappearing as everyone embarked on the Cyclone roller coaster, and a gang of toughs dunked me in America's largest salt water pool almost to the point of drowning.

My date began with wandering around the park, taking a few bland rides, and pretending to like cotton candy. I then asked if she wanted to go on the Tunnel of Love ride. Friends told me this was the lead-in for a kiss or . . . Then they laughed at what else, but frankly at this point it just seemed like a less frightening ride than the Cyclone roller coaster or bumper cars. Had I known better, I wouldn't have embarrassed myself. The car for two travelled along a track in thorough darkness, supposedly to create the mood of romance and avoid seeing any awkwardness as one made a move for a kiss. That seemed rational since I really didn't know what to do. Abruptly, after adjusting to the dark and fairly smooth ride, lights exploded through the darkness and a huge fabricated monster jumped out at us and made a nightmarish scream.

My jitters immediately turned into heart-pumping fear so great that I somehow landed in my date's lap. She could tell my heavy breathing had nothing to do with her, but rather white fear. I slithered back to my place next to her just before the next monster, but now she was prepared and held my hand steady enough to keep me from jumping back in her lap. After we exited this tunnel of horrors, we agreed to return home. It was a steamy July afternoon; the subway was hot and I decided dating was not a skill I would ever master. I could never be as smooth as the men in movies and would dedicate my life to building the best model airplanes.

Having made this decision, I didn't know what to do until I got my date back to her home. I just couldn't do what I wanted: run away. As we emerged from the Fourteenth Street subway stop, I forced myself to make one last effort at this indecipherable ritual. I asked her if she wanted something to drink, which she immediately agreed would be good. I led her into a White Castle and offered her a seat at the counter as if it were a special treat. My mind was blank and I was suffering from the afternoon temperatures in the mid-nineties. The only thing I could think of was water. So I ordered two glasses of water.

The waitress must have read my father's admonition all over my face and pleasantly served us our free drinks, leaving me with a life-long scar of shame at having been too cheap to buy a soda. The humiliation became even more devastating in that I failed to even leave a tip. I walked my date home and after her mother served us some cupcakes and left us alone in the kitchen, my date thanked me and gifted me with a hurried appreciation kiss. I walked home feeling discouraged by the logistical and emotional maneuverings dating required. I made a solemn vow of dating celibacy, which was still in effect by the time I reached Camp Hurley two years later, and prepared for my first overnight with girls, without ever thinking of seeking advice from my parents.

At Hurley girls and boys shared the bathroom, showers, and sink, but they slept in separate bunks. Murray was well aware of the rushing hormones of our age group, but rather than trying to separate boys from girls, as was common during the 1950s and early '60s, Hurley facilitated their interaction. The more experiences we shared together, he felt, the more we would respect each other and our community and the less likelihood for sexual transgressions. No camp activity excluded anyone based on gender.

From what I heard from boys at school and on the streets, I was an underachiever when it came to sexual exploits. They had experiences I hadn't even conceived of and were getting laid so often they voluntarily took time off to heal their private parts, or so they said. When Hurley planned our first overnight camping trip with a girls' bunk I feared my deficiencies would be exposed. There was some muffled boasting by a few boys about how they couldn't wait till the counselors were asleep so they could then insert themselves into one of the girls' bedrolls. That prospect ignited a thrill that was quickly extinguished by panic. I would be humiliated. I had no idea how to make a bedroll or how to slip into one without unraveling the blankets. And if I could overcome the unraveling part of two in one bedroll, I had no plan for what followed.

We arrived at the campsite and used our adolescent energy to swiftly unload the truck, build a fire, and cook an acceptable meal. The counselors told us to set up our bedrolls before dark and make sure to first lay out our ponchos to keep ourselves dry. No one mentioned where the girls would sleep and I asked Dave if I could place my bedroll next to him. "Sorry, I'm sleeping next to Leslie," he said.

"You're kidding. Where do the girls sleep anyway? Don't they sleep separately?"

"No. We can sleep where we want. Beverly told me she's sleeping next to you."

The temperature had dropped into the fifties and I was beginning to sweat. Beverly came over and told me she was sleeping near the top of the hill. "It's a neat spot and not covered by trees. We can watch stars all night." She sensed my reluctance. "Stargazing doesn't hurt and if you're scared, Ben and Harold will be near." Her broad smile was genuine; her curly dark blond hair amplified her sense of energy.

It might have been useful to have instruction from my father in the area of sex, but by now I had fully accepted my parents' methodology: inexplicable advice or dumping me on a prospective mentor. Even if I had demanded guidance I most probably would have gotten some bizarre off-the-point response such as *Avoid kissing a Communist.*

I lifted my bedroll and followed Beverly, keeping my eyes on her counselor, who acknowledged my eye contact without noticeable reproach. "Need any help?" the counselor called out. Her offer echoed through the forest and every creature within five miles knew I was in trouble.

The sun had dropped beneath the shadowy pine forest that surrounded our campsite. Even with all of our commotion I heard the sounds of lonely birds and animals protecting their turf. The pitch of their screams confirmed their ferocity. Did I *need any help*? Yes, and straightaway. The issue was defined. Which would result in more impairment to my sense of maleness: remaining with Beverly or bolting into the forest?

Beverly selected a spot about thirty feet away from another couple. She cleared fallen branches and dug out a few small boulders with the little folding army shovel we used for digging latrines and building cooking fires. After she prepared an area large enough for two, I arranged my poncho and unrolled my bedroll. "If we sleep that way, we'll roll down the hill into the campfire," Beverly pointed out. "My tarp is big enough for both our bedrolls. Let's lay them up the incline so we don't end up in flames." Beverly had not been a Boy Scout, but she knew more about camping than I did.

I lingered as long as I could before laying my bedroll next to hers. I looked around the campsite and studied how my friends were getting into their bedrolls. Some of the boys undressed down to their shorts before snaking into their constructed sleep sacks, and the girls seemed to undress while inside theirs. I tried to act nonchalant and took my shirt off, but then rapidly crawled into my bedroll with my dungarees still on.

Beverly was in her bedroll turning and tugging in an effort to get undressed. She stopped and looked at me. "You'll be more comfortable not sleeping in your dungarees." I clutched my belt and held tight. "If you don't take them off, they'll get damp and you'll feel awful in the morning. I won't look. Just get out of the bedroll. It will be much easier," she said helpfully.

I complied and slipped back into my covering in less than a second. "OK!"

She applauded. "I can't undress that fast. I'm having a hell of a time so look the other way and then I can undress outside of this stupid thing." I looked away and heard her disrobing and slipping on a nightshirt. In spite of the crisp country air my breath came with effort.

We were lying next to each other in our separate buffers. The conversations and laughter from other campers ratcheted down in volume and the forest animals had ceased hollering. I listened to the sound of the breeze and gentle stretching noises of the pine branches. A sense of safety blanketed the campsite. We talked about our counselors, other campers, and how much the camp made a difference in everyone's life. She talked about how she wanted to be a scientist.

"What kind?" I asked.

"A biologist. Think that's the easiest for a woman to get into. I want to work on finding cures for tropical diseases."

"Wow, you should do that. I didn't realize it's hard for women to go into science. Why is that?" I asked.

"The world is not like Hurley. My mother made it as a professor of biology and she says I can do it. But I have to watch out for the men who will make it hard for me."

"Things are always unfair. Guess I'm lucky I'm a boy."

"No. You'll have your problems too. Maybe they won't be as easy to predict." Talking about the future eased my tension, but Beverly got back to the present. She reached for my hand. "Talk about unfairness. In the movies we would now be together in one bedroll. Do you want to make love?" Shock overloaded my system and froze my breathing. I diverted my gaze from Beverly to a rotting log, the only means for concealing my bewilderment. Beverly seemed oblivious to the changing color of my face and exploding beats of my heart. "I'm not sure whether I want that or not, but certainly not at camp," she said. My breathing resumed and I no longer had to study the decomposing log.

"They let us have these times together. We can't ruin that for others. Hope you feel the same?" Beverly talked about "it" without awkwardness. Could I ever talk to a girl with such candor? There was a lot to think about, but it came to a sudden halt when she kissed me and I kissed back. Not a rolling-in-the-turf kiss, nor was it just an appreciation kiss. It was tender with clear hints of desire.

The kiss reverberated for a long time. My anxiety about two in one bedroll and whether I could grasp the fundamentals evaporated. Beverly raised her head onto her hand and looked down at me. "I do enjoy talking with you and love your stories and the way you ask questions." She put her head down and pulled my hand and arm into her bedroll, holding it tight, and we finally fell asleep. My last waking thoughts considered the technical aspects of fitting two people into one bedroll without unraveling the blankets.

———————

Folk music and blues competed with the songs of birds, gur-
gling streams, and cricket chirps at Camp Hurley. Singing and
listening to the music of counselors, staff, and campers expressed
our values, fears, and hopes, and pulled us closer as a community.
We idolized Pete Seeger, Reverend Gary Davis, Muddy Waters,
Woody Guthrie, and other blues and folk singers of the times, but
we admired Hurley's own talented musicians the most. Pete Seeger
visited Hurley for two days every summer. Pete devoted most of his
time listening to Hurley musicians and singers rather than perform-
ing solo. Rickey, a senior supervisor, sang "Wimoweh" as well as if
not better than Pete. One of the memorable moments occurred
when Pete accompanied Rickey as they sang "Wimoweh" on the
last night of Pete's visit. No one needed prompting to begin the
backups. Every camper and counselor took part. When Rickey hit
the high notes of this African hunting song, the camp was in
ecstasy. Tears, hugs, and laughter followed. The music was a catalyst for making us feel connected and focusing on endless
possibilities for everyone in the world.

In addition to Pete Seeger, each summer Murray arranged to
have a band from Wiltwyck, a juvenile detention center, perform at
our camp. These boys had crafted steel drums and entertained with
joy and creativity that drew everyone's attention. The music was
new to our ears and many of us danced and pretended to be
Caribbean. After their performance the band spent the day playing
softball and swimming with us, and recounting stories about what it
was like living in a "reform school."

Though I was surrounded by progressive thinking at Little Red,
our backgrounds were all similar: a focus on education, left-wing
politics, folk music, art, future careers in arts, or service to others. I
fit into that milieu, but also felt bogus because I didn't have any
direct experience with kids from what would be considered
blue-collar or poor homes. We were for the proletariat at Little Red,

but families engaged in manual labor surrounded the school rather than inhabited our community; the paradoxical exception was my father. Other than the frightful encounters with street gangs, I never got to know kids caught up in juvenile detention, or who lived in foster care, or came from working-class homes until I came to Hurley. While I was sympathetic to kids from disadvantaged backgrounds, I assumed we had little to connect us. Hurley eroded that prejudice.

During my first year as a camper, one of my bunkmates was Joel, who had a slight build and appeared more withdrawn than the rest of us. But occasionally he blurted out an observation about people or a sensible plan for how to get our counselor to change his mind. Initially we ignored his infrequent remarks, but near the end of the first week, we began to look to him as the bunk's wisest. One evening I was bitching to my bunkmates about my mother. Others joined in about their parents, and after a while we looked at Joel and waited. Joel hesitated and then added in a clipped and detached manner, "My mother was selected foster mother of the year." No further particulars were offered.

Not knowing anything about foster care, I was unclear what this meant, but to live with a mother voted best of the year seemed like exceptional luck. What prize could my mother win? Most anxious? "You're lucky. Why was she chosen best mother?"

"Guess they never asked me. She feeds her own kids better food than me, she hits me if I can't get away fast enough, and she tells me I'm pulling her down." I was stunned and baffled that Joel didn't display frustration or judgment.

"Do you have to stay with her?" I asked. "Can't you tell anyone?"

"That's why I'm here. My social worker got me this three-week vacation. I've had thirteen foster mothers and this one isn't even the worst."

"Why are you in foster care?" I asked.

"I got into so many fights that my real mother couldn't or didn't want to handle me. The last fight got me arrested. My real mother went to court, missed a day at work. Guess she gave up and then she got sick. Don't blame her. I got three sisters she has to take care of. The gangs were too much for her. She's got asthma, just like me." I found myself whipped with shame, thinking of all my trivial complaints about my parents and their intervals of bizarre behavior.

Before Hurley I had played a lot of stoopball and stickball in the streets. The competition was fierce, and winning was everything. The need to fit in made me believe that rivalry was the driving force for sports. We argued and negotiated which parked Chevy was first base, which manhole cover or pothole was second. We unleashed our most creative taunts to unsettle the opposing players and argued every close play as if losing would erase our very identities.

Hurley's ball field was spotted with wild grass that was stomped down by hundreds of pairs of feet. This was luxury compared to playing on concrete in the playgrounds or cobblestones in the streets. A good batter could hit the ball far enough for it to get lost in the forest of pines that bordered the outfield. These hits counted as home runs, but delayed the game, sometimes twenty minutes or more, while everyone, including the batter, hunted for the runaway ball. Other than one ratty base bag, the only other indication that we had an actual ball field was our aging green backstop. This relic was mostly used for leaning against, since its mesh had corroded away.

Pitcher was my favorite position. During my first week as a camper I was eager to prove my worth. Josh was up at bat. An early-life disease limited his use of one leg. When Josh batted, another camper on his team stood beside him on the first-base side and ran to first as soon as Josh hit the ball. I assumed Josh couldn't hit and lobbed easy pitches. On my third pitch, he hit a solid line drive between right and center field that advanced a runner to third and got Josh's stand-in runner all the way to second. To distract from my disgrace I protested and demanded that the next time Josh batted, his designated runner had to start on the third-base side of home so as to not have a two-step advantage.

The next batter held his hands apart on the bat and appeared hesitant as to how to stand. His counselor, Hank Hammer, helped him straighten out his stance. We needed the out since there were runners on second and third. I began to razz the batter with the taunt "Hands Apart," mostly to calm myself and encourage our team. "No hitter here," I yelled to my teammates. "Don't worry. He can't hit." That sort of thing.

Hammer, an ex-Marine, held up the game and approached me. His physique seemed like a three-dimensional chart of the body's muscles. He marched to the pitcher's area with a deliberate stride until he stood within inches of my face. In a whisper that vibrated down my knees, he asked what I was doing. I was bewildered because my goading was mild compared to what had been done to me on the streets. "Nothing." My knees knocked against each other.

"You want to win?" Hammer asked.

That was an easy one. "Yes."

"Why?"

That wasn't so easy. I stopped. I knew what teams were supposed to do. But Hammer's bearing, accented by his powerful physical presence, forced me to believe that he had a different response in mind. The emptiness caused by my silence expanded the moment. I rubbed my knees with my baseball glove, wishing this could freeze their quivering.

"Do you really want Marty to fail? Will it make you happy if he strikes out?" Hammer asked.

Sure I did. That's the game of baseball. Hammer should know. He was a Marine.

"You're up next inning. You want Marty all over you, Paul?" Hammer paused and picked up a rock and tossed it between his hands. He clenched it so hard I thought he might pulverize it. Finally, he hurled it into the woods with a force that made it ricochet off at least two trees.

I was inching backward toward center field, but Hammer wasn't finished. "I noticed you're getting help to pass the deep-water swimming test. You think it would help if Marty called out 'no swimmer in the water'?" Hammer turned to walk off the field. "Oh, and next time Josh is at bat, his runner starts on first-base side, just as before. Got it?"

I kneeled down and pretended to tie my sneakers, desperate for the solid ground to bring my knees back under my control. It worked. I went back to the pitcher's mound, designated by stomped-out grass and pebbles. "Infield back, we got a hitter here." I pounded my glove and felt like I was getting to understand Hurley's principles. I was determined to give a pitch he could hit.

Marty hit a solid shot to right field that was caught on a fly, and before I could jump with relief, I looked at Hammer and considered running to center field and into the woods. Instead, I forced myself to come off the field with the other fielders, and sure enough Hammer approached. He grabbed my upper arm and pulled me close. I detected a slight variation in his now familiar whisper. "What you did . . ." I felt no pain in my arm. I had heard some injuries are so severe one didn't feel pain. ". . . was just what Marty needed."

At Elizabeth Irwin, "capitalist" was a term of reproach, but by fifteen I had yet to meet a capitalist of the sort we roughed up in our discussions. My parents were mute on the subject of capitalists and predictably I was left hanging when it came to framing my opinion. I felt pride in the fact that my father's work as an electrician represented the working class, which my friends revered. He worked with his hands, mostly with men who, like him, had not been to college or experienced any privilege. My mother's work assisted people who were on the margins of economic dependence. So when we sang "Which Side Are You On" at camp, I had no problem identifying with the workers and those in need. Yet my father patented several inventions and tried to manufacture them. Did that make him an enemy of the working class? My grandmother worked hard to support her family through building her small store into a sustaining business. Did that make her a capitalist? Paradoxically, my first actual sighting of eminently prosperous capitalists was at Camp Hurley, which many claimed was a Communist camp.

Halfway through my first three-week stay at camp, two chauffeur-driven Cadillacs pulled up in front of Camp Hurley's small mess hall. The limousines incited unrestrained curiosity because Hurley had a strict rule prohibiting non-camp vehicles from entering the campgrounds, and most of us had never seen a Cadillac close up. The two drivers and five men in business suits, white shirts, and ties were in crisp contrast to the hungry campers and counselors flooding into the mess hall. A crowd surrounded the black luxury sedans. A few staff members greeted the men with a degree of deference I had never witnessed in camp. Someone said they must be Hurley's board members and we better be respectful.

"Who the fuck you think you are?" Without looking we recognized the rage and sound of Murray's voice. A few younger campers, who were fondling the showy rear car fins, froze. Conversations halted. Campers and staff inched forward to view the performance. Murray, dressed in his scruffy blue work shirt and dungarees, with his long hair falling across his cheeks, challenged the men so quickly they backed up against their Cadillacs. His hands flailed wildly and he pointed toward the entrance of the camp. "You don't read? The sign says *no* cars beyond that point. You drive all the way up here just to kill one of your campers? Get these heaps out of here." Our expanding circle of onlookers pulled back in fear of being caught in collateral fallout from the fight we expected to follow.

Without protest one of the suited men spoke to his driver. "It's all right, Sam. We can walk back there when we're finished."

"Bullshit," Murray snorted. He had reached his critical pre-explosive level. "Sam and the other driver are having lunch with us." He turned to the drivers. "Park these hearses up by the parking area and then come back for lunch." He turned back to the five men. "This is a camp. You come here in your limousines dressed for private clubs." Murray clenched his fists. "How the fuck are you going to wash dishes?"

The suits jettisoned their jackets and loosened their ties. Instead of socking them, Murray opened his hand and formally shook their hands. His voice calmed and he continued, "You're in time for camp lunch. But board members don't eat till all the campers have finished. Get into the kitchen and you'll wash everyone's dishes before you eat."

The suits, with their sleeves rolled up and collars opened, dutifully followed Murray into the dishwashing section of the kitchen. One man was assigned to scrape the slop off the dishes into the waste barrel, another to stack dishes into wash bins, and a third to move the bins into the dishwasher. A few campers who were serving at lunch had to show the "slopper" how to perform his task, and one of the kitchen staff, a pre-law student, demonstrated to another suit how to operate the industrial dishwasher. The conscripted dishwashers, now anointed with splatter, heeded advice from campers, who felt sympathy for their predicament. However, an eight-year-old expressed many of the others' fears. "Hope we don't get you for counselors."

The mess hall finally emptied and the suits sat down with Murray and their drivers for lunch. Anna was Hurley's cook. Her personality made us compete to peel hundreds of pounds of potatoes, or do any menial chore in her kitchen, just to be in the presence of her abounding acceptance and joy for life and food. She along with the rest of the kitchen staff joined them. "Anna, these are the guys who pay for our food. When you complain how we need to have more meat or better vegetables for the kids, it's their fault." Murray turned to the men. "This is going to be the best meal you'll eat all summer, and it's not because of the crap you force us to buy or beg from the government. It's because Anna's a sensational cook. One of your club lunches costs more than feeding 150 kids one meal here. You should be ashamed." The men meekly forked their food.

One of the suits complimented Anna on the food. "Murray's right. I'm coming here every week for my lunches."

Murray scowled at the man: "Not unless you pay."

Another suit pointed to his colleague's slop-stained shirt. "Murray, I haven't had so much fun in years. And I was worried you were going to put on a propaganda show."

"You'd rather have a show? You pay for many of these kids, but that doesn't entitle you to waste our time."

"Murray, please, we just had to see where the money is spent."

"Walk around, talk to anyone. You got two hours. Then I want you out. I can't join you 'cause I got to work with Raffety, our plumber." Murray grabbed an off-duty counselor. "Rose, take these guys wherever they want to go and let them talk to anyone. Just get them out by 4:30. Don't take any bullshit from them about leaving."

Rose was less than pleased. "But Murray, this is my day off. I was planning to go to Woodstock and the truck leaves at 4:00."

"You think I want them here? But they pay your lousy salary." Murray turned to the five suits. "You're making a mess of my day and now Rose feels I owe her big time. So before you drive back to the city, drop her off in Woodstock. Give her money for a nice meal. Call me if you have questions."

As Murray walked away, the leader of the suits called out, "And I'll tell the rest of the board we still have the same commie bastard running our camp. I can't believe it, but you give commies a good name." Murray was labeled a Communist because no one had a better term for his work to build inclusive and equitable communities. Perhaps he even had been a Party member at one time. He dared to bridge our ideals with whoever would help, regardless of differences in ideologies.

Labels acquired from ordinary life had no meaning in Camp Hurley, where I learned the importance of community as a means of letting people flourish and nurturing self-confidence. In this environment of camping, working, living with strangers, sharing music and the passion for social justice, in an oasis free of judgment by physical ability, lifestyle, or background, I was at my best. The life resonated so strongly with me that I felt myself straighten up figuratively as well as physically. Finding a place where I truly belonged made me feel stronger in belonging to myself.

CHAPTER NINE

At home, there was no formal conference or letter of agreement passed amongst us, but it was clear that my mother, father, and I agreed that my training wheels were off. If I needed emergency rescue they were there for me, but given my father's wacky advice and preoccupation with renovating our home and my mother's preoccupation with her new career as a professor of social work, I had to rely on my own experiences to figure out how to get on in life.

Beginning my second year at Stuyvesant I knew academics were a lost option for fitting in. It all seemed like Greek. The majority of students at Stuyvesant were headed for Ivy League or first-tier college educations and I resigned myself to finding other ways of distinguishing myself. Even back at Stuyvesant, however, my emotional attachments were with my Hurley community. Perhaps I was never suited for the style of Little Red or the relative homogeneity of our class. Or perhaps the emphasis of identity on our parents' politics at Little Red never allowed me to feel fully connected there. Or possibly the abrupt extraction from Little Red/E.I. curtailed what could have blossomed into a strong sense of belonging once I had tripped fully into my adolescence. Perhaps the switch to public school at a critical age was a mistake. I'd easily lay the blame on my parents, yet it was my mother's instinct and ability to dump me into new experiences that introduced me to Hurley, a pivotal experience of belonging that affected my entire life.

Sunday at Washington Square Park was my favorite day of the week. The park was the common assembly point for the Hurley community. Most of my camp friends travelled from other parts of Manhattan, the Bronx, Queens, Brooklyn, and Long Island. It was my luck to live a few blocks away. A camper from Hurley would stand on one of the monuments that connected the circle surrounding the fountain, serving as a beacon for us to gather amidst the congregations of folksingers, poets, and artists. Banjos and guitars were ubiquitous. We sang old songs and never missed opportunities to learn new ones from strangers and new friends. We embraced each other as if we had just returned from six-month trips rather than a six-day separation. Quick updates about what seemed a disconnected week at our schools were exchanged, but the vital conversations related to our plans for ending nuclear testing, the meaning of life, making arrangements for attending civil rights rallies, films, books, and parties, and counting the days till we returned to Hurley. Before everyone walked to the subway, we clasped hands and swayed back in forth in a huge circle singing "We Shall Overcome."

Years later, in 2009, at Pete Seeger's ninetieth birthday bash at Madison Square Garden, I bumped into some Hurley campers. They looked much older, yet rather than showing age lines that represented the competitive struggles of life, their faces and posture reflected a sense of softness and a thrill with continuing to make or hope for justice and equality. We sang the songs with the same gusto as when we were campers a half century earlier. It was almost silly shedding tears in Madison Square Garden, the iconic arena for the toughest of competition, yet I did, realizing that Hurley had been one of the more significant touchstones for my adult life and still was. I recalled Hank Hammer introducing me to the unusual idea that winning wasn't the most important thing, or Dennis reminding me that struggles were just natural and empathy was more important than status and riches. And Mac, who despite life-long rejection because of the color of his skin, would never give up hope. And Mickey, who gave me the means to share my inner dialogue with another. And Murray, who created a community we would never have dared to fully believe could be a utopia, but nevertheless came as close to it as any of us would ever encounter. If I am truthful in looking back, I realize that throughout all my careers I worked to find or create microcosms of the Hurley experience, forming groups to achieve collective goals, perhaps an offshoot ideal of socialism or even communism with a small *c*.

We rarely know at the time which early life experiences will have the most significant effects and carry forth throughout a whole life. Even though I sensed the positive powers of Hurley I had my doubts too. When I was a camp counselor I would talk way into the night with Murray about the effects of such a safe and nourishing environment on the kids who had to return to foster homes, poverty, and the continuing struggles of life. Whether this too-brief oasis in a life could actually make things harder for most of the campers to go back to their more challenging environments. Weren't we creating an ideal that could never be found in the world beyond our campgrounds? Obviously Murray refuted this notion. What I didn't realize then was that this distinctive contrast had significant impact on my life as well as that of the less fortunate campers. Throughout my life, I felt heightened frustration and less acceptance for conditions that couldn't rise to the level of Hurley's progressive ideals and ability to implement those ideals. It made me too impatient, even too judgmental, when systems and others thwarted the drive toward justice and equality. But back then, while I thought I recognized the grandeur of this experiment, I couldn't realize that I knew very little of how the experiences would shape my life.

I could mostly give up my anger and resentment for having been pulled out of E.I. Strangely (for me as well as my parents) I didn't fall apart when removed from the shelter of private school. Public school was not comfortable, but no longer was I caught in the middle: defending my teachers' and friends' politics to my father while covering up his politics to my classmates and teachers. And I no longer had to feel guilty about the costs. I was left alone except for report card periods.

My academic skills contributed to the left side of Stuyvesant's bell curve. My report card produced peculiar results at home. From my father there was little evidence of passion when he reacted. "Paul, you can do better than a C-minus in chemistry. You ought to work harder." Perhaps a line he heard from *Father Knows Best*. I favored my mother's interpretation: "Paul, that's wonderful, a C-minus from Dr. Lieberman! He has a PhD and is a demanding teacher. C-minus shows you must really be working hard."

Mr. Herbst, an English teacher and faculty advisor for the student government, approached me out of the blue. He seemed unaware of or uninterested in my academic shortcomings, and thus I accepted his offer to volunteer to work for the student government. Mr. Herbst helped me make friends with the school's student leaders.

David, the current school president, Frank, the vice president, and Herbst brought up my political future. Frank laid out the path to becoming school president in my senior year. "You must run for school secretary when you are a sophomore. It's the only school position you can run for. Forget running for class offices. They mean nothing."

Secretary? I couldn't spell and couldn't read my own handwriting. Thinking the job consisted of taking notes at meetings I rebuffed the advice.

"Trust me. You need this to get into an Ivy League school." This was a preposterous target since, despite my mother's assessment, I was barely passing half my classes.

The three of them directed me to collect the three hundred signatures needed to run for school secretary. Considering I spoke with only eleven students in the school, this seemed ludicrous, but oddly, this diminished my sense of panic inasmuch as my failure to collect the necessary signatures would prove I was not the political operative my support team believed me to be.

Meanwhile, the New York State Regents exams were plunging toward me and I feared statewide humiliation. How supportive would my mother be when I failed chemistry? A practice Regents exam was given in chemistry class. Dr. Lieberman passed back the graded exams in order of performance. The third student to receive his exam had a 98. Before too many other exams were passed out, that student protested. "Dr. Lieberman, question three is correct and you marked it wrong." A fifth student, who received a grade of 97, interrupted. "Question twenty-one wasn't clear. That's not fair." The seventh student complained to his neighbors and encouraged them to get their parents to register protests with the principal regarding Lieberman's inability to prepare us for question seventeen.

After twenty-six students received their exams I was handed mine with a red 66 circled, just barely passing. The four students after me failed. They were part of the smaller group of school toughs. How and why they were in this school were mysteries to me, but given my grades it was a mystery why I was there. Maybe they had mothers like mine.

"Swenson, you'll never pass the Regents." Dr. Lieberman said this to one of the four as a fact rather than reproach. Swenson tormented many of us in the lunchroom and sometimes threatened to take our lunch money. He was brawny. His physical power was in stark contrast to the bearing of most of the school's students, including my own. I once had a minor altercation with him when he grabbed my shirt and jerked me away from an empty lunch table I had chosen to sit at. "Don't you know my table is reserved for me and my guys?" he goaded.

For some reason I challenged him. I had in mind my mother's ability to talk the behemoth at Macy's into giving her credit for dresses she bought at S. Klein's and my father's ability to persuade a judge he hadn't gone through a red light when he did. "I know you can beat me up and there's nothing I can do about it. But just because you can beat me up doesn't mean it's fair." I flinched before he swung at me.

Unexpectedly Swenson recoiled. He shoved me back into my seat. "Just don't take my favorite chair." When his buddies showed up and were about to thrust me from my chair, Swenson intervened. "Think of him as our new mascot. Leave him alone."

"Who's going to help Swenson pass the Regents?" Dr. Lieberman demanded. There was silence. I wanted Lieberman to find someone to help me, but was too embarrassed to ask. "Goldstein, you got a 99. Why don't you work with Swenson? We can't have one of ours not passing the Regents."

"Dr. Lieberman, please. I have to get my grades up or I'll never get into Brown," Goldstein answered.

Lieberman wouldn't be discouraged by this scholar's response. "Stiles, you got a 95 and you certainly know your chemistry. Come on. It'll take you just a couple of hours."

Stiles squirmed, glancing at Swenson. "I'm with Goldstein."

"Pitcoff." I was startled and assumed Lieberman was now matching me with a tutor. "Pitcoff, you help Swenson."

"But Dr. Lieberman, I'm barely passing. If I help Swenson he'll fail and then he'll—" I stopped as my future turned bleak. I would tutor Swenson, he would fail, and then he would beat me up.

"Make time to help him," Dr. Lieberman ordered and went on to do his postmortem of the practice test. Swenson was even more alarmed than me at being forced into a shotgun tutelage, but we both had to do what Lieberman wanted or else neither of us would pass his class.

While I studied chemistry with Swenson, Mr. Herbst pestered and encouraged me to gather the courage to stand by the front door of the school and collect the remaining 289 signatures from arriving students. Streams of students divided around my tense and mostly frozen body as they entered the school. I woodenly reached toward one of them who'd been in a few of my classes and timidly asked if he would sign my petition. "I don't sign petitions," he groused.

His attempt to move on was blocked. Swenson appeared from the multitude of adolescent boys, seized the petition out of my hand, and thrust it back at the recalcitrant student. "Hey pal, you'll need a pen. Here." He thrust my pen into the student's hand and studied the petition. "Aren't you lucky, you're number seven to elect Pitcoff secretary. Sign." Persuasion came easy for Swenson. He mashed the petition against the student's chest. The student rapidly signed and seemed pleased to be able to walk away in one piece.

Swenson snatched back the petition and looked it over. "What's this about?"

"Well, I'm thinking of running for school secretary, but I need three hundred signatures. Doubt I'll get that many, but want to try. So if you could—"

Swenson ignored signing it himself. "You gotta have a better approach." He looked me up and down and continued, "Nah, you'll never get shit. I'll do it."

I was mystified and Swenson saw it in my face. "Pitcoff, you were the only one willing to help me in Lieberman's class. How about I get you your signatures at lunch period. You know, payback.

OK?" He seized the petition and was swallowed up in the herd of last-minute students swarming into the building.

After sixth period Swenson waited for me to get out of homeroom. The petition was a bit crumpled but complete. "I got 357, just in case. Many of the guys don't know who you are. You got to get out there. Anyway, I kind of encouraged everyone; you know what I mean. You'll win." It felt eerie and unethical to learn that students who had no idea of my very existence were signing the petition.

When the campaign officially started, Dave told me to make dozens of campaign posters to acquaint students with my platform. One poster I prepared had a picture of Sputnik with the line "We Can Catch Up—Vote for Pitcoff."

"Why so nationalistically competitive? Isn't this just a position for school office?" my mother asked. I kind of liked the Sputnik link because everyone was talking about it, and the school had changed its curriculum based on its recent launch.

"You shouldn't be giving credit to the Soviets. It panders to the Communists," my father added.

"Dad, this is Stuyvesant, not E.I. Believe me there're no Communists at Stuyvesant."

Their comments were merely background static. My new anxiety fixated on how I could secure prominent hallway spots to hang my posters. I applied and received a hall pass for fifth period, my lunch period, to walk the halls to hang my posters. My two opponents had already hung their slick posters in prime spaces where most students congregated. I was juggling my posters and pins and tape for hanging them, while searching the hall for empty spaces, when Swenson came from the assistant principal's office. "Guess I'm too late to get any good spots," I said. "I couldn't find space on the first and third floors either."

Swenson said some teacher had it in for him and he wasn't going back to his class. "Give me those posters. We'll do it sixth period when my guys have lunch."

"But how will you get hall passes?"

Swenson popped a whole bunch of permission slips from his pocket and fanned them in front of my face. "See how they have the official stamped signatures? All I have to do is fill in my name, date, and a period. See, just the same as your pass. Bet you had to ask the assistant principal to get yours signed. Here, you may need a few." Swenson understood systems better than me and there was no doubt he would be a more effective school officer, but I sensed he thought it was a waste of time.

After last period I checked the halls to see if Swenson and his gang had done what he offered. There they were: "Vote for Pitcoff for School Secretary," with some simple tag line such as "He's the Best," "He Won't Let You Down," "A Way Forward." Something struck me as strange. My posters were in the most prominent places in the school, and while I climbed every floor I could not spot a single poster for any of my opponents. It looked as if I was the only candidate. Swenson won the election for me. I was too young to recognize I won the election in the traditional American manner of a bit more than robust campaigning itself. Most likely my opponent lost because he had no visibility as a result of Swenson. Not much to build my pride on, yet I did feel a new injection of confidence.

Swenson and I played life from sharply different perspectives. While I was searching for ways to project my fledgling idealism, he had long developed a sense that such sentiments masked accepting the realities of life. Yet with Lieberman's nudge, we eliminated what divided us and found ways to help each other. Hurley and now this experience made me sense that I could transcend gulfs of differences. I would not be confined to cocoons with people who looked and acted like me. I didn't note this as a talent or something that would later be of enormous help in my multiple careers and social life, but at the time I sensed its necessity for broadening the theatre of my life. I may not have mastered the structure and properties of matter, but Lieberman's chemistry class brought new insights about politics and life. Ideas and philosophy were OK, but allies were crucially important too.

CHAPTER TEN

Since my first summer at Hurley I had emerged progressively from the molasses of adolescence insecurity. Official recognition came with a "promotion" from plain old camper to responsible work-camper in my second summer. Work-campers were around the age of sixteen and not supervised like other campers. On a daily basis girls and boys were given work assignments for maintaining and improving camp facilities by our supervisor, George McCracken. We were mostly on our own to perform our tasks during the day.

The guilt my mother experienced in working so hard at her career must have been eased by the outside reinforcement that I was of an age that needed far less supervision. Perhaps the elimination of the camp's fee also gave her hope that in the future I might no longer be a dependent.

Work-campers washed at the same outdoor trough sink used by teen campers and their counselors. The second week at camp I carried my toothbrush, towel, toothpaste, and leaking collapsible tin cup for my final washing of the night. The sun had retired hours before, the evening had a Catskill chill woven into the light air, and only the familiar outlines of buildings and trees were visible in the darkness, punctuated by an occasional sweep of a distant flashlight. Hysterical moths attacked the two bare light bulbs laboring to ward off the darkness around the sinks. It had been a satisfying day of physical work, conversations with friends, a few innings of baseball, and a swim. All that remained was the five-minute walk back to my bunk, some concluding gossip with bunkmates, reading a few pages of *Dissent*, and ultimately sleep.

Across the sink was a pleasant-looking girl, wearing an open flannel shirt over a blue denim work shirt. A towel was thrown over her shoulder. Her face bobbed in and out of view as she rigorously brushed her teeth. She lowered her head to take in water directly from one of the six cold-water faucets, which she would spit out and then repeat the process. The aroma of Colgate toothpaste masked the scent of the pine forest. Each time her head appeared above the faucets she sent a toothpaste smile my way, chuckled, and encouraged me to get to work on my teeth. Her dark blond hair was cut short and she seemed comfortable with allowing it to do its own thing. Her lighthearted humor made me assume she was a camper and younger than me. I nodded and she smiled again and mumbled a greeting between her closed teeth. Finally, she spit out into the sink.

"Hi. I'm Mickey, Mickey Brodsky. You're in Mac's group, right?"

"Yea," I answered. Mac had already gained the affection and respect of all the work- campers. He was tall, in his thirties, had an athletic body, deep chocolate skin, and penetrating eyes. Accepting and charismatic in his leadership, George McCracken was from Chicago and completing his master's degree in social work. Leading the work-campers was a senior position at Hurley, because one had to provide freedom to adolescents and at the same time ensure their safety. My only problem with Mac was envy. The girls talked about him as their ideal man. I hoped they could only wait and see me when I was his age, although I knew I could never be as strong or good-looking. His model, empathy in a strong male, echoed my father's, and I was heartened to see that girls appreciated it, hopeful that these traits might show up in me.

I fumbled for some words. "You must be in Charlotte's upper teen bunk." Charlotte was the lead co-counselor for the oldest girls' bunk.

I didn't see anything humorous in my comment, but Mickey laughed and then ducked her head under the faucet again for another rinsing of her mouth and said, "Well, thanks for the compliment, but I'm a counselor for the fourteen-year-olds."

"Sorry. Just thought you seemed like a camper." I paused and then added, "How could you be a counselor?"

Mickey dried her face with the kind of purpose that for the first time made me consider she might be more a woman than just a girl. There was no accusation in her tone, but she responded with a considered seriousness. "You think I'm not ready to be a counselor?" She paused as if to hear my answer, but the only sound was of my toothbrush scrubbing away at my teeth.

She continued, "I'm starting City College in the fall and last year I was a counselor in training. What do you think I need to do to be a real counselor?" She noted my perpetual teeth cleaning and thus didn't bother to wait for my response. "Should I wait till I finish my master's in social work?" She packed up her toiletries and reached across to shut off my flowing faucet. "If you continue brushing your teeth, you'll need a new brush and the camp will run out of water."

"This fall I'll be a junior in high school." The words "high school" echoed through my head.

Instead of dismissing me with "I'll see you around," she continued, "It might be fun for you to visit one of my classes this fall. See what college is about. I did that last year when I was in high school." The "high school" reverberation throbbed in my head. Mickey pointed to my buttons. "I think they don't match up. That's why I always button from the top." I was mortified and quickly redid the buttons to line up. Mickey was without guile and I thought I had found my older half-sister even though she hadn't appeared from an airplane, as my half-brother came into my life when I was four. Oddly, I found myself disappointed in this thought. If I could figure out how to gain two more years and how to button evenly, maybe we could be more than sister and brother. This thought came from nowhere. Without thinking, I refueled my toothbrush with a dollop of toothpaste, which I directly swallowed, causing me to choke.

Mickey cocked her head and looked puzzled while I coughed. The warm color light bulbs intensified the hues of my reddening cheeks. "Swallowing toothpaste is not such a good thing," she said. I managed to stop coughing and joined her in laughing at my misfortune. Perhaps she feared I would choke to death if we stayed any longer and guided me away from the sink toward her bunk. Mickey talked about her experiences two years ago as a work-camper, and how Mac helped everyone discover what they were good at. "He's one of those few people you can talk to about any-thing. His warmth and care made me feel I could fall in love with him." My affection for Mac waned.

"You come wash at this time every night?" I asked.

Mickey's eyes followed a tall pine tree into the sky. She let my question hang for a few moments. "Remember, I'm a counselor and when I'm on duty I don't get here till late. I'm sure we'll bump into each other again." She chuckled. "You know you are technically still a camper."

There was a no-fraternizing rule between campers and staff, but was a work-camper considered a camper? Some rules never seemed to have clear answers. What was she really telling me? Would it be wrong to brush teeth together or talk more? Was she just being pleasant and assuming the role of an older sister? I was sixteen and she had to be eighteen or older. Did eighteen make a girl into a woman? Sixteen certainly made a boy. Where could I get two years, fast?

When we reached her bunk, we agreed to meet at the sink in two nights at 10:00 p.m. We didn't even shake hands. I turned and jogged back to my bunk fantasizing about enrolling at City College and beginning a new life together with Mickey in the fall. I swatted off thoughts that we were destined merely for a sibling-type relationship.

Work-campers repaired bunks, constructed steps from logs for steep footpaths around the camp, and built a large lean-to for those who wanted to sit outside in the rain. Work-campers didn't pay to attend Camp Hurley, but our labors were rewarded by a six-day camping vacation led by Mac to wherever a chartered bus could take us within five hundred miles. As we boarded the bus, we envisioned travelling as an exotic journey in a foreign country, filled with joyful experiences and camaraderie we would never forget, even if it was only Canada.

Our group was racially mixed: a black leader, along with nine white and three black campers. It was 1959, a year before sit-ins began in the South. Now, five years after the Supreme Court school desegregation decision, most segregated schools had not complied. My friends and I felt tormented by the plague of racism that barnacled our country. In Canada we would be welcomed regardless of our race.

Our friendships had been tested by time and were made stronger from the physical work we'd been doing together. We camped near Niagara Falls on our first night, which reminded me of how happy my parents were when we detoured there on our return from our cross-country trip. I missed Mickey, but felt happy to be with

friends. Late in the afternoon of the next day, we reached
Algonquin Provincial Park. Mac left the bus to arrange for a large
group campsite. We were worn from the day on the bus, but were
eager to enjoy five days hiking and camping in a great wilderness
area. Mac was gone a long time and Roy, the bus driver, worried
there might be some problem.

Mac returned and called for us to get out of the bus and hold
off on unpacking anything. We needed to have a meeting.
Apparently the park wouldn't accept Negroes sleeping overnight.
No matter how Mac explained it to the park officials they were
steadfast in their refusal. The manager was sympathetic, but said
he would lose his job because many of the park's campers would
complain. He did offer a solution. Mac, along with three black
campers, Lorraine, Marvin, and James, could stay at rental cabins
off the park grounds. The park manager assured them that the
cabins would take "anyone." They would be free to come to the
park during the day; they just couldn't sleep there. Mac's facial
muscles must have collapsed because he looked more like fifty
than thirty. His dark brown face almost turned pale white. "Sorry,
I should have checked before. Somehow I thought Canada would
be different from Chicago or D.C."

Felice and Judy started crying. Dave and Phil asked me to
come with them and try to change the manager's mind. "You have
a mouth, Paul." Mac didn't want us getting into a fight. We
weren't in our own country and who knew what rights we had or
didn't have.

Roy blared the bus's horn for a long thirty seconds. He was
from Arkansas and in just two days had become a member of our
group, choosing to camp out with us at Niagara Falls rather than
stay at a motel, which his bus company would pay for. Roy's deep
southern drawl, good nature, and curiosity made him a charming
and much liked older addition to our group. After exhausting his

rage on the horn, he finally spoke. "Let me talk to the son of a bitch. I don't care if they lock me up. My company will bail me out, just so they don't have to send another driver up here." He rolled up his sleeves and pulled out a long lug wrench from the cargo compartment.

"Roy, put that away. If we lose you, we'll be stuck here." It was the first time Mac cracked a half smile. "And I don't want to be stuck here." He turned to the group. "Look, if it's all right with James, Lorraine, and Marvin, we four Negroes will have a pleasant night with a warm shower and no bugs. We'll meet up with you in the morning."

There was a chorus of noes and everyone boarded the bus and demanded that Roy get us out of such a repulsive situation. The public park policies had degraded our leader and fellow campers. We, who had a free pass to general acceptance in the outer world, could do nothing. Someone overheard Mac mention to Roy that the real problem was not having a few Negroes in the park, but that we were a mixed group.

We headed for Ottawa, not knowing whether we would find anyplace that would take us in. The silence and the dimness of the bus seeped gloominess into every crevice of our minds. The pine-scented air from the open windows had lost its power to raise spirits. We couldn't overcome our personal sense of powerlessness. James smirked at our naiveté. He told stories about restaurants and stores in New York City that barred his entrance because of his color. Lorraine sat still and stared out her window.

In Ottawa, a YMCA director graciously accepted our group. We arranged our bedrolls on the indoor basketball court and went out looking for dinner at 9:30 p.m. No one was on the street and only one or two cars drove by. Ottawa looked like one of those cities in a sci-fi movie that had lost its population. Eventually, we found a café that was just closing, but welcomed our unexpected business.

"Where is everyone?" Dave asked the waitress.

"What'd you mean?" The waitress was caught off guard, but then looked out onto the street where Dave was pointing. "Oh, it's Tuesday. People got to work tomorrow. They're all home, probably asleep."

Growing up in New York, D.C., and Chicago, we never imagined any city could close down at night. The revelation diverted our thoughts, except for Mac, Lorraine, Marvin, and James. They seemed to be lost in their thoughts, far removed from our group. Roy was attracted to the waitress. She was slender, not much older than forty, had straight dark hair, and made us feel as if she were our caring aunt. She introduced herself as Judi, underscoring the "i." After Roy told the story of being refused entry into the campgrounds she became agitated. "Mr. McCracken, your meal, and Lorraine's, Marvin's, and James's, is on me. Want you to remember Canada in a good way."

Roy exaggerated his southern drawl for the Canadian waitress. "I grew up in Marianna, Arkansas. Just assumed coloreds were second class and nothing to it, till I got this driving job. Been around the USA and even Canada. It ain't right. Got to get along is what I learned. After a while, every passenger is just a passenger and some are pretty special. Never seems to matter what size, shape, or color." Roy turned to Mac. "Mr. McCracken, why don't you and I go out with this pretty waitress tonight? I'm sure she has a friend. These kids are all right and they can take care of themselves. Don't need us."

Mac smiled with amusement. He thanked Roy and Judi. Our group remained subdued. Mac turned toward everyone and said, "This stuff happens. Lorraine, Marvin, James, and me will never get past it, but guys like you are going to make a difference for my kids." He turned back to Roy and Judi, who'd already told Roy that all her friends were probably asleep. "Thanks, but our group stays together. You two go and have a good time." Roy excused himself in the same way to Judi, explaining he had to return to the Y, but took her address and phone number and said he would be back on his next trip to Ottawa.

Our excitement and hopes for our trip evaporated. The next morning we ended our trip early and headed back to Hurley. I thought of the time when some men tried to beat up a black man for eating at Horn and Hardart. My father interceded by inviting the target of racism to eat with us. Even at six I detected in this stranger's face a look that fused anger, humiliation, and shaken pride. I recognized similar looks now in the faces of my friends who had just been victims of racism. I ached to get back to Hurley, a harbor of fairness.

When we returned to camp, Mickey and I found ways to meet every day. We wandered into the woods and made our own trails to eventually nestle together in luxurious carpets of pine needles. Anything that popped into our minds became a fount of conversation. Thoughts I had long held in my mind seemed fresh and different when I heard them come from my mouth and had someone interested in asking questions about them. As the relationship grew and blossomed I feared it might be too late to reveal some of my more shameful truths about myself. "I can't spell. I don't know how to spell and don't think I can learn."

She threw some pine needles at me and laughed. "I knew you were covering up. There's a secretive nature to you. Didn't realize it was around such serious matters. I can teach you some simple rules, if you like," she said. "Now I'll tell you a secret." She leaned backward on her arms. "A few men asked me to sleep with them, but I haven't."

And my big secret was spelling! "Were they your boyfriends?"

"No. Just knew me. I kind of understand. You actually know some of them. I didn't take any offense, just said no. I wanted to be in love the first time. They weren't that upset, and we're still friends. They felt it would help me once I found someone I really loved. You know, be more experienced."

Hurley was a well-protected world, but what would our relationship look like back in the city where I would return to *high school*? I couldn't silence that echo. A sixteen-year-old boy dating an eighteen-year-old woman just seemed too overwhelming to turn into success. In the city I would have to travel to Pelham Parkway, a foreign neighborhood in the Bronx, a far-off country over an hour away and thirty or more stops on the subway. How could I tell an eighteen-year-old that I had to be back home to study for the New York State Regents exams? And there were all those guys old enough to go to bars who had cars and were interested in her, while my only experience in dating had been taking a girl to Palisades Amusement Park and a drink of water at White Castle.

———————

Near the end of summer Mac arranged for the entire camp to meet in the rec hall just before the younger campers had to go to sleep. Everyone had heard how we had been prohibited from camping because we were an interracial group. He believed it would comfort the camp community to talk about our ordeal. Mac had noticeably regained his sense of purpose and hopefulness, but he seemed to consider his words for a few extra beats before letting them loose. He leaned against the little performance stage flanked by James, Marvin, and Lorraine and a few other work-campers.

Mickey and I leaned against the wall. The excitement of being part of a larger group, politically conscious and taking responsibility for social justice, caused us to inch closer to each other and brush hands, which set off both romantic and political charges. My mother fell in love with my father when he was standing on a soapbox, organizing workers. As Bill Kunstler, the radical lawyer and civil rights activist noted years later, politics ignited romance.

"Guess it's no secret that Lorraine, Marvin, Dennis, James, Anna, and a whole bunch of us are Negro," Mac said. One of the eight-year-old African American campers held out his arm for his bunkmates to see it was the same color as Mac's.

"At first I didn't realize I was different," Mac said. "Growing up in Chicago I quickly learned that some people hated me for what I looked like." Mac's words had a solemn quality that created suspense as to what he might propose we do.

Mac took time to make eye contact with as many of the campers as possible and continued, "I joined a gang and was going to beat up those people who hated me because of my skin color. I was sixteen when I met Murray. He was doing his social work internship at my housing project." Murray, uncharacteristically quiet, sat on the floor in the very back of the room with his arm around Anna, our cook, and his other arm around a nine-year-old camper who was having a difficult time preparing to return to her foster care home. He made no acknowledgment that Mac had mentioned his name. Mac didn't look at Murray. "Murray told me he tried to beat up all the Irish kids who taunted the few Jews in his neighborhood when he was growing up, and he joined a gang for protection."

Mac paused as everyone turned to look at Murray. Many of us couldn't imagine him in a gang although the idea that he could beat up someone didn't seem far-fetched. "He told me there were more of them than him," Mac continued. "So he had to give up before he got killed. Murray ended up going into the Army and then college and then helping Irish kids find jobs. I think he found a job for one of the kids who beat him up."

Mac allowed a slight whiff of a smile at this recollection. "I decided college might be easier than taking revenge on white kids. Dennis, James, Anna . . . none of us can change what other people think when they see us. It's just a battle we have to deal with. Change will come." Mac's words were the only sound apart from a distant cow bellowing about some issues in her own life.

"For me, living in this integrated world at Hurley, where we come from different backgrounds, makes sense. I've had time to meet you, talk, understand the feelings we share and those we don't share. I'm a different person now. The anger I've towed since I was first conscious of my color will never disappear, but here it has been tempered and someday—" Mac coughed to smother the makings of a sob. He smiled with the acknowledgment of what we all saw. "When we go back to our neighborhoods we must remember these times together because anger alone will never move us forward. It's the small things we can and must do that will change things."

Tears glistened on Mac's cheeks. "If we make an effort to listen to each other, things will change." He crossed his arms and took hold of Lorraine's hand on one side of him and Marvin's hand on the other and everyone got up, joined hands, and sang our peace hymn, "We Shall Overcome."

———

Returning to the city was a shock. I was homesick for Hurley. Way out of my neighborhood comfort zone I began taking the fifty-minute IRT ride to Pelham Parkway, and often an hour and a half back at night when trains ran less frequently to meet Mickey at her family's apartment. Her parents couldn't support her, so she had to get work to pay for her living and college expenses. Her family lived in a one-bedroom apartment and Mickey slept on a hideaway in the living room. Occasionally her younger sister, who was in and out of mental health institutions, slept in the living room with her. Her parents were upset that Mickey didn't get full-time work to help support the family. She felt there was a good chance she wouldn't make it through college because of the living expenses and having to work while studying.

"Maybe it's not right for me to abandon my family just so I can live better than they do." Her eyes lost focus, as if she were being pulled away from our moment. "What if I can't even help anyone else, once I become a social worker?"

We sat on the roof of her apartment house one evening, looking out onto Pelham Parkway and talking about our relationship. Mickey pulled her winter coat tight around her and doused my anxieties about our age differences. It was 2:00 a.m. and the subway wouldn't get me home till after 3:30 a.m.

"I have too many other things to think about in going to college. We just have to make it work out." Thinking about our relationship exhausted us and we turned to singing camp songs: "Which Side Are You On": "My daddy was a miner/And I'm a miner's son/I'll stick with the union/'Til every battle's won." And then "Oh Freedom": "Oh freedom, oh freedom,/Oh freedom over me!/And before I'd be a slave/I'd be buried in my grave/Oh freedom over me." We ended this, as with all our private songfests, with "We Shall Overcome": "We shall overcome/We shall overcome/We shall overcome someday/Oh, deep in my heart/I do believe/We shall overcome someday," with Mickey taking the high part of the harmony. We felt blanketed with hope. We reminded ourselves of how much Mac had done to change his life and get his master's degree. Our love made us feel we had the power to face all the challenges ahead of us.

Our exclusive relationship went on for two years. Every experience we shared took on a vividness that increased our desire to spend time together. No feelings were caged and we shared our enjoyments as well as our worries. Doing anything together packed our agenda of things to talk about. We rarely planned our times together. We rushed to see the latest foreign films. We roamed bookstores for hours, attended free lectures, or if we couldn't find anything particular to do, we walked new neighborhoods. A big event was attending the 1960 SANE (National Committee for a Sane Nuclear Policy) rally at Madison Square Garden, where Harry Belafonte sang, Eleanor Roosevelt spoke, and most of our friends from Hurley gathered along with 17,000 others because we believed we could end the nuclear arms race.

The age disparity had its effects and was made painfully evident at parties held by Mickey's college classmates. "What year are you?" "I never saw you in any of my classes." "Oh, I didn't realize you were still in high school." "What're you doing here? Are you Mickey's kid brother?" Parents and friends more than whispered that we were too young and inexperienced. Direct and indirect advice was one-sided: "You shouldn't cut yourselves off from other experiences and romances."

We knew different. We were awed by how quickly our intimacy shattered boundaries. Only a few months back from Hurley we made love and felt bathed in an everlasting relationship. We were determined to make our love affair the best creation of our lives. We devoured Erich Fromm's *The Art of Loving*.

"I'm not sure I understand Fromm," I said. We were on a bus in the Bronx coming back from seeing a movie at the Loew's Paradise on the Grand Concourse and Fordham Road. It was after midnight and the bus was empty except for another teenage couple entangled on the long and battered back seat. The bus swerved to miss a pothole and shuddered when it hit another, causing the couple to fall onto the floor. They quickly returned to their seat and resumed petting.

"I know. I started to reread it," Mickey said.

"The part where you can't really love anyone until you love yourself first. That doesn't make sense. I love you more than myself. Otherwise I would just be selfish." It was one thing to be in love and feel the romance, but reading Fromm made it much more complex and gnawed at my confidence.

"I think he's trying to explain that if we can't love ourselves for who we are, rather than how others see us, the love for anyone else can't happen. The art is how to love ourselves and not be seduced by what others expect. He combines much of Freud and Marx."

The bus driver yelled, "Hold on, you lovebirds, here comes another." We hit a huge hole and the couple in the back was thrown onto the floor again and this time just remained in a tight embrace without bothering to return to their seat.

I used my thumb to point back to the lovebirds. "Doubt they're Marxists." I felt smug. I was puzzled and a bit hesitant to learn that true love had a Marxist element to it. Did that mean I was becoming a communist? When I wasn't fooling myself I suspected that both concepts were beyond my comprehension. Nevertheless, I felt quite sophisticated to be discussing Fromm with an older woman.

Our affection was heightened by many constraints and few opportunities to be alone. The roof of Mickey's apartment house offered us a romantic setting, after returning from the movies or a party in Manhattan. The bleak, cold tar roof surrounded by a tired brick parapet, oozing out its mortar, was our castle above the traffic and people on the streets, a bit closer to the stars if we could see them through the city haze. Amongst the various vents and pipes that protruded through the roof we were alone unless someone heard us and called the janitor or sometimes the police. One night we quivered in panic and escaped in time to hide behind the boiler chimney as two weary cops banged open the roof door flashing lights around the roof to the demands of a suspicious tenant. But they wouldn't go further than the doorway to inspect behind the chimney. Maybe they were drained from the end of a long shift or perhaps they were romantics in police uniforms out to protect the cravings for lovers with no place to go. One of the movies we saw, a

Polish–West German film named *The Eighth Day of the Week*, unfolded during the housing shortage in Warsaw and depicted the shortage's emotional effects on a couple who search for somewhere to be alone. When they are accidentally locked inside a department store that closes, they soak up the uninterrupted seclusion. We longed for such a place.

———

Hormones, Hurley, and even Stuyvesant propelled me into a life separate from my parents. Except for family meals during the workweek, we absorbed each other's lives from incidental eavesdropping rather than through catch-up conversations. On weekends I'd get home no earlier than two or three in the morning after riding the subway from the Bronx. Neither parent acknowledged how late I had been out nor questioned me about my relationship. I don't remember if I had revealed our age difference and it appeared that neither parent had any idea how intense my relationship with Mickey had become. Yet they didn't feel completely comfortable to leave me alone in the apartment on the very rare occasion they stayed overnight with friends. They had my grandmother sleep over, which I probably misinterpreted as a gesture to have her spend some time with me on Sunday morning.

When I got home close to three in the morning, my grandmother was crying, worried sick that something had happened to me on the subway or in the Bronx. I was dumbfounded. "Mom and Dad never get upset when I come home at this time every weekend. They always sleep fine. Why are you so upset?" My grandmother became fiery with my mother when she and my father returned home Sunday afternoon. Yet even after the revelation of how late I stayed out, I kept to my early morning returns and nothing seemed to be noticed or even overtly suspected about the intensity of my relationship with Mickey. My mother was fully absorbed in developing her new academic career as a professor of social work. My father was absorbed in struggling to bring to market a combination roll-up storm window and screen he patented. At our family dinners, there was much arguing about politics followed by calming my mother's anxiety about her new teaching and research position.

We'd watch the news at the very beginning of dinner and after fifteen minutes my father would turn off the TV and we'd begin serious eating and conversation. "The country is not reckless enough to elect Kennedy," he proclaimed as if it were obvious.

"Bob, everyone at work is against Nixon—his grandstanding with HUAC and support of McCarthy." My mother blotted a stain on her dress with a wet napkin. She looked pained, but couldn't let things go. "You're not being open anymore."

"Listen, Florence, that's history." He tapped the table in sync with his next few words. "Soviets can never be trusted and Nixon knows that. You can't expect someone like Senator Kennedy, with a father who encouraged Hitler, another fascist like Stalin, to deal with the Soviets." My father pushed his fork forcefully against the half-cooked baked potato.

My mother sensed the peril in continuing on this track. "Paul, how's school? You never talk about what's going on in your classes."

"Well, I don't think I'll pass French."

"Sure you will. Maybe I can help you after dinner." Even after such long experience with the lack of conversational transitions at home, I had yet to develop the talent to keep focus on my own issues or prevent the feeling of whiplash as she turned to my father. "Bertha is pushing the dean to let her take over my casework class for next semester. If I have to teach anything else I'll go crazy." Whiplash again as she turned back to me. "It would be like your panic of failing French." She looked distressed and turned to a spot on her dress, which bloomed with little napkin shards as she roughed up the stain. I misread her distress as related to my failing French. I was hopeful that she would express more sympathy or advice about my French dilemma, as she looked up at me and continued her thoughts. "I need that class. I've worked so hard to perfect it." I gave up, knowing that my father would come up with some specific political advice for holding on to her class, which in turn both my mother and I would learn from. I would have to deal with my French failure on my own.

"Florence . . ." My father thrived on proposing interpersonal tactics. ". . . you need to make an appointment with the dean tomorrow and tell him how much you admire Bertha and hope he can encourage her to give you some help." My mother looked resistant and was about to protest. "Then tell him that preparing for that casework class will help you write your speech for the National Council of Social Work conference." My mother looked confused. She dabbed another napkin with water to work on another stain. "The dean will understand the advantage to his school of you speaking to a national audience."

"How do you figure these things out? I think the dean's going to know I'm getting tutored by an expert—you." She smiled and so did my father. Miraculously the cold war conflict had vanished and developed into one of the many professional counseling sessions my father gave my mother, which I attended as a non-matriculated student.

My parents' benign neglect came to an abrupt halt one Saturday morning in November of my senior year. It was 8:30 and oddly, my father hadn't begun his weekend renovation work on the house nor had my mother spread out her papers for work or planned a shopping trip. My intention was to do some homework and then go to the park for a few hours to play ball and then meet Mickey at the Art movie theatre on Eighth Street to see *Shoot the Piano Player*.

"Paul, we need to speak to you." My mother seemed nervous. Her hair was pinned up in her formal style, unusual for a Saturday morning. I could sense she was forcing herself to project assuredness and professionalism, a pattern I noticed when she tried to ward off anxiety. "Mickey's mother called. She's hysterical. It's the first time I ever spoke with her. She's afraid Mickey will get pregnant." She tried saying the word in the most professional atonal manner, but her eyes betrayed fear, which I assumed was over me, and yet her look had a hint of distraction.

It took years for me to figure out my mother's related experience to the position I was in. Growing up she more than once told me, and I overheard her tell others, how she had to assume the role of surrogate mother for her three younger siblings, while my grandmother Mollie was fully absorbed with working in the store and being a wife. Mollie became pregnant at sixteen with my mother. In reminiscing about her childhood, my mother highlighted her own lack of preparedness for taking responsibility for infants and young children when she herself was so young. With the slightest hint of victimization she recalled a particularly traumatic experience when she was five and hit by a soda bottle thrown off a roof of a tenement, forcing her to find her own way to get herself to a hospital. I am sure this story was her metaphor for how teenage parents were ill prepared to give the needed attention to their children. She never stated whether Mollie was married when she became pregnant, and neither did anyone else ever talk about Mollie's wedding with Jacob, and thus I came to assume they didn't get married till after Mollie became pregnant. Thus the discovery of the intensity of my relationship with Mickey must have triggered memories my mother wanted to suppress and added to her fear that I might be headed on a path to repeat her own family's trials stemming from teenage pregnancy.

My mother couldn't hold off long enough for me to respond. "We must forbid you from seeing Mickey. Sorry, I know it will hurt very much and be hard for her and you, but—" She stopped as if watching an approaching train wreck she couldn't prevent.

My father's silence implied I had no ally.

My mother looked at my father as she spoke. "You must stop seeing Mickey . . . now." My mother's discomfort, panic, and frustration said more than her words. She glanced toward me without making eye contact. "Call her and tell her. Her mother's threatening to kick her out of their apartment and that would force her to quit college. You don't want to do that." Smoke from her cigarette surrounded her face and uncharacteristically she didn't wave it away from her eyes. I thought of the Second World War destroyers, which used smoke screens for the same purpose.

My level of defiance and hurt frightened me. I had no resources to ward off this invasion into my life. "I won't stop," I said flatly to cover my fury. "There's nothing you can do. And Mickey won't stop. She'll move out and get an apartment. I'll move out if I have to, but we . . . I'm not stopping." I was demolished and screaming with rage just as I did at age five when my mother left me with Bernice for the first time. I felt frozen even though sweat poured from my skin.

My mother lost all hope of stopping me and excused herself to go wash dishes. Things had to be pretty bad since my father and I usually did the dishes.

"Paul." There was no twinkle in my father's eyes, his face was colorless, and his *New York Times* was not close at hand. "Paul, you need to know . . . I made some serious mistakes in my life," he said in a manner I had never witnessed before, clipped and severe. My mind tumbled from Mickey to trying to comprehend what my father was acknowledging. While he readily admitted mistakes in doing his construction work or even misunderstandings between us, he had never admitted to a *big* mistake or aired regrets about his life. I wanted to get back to the preposterous "forbid" issue, but his acknowledgment upended my self-focus. His pause lingered and I suspected he was thinking about his regrets and not me. The length of the silence heightened my concern as to what possibly could be his "serious" mistake. As if some force compelled him to continue, he added, "Mistakes in judgment. Unfortunately we all make them."

I waited for an explanation to follow, but he remained quiet, as if he were now in another place. Up to that moment I had never seen him appear so passive or depleted. He wasn't a religious person, but he acted as if a force as big as God was pinning him down. I sensed that his regret was shattering and didn't dare ask for clarification.

My mind wobbled and then went dark. I lacked the experience or examples for how this invasion into my life would play out. My father went off to do his work on the house and my mother left to go dress shopping for her upcoming speech at a conference about child development. I went out to a phone booth and commiserated with Mickey, who was in equal shock having been threatened with expulsion from her home if she continued to see me. We met surreptitiously for the next six or eight months, and Mickey found a room to rent to avoid her parents' scrutiny and continue with college.

Naively, I assumed if I could earn income, I might be able to quickly gain my full independence. I had no idea that this plan would fail in supporting my independence, but unexpectedly would highlight my father's reference to "serious mistakes" in his life, and raise my anxieties about what I might discover if their secrets were revealed. The strain of continuing a covert relationship competed with a sense of denial that our dreams could be achieved. Denial was further assaulted when it became clear, even to me, that fifteen or twenty dollars a week would not support my independence.

Before the next summer Mickey decided it best not to return to camp and got a better paying summer job in the city. We accepted that our relationship had to be put aside while we caught up with the needs of our lives. She had to prepare for her junior year at college, and I had to get myself graduated from high school. Our differences in age and life stages were hard to ignore. Finally, we deserted our fantasy. It felt as if we were doing surgery on ourselves without anesthesia.

One afternoon, after our summer separation and during my first year at college and living in the dorms, we met at a local coffee shop on the Upper West Side of Manhattan. I thought I was more mature than when I first read Fromm a few years earlier. If I could just get my final basics of adulthood, maybe we could get together again.

"I'm going out with a very nice guy. I think you would like him. I think we're going to get married," she said.

I didn't say anything. I surveyed the customers. Each one effortlessly played the role of adult. Where was I on the spectrum of adulthood? How was it they allowed me into a coffee shop without checking my age? I didn't belong in this grown-up place talking with an ex-girlfriend about her intended marriage. I worked to sound mature. "Why don't you wait till you finish graduate school?"

She smiled and touched my hand. "It's just too hard on my own. He'll be good and we . . . Let's not talk about it. Maybe we can meet for coffee again. Soon."

It was the last time I saw Mickey. A year later, when I was visiting my parents at home, I received a call from one of Mickey's close friends. "I have a dreadful thing to tell you. Mickey died," he said.

I froze, and dug the phone into my ear for what may have been ten or fifteen minutes. Eventually my mother noticed I wasn't talking and my face had slumped. She asked what was the matter. I felt I couldn't breathe. In a fog I spoke, repeating the word *dead*. My mind and memories of our times together caved into a heap of unrecognizable fragments. *Dead*. Was I thinking of Mickey or myself? Fuzzy images of Bernice, Wyn, and Mickey drifted into my mind. They were my mentors. I was abandoned.

At the funeral the situation was unmanageable. I became unhinged. One of Mickey's friends had to keep me on my feet. He disclosed that the cause of death was natural, but no one knew exactly what that meant. The horror felt catastrophic.

I had driven to the funeral by myself, but sometime after the service I sensed my mother's presence. Apparently she had taken the subway and bus to the Bronx, which in itself was an unusual feat, especially since Mickey was the person she had forbidden me to see. Her presence fueled my rage. She became the lightning rod for my anger and guilt and I didn't hold back my anger at her forbidding me to continue my relationship with Mickey, in spite of being in public. I yelled something unintelligible even to me, intended to blame her, turned my back, and left her to get back to Manhattan on her own. I suspect she knew this would be her role and it was a deep, loving self-sacrifice she voluntarily accepted.

CHAPTER ELEVEN

MY PARENTS' INCURSION INTO MY RELATIONSHIP with Mickey was an uncharacteristic intervention into what I had come to assume was my own life. My sense of hurt and rage at my parents festered, yet we all managed to go through the normal routines of relative peaceful coexistence, although now I was an equal participant in holding back secrets from the family. The period of keeping my continuing relationship with Mickey covert spread to a new era of keeping other events of my school life and relations with friends bottled up from the flow of family discourse. At the same time, my father's reference to the big mistake in his own life, without disclosing its nature, unintentionally reconfirmed that my parents harbored substantial secrets. His new acknowledgment made me think more seriously about the FBI visits. "Happened to be in the neighborhood" no longer washed. I was in a family of secrets and the unwritten rules became more manifest; none of us would venture far enough to pursue each other's secrets. This heightened awareness amplified my sense of alienation and renewed wondering if I would have been better off in the "Anderson family," devoid of undercurrents.

My desire for independence and lack of success in the academic arena propelled me to eliminate senior-year electives, get out of school by noon, and try to find a job. My second interview was a hit. I was hired at a travel agency as "senior messenger" at ninety cents an hour, working from 1:00 to 5:00 in the afternoons after my school day was over. On my first day, I learned I was also not only the lead courier but the only one. My duty called for delivering airline and steamship tickets to apartments and upscale businesses. The particular skill requisite was mastery of the subway lines in Manhattan.

On my first day I had to pick up tickets at Cunard Lines. I entered their downtown ticket building and froze. The elaborate wall and ceiling murals made me feel as if I had entered a seat of world power rather than a transaction center for steamship tickets. The volume of interior space took on a sepia hue from the marble counters and wood paneling that swallowed most of the light. My ninety-cents-an-hour delivery job had given me a passport for my first trip to the world of elegance. I picked up the steamship tickets and brought them directly to Amtorg, the Soviet Union's trading organization on Thirty-Ninth Street.

Completing my missions without mishap on my first day of work would be strong evidence that I was ready for independence. A tenuous detente had developed between my parents and me, despite my remaining bitterness. I looked forward to dinner and sharing my first day's experiences. "Work was great," I enthused. "Look, they gave me a Cunard Lines bag to carry tickets and visas in." I showed off the bag as if it was a critical tool of my new trade.

There was no doubt that they were proud of my becoming a member of the working class. My father tore a piece of bread off the French loaf and poured wine for me.

"And Dad, guess where I was today." My father and mother exchanged unrestrained smiles and turned their full attention to my pleasure. "Did you ever hear of a place called Amtorg? It's not that far from here. It's the Russian—" My father's face drained of color with such unexpected speed that it stifled my next word. My mother flinched and her smile dissolved as she watched my father.

"Paul, you're never, do you understand, *never* to enter that building again," he said in a commanding voice with an intensity and terror I had never witnessed before. He poured more wine, slightly overflowing his glass.

"But Dad, they were really nice. They didn't seem like Communists at all, just regular New Yorkers. And there was one man who spoke Russian to a few older guys. All I did was deliver tickets. I didn't do anything—"

"Paul, tell the travel agency you can't deliver there. Otherwise you can't work for them." He reached for the loaf of bread, but then pulled away from his favorite food.

My mother tried to intercede. "Bob, no one knew who he was. He's just a delivery boy to them. He doesn't have to give his name." She looked to me to confirm her statement.

I nodded and protested, "I thought you'd be pleased. I didn't do anything wrong and didn't mention my name, although I told the receptionist my father was from Russia."

My father abruptly pushed hard on the dining room table to leverage his retreat. The table wobbled back and forth while he thundered toward the doorway, turned and barked at my mother. "Florence, he can't go there!" He disappeared. My father's politics were no longer theoretical. My career and livelihood were in the balance.

"Do you have more deliveries to Amtorg this week?" my mother asked.

"I don't know. It sounds like tomorrow it's all uptown deliveries. How can I tell them I can't go to certain places? They'll fire me! And they told me if I do a good job for six weeks they'd raise my pay to ninety-six cents an hour. I like the job."

My mother suggested I just continue working at the travel agency without mentioning Amtorg and count on never having to deliver there again. If I was assigned Amtorg, I was to make some excuse, since it was close enough to the travel agency for someone else to deliver to it.

I assumed that my father's attempted injunction on my innocent delivery of steamship tickets stemmed from his hatred of Communism in general. I had no idea that somehow I had tripped into the very epicenter of the world he had spent the rest of his life physically, emotionally, and politically fleeing. I was shaken from witnessing the fright in my father's face. I quickly repressed the scene rather than ferreted out the truth of why he had become crazed, and Amtorg receded as a confrontational issue at home, since I never was again called upon to deliver tickets to them.

As I approached eighteen, the legal age to drive, my hunger for the freedom of the road became my singular passion. In spite of the indelible memory of experiencing the passenger door fly off my father's car when I was three or four, I wanted to drive more than anything else. I had waited much too long. Owning my own car would be the culminating event for escaping adolescence and entering the world of adulthood. I squirreled away my messenger earnings to purchase car insurance. I now needed a car and lessons. I would be eighteen in May and working as a counselor at Camp Hurley for the summer. Having my own car for nights and days off was a fantasy that I could finally make into a reality.

Not often did I surprise and please my father as much as when I presented my bank passbook with a balance of $124.90, enough to pay for a full year of car insurance, more than the cost of any Pitcoff family car. Impulsively, he changed his mind about junking his eleven-year-old 1950 Sunbeam-Talbot, which he had bought two years earlier for $85. The car had no heater, a badly corroded exhaust system, droopy headlamps, and clutch linkage cobbled from a twisted shirt hanger, but it was still reliable seventy percent of the time and it was to be my first car.

In preparation for my driving test on my eighteenth birthday, my father gave me two driving lessons in April. On our concluding outing he decided to have me drive in the city rather than the empty parking lot at Riis Park in Queens. I was obsessed with whether my right front fender was going to hit the parked cars as I lurched down West Eleventh Street in first gear. An irritated driver close on my tail made short beeps of his horn. "Dad, do I have any room on your side?" Panic was radiating through my body and I wanted to stop and hand the driving over to my father.

"Don't worry about your right side. As long as you're clear on the left you'll be fine," he said.

I made the bold move of shifting out of first into second as I pondered his illogical assurance, but hadn't the courage to go fast enough to avoid stalling. Before I re-fired the engine he spotted my distress. "Let's stop for the day. Pull over at that hydrant. This is going to take more practice on your part." His forced calmness was obvious.

I was relieved. I restarted the car and turned into the open space by the hydrant. The car behind us zipped by and gave us a long and unfriendly horn blast. I waited for my father to unveil a more sensible plan than practicing in the city. "You don't need me anymore," he said. My formal driving lessons ended at the fire hydrant.

I scooted over to the passenger seat and he quickly came around to the driver's seat. I sensed his frustration as he added, "I'll drive the car up to camp this summer and when you have time, teach yourself how to drive." Why leave it to me and not ask my uncle, or even a driving school, to teach me? Even in this critical learning area my father held to a belief that one must learn from experience rather than formal lessons.

My father drove the Sunbeam and me to camp and immediately took a bus home. On nights when another counselor was in charge of my bunk, I sprinted to the parking area outside of the campgrounds. I verbalized encouragement to my car, pressed the starter, and the Sunbeam coughed to life. I was never sure whether it was the Sunbeam or me that was more surprised when I tentatively released the clutch and we began to move down the mile-long dirt driveway to old Route 28. The Sunbeam suffered from losing various basic parts along the road, but in my ecstasy of propelling myself on the open road, I remained indifferent to her travails, despite the uncertainty as to whether we would make it back.

Dave, my closest friend at camp, was eager to ride shotgun. His father bought only new cars and the Sunbeam's dependable breakdowns provided opportunities to learn car repair. This benefit also added a sense of risk that he missed in his daily life. Often, when black smoke wafted across the windshield and seeped through the firewall into the compartment, I was compelled to pull off the road. These incidents were usually caused by oil spills on the engine block when I forgot to fasten the air filter properly. At other times the Sunbeam backfired and shuddered even after I killed the ignition. Despite Dave's recent familiarity with the car's obstinate resistance, one particularly loud explosive backfire followed by a billow of black smoke from the hood caused him to jump from the car before we came to a stop and bolt into the woods to avoid being blown to pieces.

It turned out that the backfires were caused by my compulsive desire to adjust everything under the hood. Relentlessly I cleaned the spark plug wires and polished their electrodes, never appreciating that when I replaced the wires they had to be arranged in a particular order. My abused Sunbeam valiantly tried to fire its four cylinders even after I caused havoc to the proper firing order.

The battery often lost its charge after a breakdown, forcing Dave and me to get out and push it fast enough to gain some momentum, jump into the moving car, shift from neutral into first gear, and pop the clutch to start the engine. One night, we were stuck going up a hill. We searched the trunk for a flashlight to walk back to camp in the dark; instead we found a few wrenches, hangers, an assortment of clamps, screwdrivers, pliers, rags, and a long steel pole with a handle on it. We discovered it was a crank, like the ones used to start old-fashioned cars. Sure enough, there was a hole in the front bumper that allowed the crank to be inserted into the engine. We started the car by cranking, even with the dead battery.

Why hadn't my father told me about the crank or specifically how to get the car going after breakdowns? Possibly he hoped I would experience the same thrill and satisfaction he did from learning on my own. His approach made me nervous, but he believed insecurity was the price for avoiding orthodoxy. It was my responsibility to find experiences that would give me a stockpile of life lessons.

My parents were slowly diminishing in size and influence in my life. It was a bit like sailing off from a dock in a large slow steamship. They remained the same, absorbed in their lives, while I was moving away on my own journey. I was teaching myself how to start a car with a crank, making important decisions as a counselor to help children, and planning my course schedule for my first year in college. This new level of decision-making opened doors to new friends and new experiences. My Sunbeam broke down often enough to make me an expert in finding ways to get it going again. This served as a touchstone for taking on anything in my life that might need fixing, which would be just about everything.

Parents while enjoying more freedom from taking care of me

═══════

Eight months into John F. Kennedy's presidency, politics had taken on a romantic, hopeful tenor for me while my father feared Kennedy wouldn't be able to handle the infectious spread of communism throughout the world. The Vietnam War and showdown over Cuba were future events I couldn't have predicted. I was at college only thirty-five miles away from my parents, but felt my independence expanding and at times felt more conversant with my own personality. Like a falling leaf flicked by the changing currents of the wind, I was absorbed more by activities than by achievement and thus easily floated in new directions. My experience with uncertainty at home softened the anxiety with being one of the few students without a clear bearing toward their future.

"Take sociology your first year. It's an easy A and it's fun." This advice about my first year of college came from an impeccable source, a cheerful sophomore with curly brown hair, a green three-ring notebook with dividers, and a pencil in her hair. Even without her notebook, "Curly" was my ideal of a college coed.

"Sounds good, but what is it?" I said.

"You know, it's about people doing things. You'll love it. You can say anything and it's always right."

Perfect. It wasn't academically demanding, and it sounded like something I already enjoyed: studying people. However, Curly neglected a critical fact. Not all sociology students performed at her level.

Dr. Frank Lee, chairman and professor of sociology, entered the classroom wearing a worn tweed jacket and bow tie. He was tall and slimmer than most middle-aged professors. Although I couldn't be certain from the back row, I was confident that his jacket had the aroma of a library's aging, yellowed pages. He ran his long, graceful fingers, which looked like a musician's rather than a scholar's, over the piles of books on his desk. They had slips of creased paper sticking out from the pages, some with writing, others blank. "If you read these books you will learn much about sociology." He pointed to the first pile. "Aside from the text, you must read these five books. The names are in your syllabus.

"This next group"—he pointed to the middle pile—"you'll need to read if you want a decent grade."

He fingered the third group of books as if they were precious first editions. "The last group is for anyone who expects to take a second class in sociology. You'll take a lot of subjects in college but unless you understand sociology you'll risk squandering your individuality to the power elite."

I looked around to see the reaction of others to this politically charged statement. Politics was an invisible magnetic force I couldn't escape. I longed for the certainty of identification with a particular political leaning, yet felt an opposing force preventing me from declaring allegiance. My parents' immersion in politics made me want to be involved, and yet my father's fundamental loathing of Communism rattled me. Socialism, Communism, even the progressive left of the Democratic Party, seemed too doctrinaire. Controlled capitalism in the Republican mode seemed too heartless as well as doctrinaire. I feared my destiny was as a political agnostic.

Dr. Lee continued, "Unless you are prepared, you will be subsumed into groups and political orders you don't believe in. There is much at stake." He paused to see if we were paying attention. "We have fifteen weeks and won't waste any time."

During the semester I read and reread the textbook, all the books in pile one, and three in pile two without fully grasping the meanings in any of them. This didn't stop me from mouthing off in class. Dr. Lee was masterful at refuting my clever conclusions, while concealing his own conclusions on the same issues. He created an inviting atmosphere to explore any hypothesis. I typed and retyped my sociology papers as if they were destined to change the thinking of the Western World. My pristine black-and-white papers were returned with reddish hues. Every assumption I presented was questioned and my sloppy research noted in red handwriting.

By the end of midterms my papers and tests averaged Cs and he made it clear that even a C– would be a generous end grade from what he saw of my work. Most teachers at Stuyvesant, and so far in my first year of college, avoided talking with C or even B students. They shunned us as if our poor class performance could infect the intellectual atmosphere and taint their A students. *Apply yourself harder* was the most encouragement I could expect. This cliché contained the same level of passion and interest as the women at the telephone company who announced the time when one called to find out.

A month before the end of the semester Dr. Lee invited students in our class, along with some from his advanced seminar, to his house for wine and cheese. He made an effort to seek me out and asked my views on his class. I was unprepared for his solicitous manner and merely blurted out what was running through my head. "I'm surprised you invited me. I'm your worst student. I've already prepared my parents for a D, although I hoped for a C."

Dr. Lee handed me a glass of wine and straightened his bow tie. "You must learn all those terms in chapter eight to pass the final. I know you'll pass. But you are not one of my A students." I took a sip to hide my embarrassment. "And that's not bad." He motioned to Curly, the brunette who had hustled me into this "easy A" class and was in his advanced seminar, to join us. I tried to appear casual, but the combination of brushing against a revered professor and Curly made me feel as awkward as the time my voice and everything else changed.

Dr. Lee continued, "This is Diane. Get to know each other. She could learn how to take risks from you in her analysis and you certainly could learn how to be more careful in your research."

Dr. Lee asked a question as if he didn't know the answer. "Diane, do you think Paul is a poor student? Do you think he doesn't belong in my class?" He patted my back in a reassuring manner.

"Come on, Professor," Diane teased with a light laugh. "If you don't mind me saying, you are too demanding. And I dare say rigid."

Dr. Lee fingered his bow tie again. "First of all, we are not on campus, so call me Frank. Second, you may be correct, but if you're going to make a difference in the world, you have to be more educated and more equipped with knowledge than those who control things." He pulled more students into our group and refilled our glasses of wine, ladies first. None of us dared to speak until he had time to formulate his next thought. "What makes a great student?" he asked and then walked toward the kitchen to help his wife put out cheese and crackers.

The group discussed the issue and moved into the subject of grades. Diane said, "Grades are important. They give us feedback on our progress and mastery of a subject."

"Bullshit. Grades are just a way to maintain hierarchy," Ray fumed.

Dr. Lee returned to the group and hung his long arm around my shoulder again and made his point as if he had overheard our discussion. "Look, I hate grades too. They reflect little to nothing about a person. I admit I'm a coward because I grade based on performance on certain established parameters. But I confess . . ." He paused to look at Diane and a few other A students. "Don't take offense, but often I find my C students more interesting and more willing to take intellectual risks. I admire their ability to look at the world from a perspective different from a customary formula."

We all knew the moment it was appropriate to help with the cleanup and leave. When Diane expressed appreciation for the evening, Dr. Lee moved us aside and noted our discontent with the lack of political activities on campus. "What would change that? What kind of political activities does the campus need?" he asked.

The NAACP popped into my head and out of my mouth. Camp Hurley had honed in on racism as being one of the biggest hurdles to social justice. There were only a handful of African American students on our campus and the Supreme Court integration decision of 1954 was still prominent in my mind.

"Why don't you two go to the dean and recommend that the college open an NAACP chapter," Dr. Lee offered. "You can tell him I'm willing to be your advisor . . ." He paused and added, "Although I'm not sure if that will help."

The stigma of being a C student had led me to believe I would remain in the background of this social evening at an esteemed professor's home. Instead a klieg light had been aimed at me and Professor Lee was suggesting that I might be an intellectual risk-taker and bring Curly, his esteemed A student, along with me. Nothing was certain in Dr. Lee's presence, which was a bit like home.

The next day Diane decided that we had to get to know each other better before meeting with the dean. I wasn't sure if we were dating or doing homework together, but we began going into New York City every Friday to the main branch of the New York Public Library on Forty-Second Street. Her reverence for working in the Great Reading Room became infectious. After finding likely books in the purposeful and elegant card catalogue room, we entered the Reading Room, the largest single room in the city. I submitted my requests with a formal reverence, which were returned with particular call numbers. The request slips were bundled into canisters for the pneumatic tubes that sent them floors below to the closed stacks. Diane and I waited at one of the long wooden reading desks and watched a large screen that displayed numbers. When my number ultimately lit up, I dashed to the counter, thrilled at being handed a first edition or rare book on the subject I was interested in. At the Main Library I found materials that no other students had uncovered. The hunting of facts and clues to other facts caught my fancy; although it may have been that I fancied Diane better.

A month later I sat in the dean's office. Sunlight blasted into the room from the two large windows behind his back. Diane and I were forced to squint. A few worn ivy leaves peeked through the window, mocking our decidedly un–Ivy League status.

"We have no problem here, and we'll keep it that way. There is no need for an NAACP chapter on campus or that kind of trouble." The dean took time with each word to squeeze out as much condescension and intimidation as possible. My passion for racial fairness intensified proportionately with his mounting resistance. He leafed through a file on his desk. "Paul, I see that Dr. Lee, your collaborator, has given you a C. Perhaps the two of you should be thinking more about improving your grades." He flipped a page back and forth, leaned back in his plush chair, and smiled. "I'm pleased you came to see me. This gives us a chance to evaluate your first semester's midterm performance. It might be in your best interest to put you on academic probation." The threat crushed my momentum. Diane put on her sunglasses.

Puffed up by the effects of his power, the dean stood and walked around his desk. "It's agreed you have no time for extracurricular clubs, and certainly our hardworking Negro students have no time for them either. Thank you for coming." He continued to the door and held it open for our exit.

I found my own passivity maddening. I ached for the power to tell the dean to go to hell. The next day I confessed my failing to Dr. Lee. He too had heard from the dean, who warned him that association with Diane and me would confuse the Personnel Committee when Lee's tenure application was reviewed next year.

But, he said, "There is a way around this. While we can't have an official chapter or club, couldn't we form an ad hoc group? When we get enough members the dean won't be able to stop us." Dr. Lee startled me with his audacity and creativity.

In a week Diane and I recruited a dozen students to begin an unofficial political group. Our first meeting was held at the home of a student who lived off campus. We agreed to meet every three weeks to discuss political issues and invite speakers to inform us about various ways to take political action. Our plan was to decide on specific actions our group would take within a year. We named ourselves "Outlook." Dr. Lee attended the meeting as our consultant. He emphasized the importance of our mission to exercise free speech. Within a month Outlook expanded to over twenty women and one other guy. I was elected president and Diane vice president. Though feminism as a movement had not yet touched the campus, nevertheless it was made clear by the group that my male status entitled me only to be a figurehead. Power would reside with the women.

Dr. Lee suggested and helped us engage Norman Thomas, a three-time Socialist Party presidential candidate, as our first speaker. We were disappointed with the turnout of sixty students and fifteen faculty members, but Lee was encouraged, especially since the dean had tried to squelch the presentation by withdrawing permission to use a campus room. Diane used her charm and at the last minute arranged for a fraternity to lend us their space.

The next speaker we engaged was a representative from Students for a Democratic Society, SDS. This was October 1962, just before many campuses were radicalized. Ours was still strongly rooted in fifties establishment contentedness. However, the Cuban missile crisis was reaching a danger point and there was mounting fear that the confrontation with the Soviets would erupt into a short cataclysmic nuclear Third World War. Much of the country was panicked as Soviet freighters carrying nuclear missiles steamed toward Cuba. When I introduced the speaker I looked out at over 150 students and faculty in a space meant for 80. They streamed like dominoes out into the hallway.

This event reminded me of the stories my parents told of their first meeting in 1933. On a lunch break from her job at S. Klein's Department Store as a theft lookout, my mother walked across the street to Union Square Park and joined a small crowd of workers standing around a man on a soapbox. She immediately fell in love with that man, my future father, who was giving speeches about the need for workers to organize. For me, organizing and leading this discussion about how our government could so easily lead us toward war, perhaps a nuclear war, as the missiles steamed closer to Cuba, seemed like the most natural thing to do. My parents protested against orthodoxy and refused to remain silent. Without telling me directly, I was irreversibly attached to their engagement in political activism and distance from group orthodoxy. My organizing work at Outlook was part of a legacy that connected me with my father. My indoctrination into this path most likely came from the progressive political milieu I was dropped into at Little Red and Camp Hurley, overhearing and participating in my parents' political arguments, listening to their friends and my friends, attending peace rallies, singing protest folk songs, and mostly hearing the few stories about my father's actions for social justice, told by my mother.

My formal education was much less directed, perhaps with the exception of my father's urging me to read certain books. I read about Clarence Darrow, a famous defense attorney who fought for justice for workers; the Sacco and Vanzetti story about how easily a mob of fearmongers and apathetic citizens could allow two immigrant anarchists to be unfairly executed for murder; Lincoln Steffens, who exposed government corruption in a series of national

articles; *Crime and Punishment*, as a means of feeling the desperation of poverty; the court-martial of General Billy Mitchell for
publicly criticizing the establishment army, and other such books,
all offering examples of divergent thinking and focused on righting
injustices.

When the speaker and discussion was over, the head of a
fraternity approached me. I was taken aback, since I was known to
have refused to pledge any fraternity. He offered a hearty welcome
as if we were brothers sharing the secrets of the world. I was pleased
since I hadn't expected a turnout from the fraternities. "We need
you to join us."

I was flattered that I had touched his political core. "I guess I
could consider it, but I would refuse going through your degrading
and sophomoric pledging process." Now I was emboldened enough
to speak my truth.

"Fine. Anyone who can attract this many girls to an event is
needed by our brothers." I was stunned. I never thought of myself as
a girl-gatherer, rather the opposite. The world was about to blow up
because of the nuclear arms race and bad political decision-making
and all my intended brother was interested in was whether I could
lure girls to his fraternity.

The large turnout elevated my self-confidence. My group had
gathered students not so willing to leave control of their future only
to politicians. In a few months Outlook had made its presence
known and valued and the dean had lost his power to stop us. The
success of the event made me hopeful about the prospect of organizing more students to speak up and perhaps take action.

———————

We learned our grades from postcards sent out by our professors
several weeks before official transcripts were received. None of mine

had a kind word or even the first two letters of the alphabet scrawled on them. On an overdue visit to my parents I sought to divert any attention from my grades. Not that I was now lacking in self-confidence. To the contrary I offset my setbacks on the academic playing field with the considerable confidence I had gained from my work with Outlook. Yet in this topic I dreaded my father's truculence about Communism. He believed that any left-wing organization was either a pawn, acting for the Soviets to spread Communism, or would eventually be infiltrated by Communists. Outlook might set him off, but my poor grades were a topic I didn't want scrutinized. If I could anticipate my father's concerns maybe he would temper his political suspicions. My plan was to emphasize that Outlook's members weren't Communists and we were determined not to affiliate with any other organization. This might cork his objections. If not, I had a backup plan. I would justify Outlook as merely a means for the social life I was missing by not belonging to a fraternity.

We sat around the dining table and my father poured his favorite one-dollar Beaujolais into three glasses. He enjoyed the idea that we could drink together. My mother had successfully broiled a steak without the customary smoke and fire.

"You had dinner with Norman Thomas?" he said. "I got to hand it to that guy. He never gave up running for president even though he couldn't win. You know he was never a Communist. He knew the difference between freeing workers and totalitarianism. A good man."

With mounting courage I revealed we had recruited a speaker from SDS, an organization that advocated the unilateral end to the Cold War and cooperation with the Soviets.

"SDS is another radical organization the Soviets will infiltrate if they haven't already," he said.

"Dad, not everyone is a Communist. The SDS speaker spoke

out against totalitarianism, but he also thinks the anti-Communist movement has crippled any chance to make peace with the Russians. I think that makes sense." I couldn't find the slightest softness in my father's grave expression. I continued, "You would have liked him. He emphasized the importance of empowering workers." I was surprised that my voice remained calm and hadn't yet reached the upper pitches and faster cadence that usually accompanied my defensiveness.

"Doubtful they haven't been duped by the Communists. You got to be careful with your group." He watched my reaction with a similar scrutiny I gave to his.

"Bob!" my mother broke in. Her look filled out the sentence. There would be no escalation tonight.

My father drank some wine, looked at her, and turned to me. His eyes glistened and his facial muscles loosened. "When I was . . . If I was in your shoes I would be doing the same thing."

He poured more wine even though I had barely taken a sip. I looked at my mother for assurance that my father meant what he said. She was unusually relaxed and seemed to enjoy his endorsement in such a politically perilous zone. "Like Dad, I'm impressed. And getting a non-tenured professor to risk being your advisor is such an achievement."

I had muddled my way into their manifest respect. My back straightened with courage. Without further hesitation I revealed my poor grades, promised better results next semester, and awaited their reproach without fear.

My father jumped in before my mother went on. "It doesn't matter if you fail a couple of courses." My father cut the steak into three pieces and complimented my mother on how it was cooked. He tore off two pieces from a loaf of French bread, his and my favorite food, and handed me one. "Passion with reflection, that's what's important." He buttered his piece and took a large bite along with a swig of wine. The crusty feel and aroma of the bread added to my increasing enjoyment of the occasion. My mother remained attentive. She knew there was more to come. "Individuals make a difference. You can make a difference," he said. This was getting too good. I reconsidered my policy of limited home visits.

"Even failing at something is OK if you don't lose your passion. Failing is always a good experience. You learn you can survive. You failed French and almost biology . . . you'll just have to learn another language, and by the time you get out of college, biology won't be the same."

CHAPTER TWELVE

I VISITED HOME FOR A WEEKEND during my sophomore year. My mother and I were sitting in the living room scouting out areas of conversation that wouldn't invade my emerging independence or bore us to death. "Meet any interesting girls in Outlook?" Since my forced breakup with Mickey, I kept my romantic life a family secret and shrugged off to a new topic. My parents had been good tutors in guarding one's secrets.

"Any time to help Dad with the house?" I devoted many weekends, and even included friends, in helping my father build a simple house on Fire Island, a barrier island close to New York City, but resented that my mother always wanted me to do more. I forcefully shrugged off this topic too with an exasperated "Mom."

She was indomitable and switched to C. Wright Mills and if I was reading him in sociology. I knew she would enjoy getting into a debate about his theories of power, but I needed a respite from academic thinking and got up to leave the room. My mother's attempts at connecting with her college son were failing and perhaps she was searching for something more dramatic or less expected to keep me engaged with her. "Since you learned how to use the microfilm archives, you might look up Dad in the October 15, 1939, edition of the *New York Times*," she said as if suggesting I might pick up some oranges when I went out to get her a pack of cigarettes.

Now that I had a footing into my own life, I was less curious about my parents' past. Their secrets could rest as far as I was concerned. I didn't rush to the library or even contemplate that I might learn something I didn't already know or much cared about. Yet I felt some obligation to affirm my mother's pride in my father as well as my own. A week later I found myself in the university library spinning the wobbly microfilm crank to the article about my father, most likely about his wiring the mast of the Empire State Building.

I was fully unprepared for a far more alarming discovery. The article contained three columns, with a headline stating that my father "SAYS AMERICANS ACT AS OGPU SPIES." Emotions passed through me almost at the same rate as I had been reeling the microfilm. Initially I was fully disoriented, as if my father's name and picture had just fallen into the wrong article. I could feel my denial at work as I tried to cover up my hurt and anger over having such facts withheld from me for nineteen years and then so cavalierly revealed. Alienation took over, as my sense of family dissolved. Overtaking these fleeting emotions, I settled on shock at learning that my father had testified before the House Un-American Activities Committee, then headed by Representative Martin Dies from Texas, who was succeeded in malevolence by Senator Joseph McCarthy a decade later.

Beginning at eleven years old, when my family watched Edward R. Murrow on *See It Now* expose Senator Joseph McCarthy's evils, I began to build a fear and hatred of HUAC, which was closely associated with McCarthy's demagoguery, successful destruction of innocent lives, and suppression of freedom of speech. Everything I learned at Little Red, from friends of my parents, and even my own parents, was that the greatest threat to freedom in the United States was epitomized in HUAC. My emotional shuddering as I read the subhead, "Former Amtorg Aide Testifies It Assists Espionage Under Commercial Front/FACTORY SECRETS STOLEN/Dies Witness Declares Two Russians Here Disappeared in Stalin Purge of 1930," produced a series of emotional aftershocks that choked off my comprehension of the information in the article. The man in the photo seemed an impostor taking my father's identity.

The photograph was from twenty-two years before, yet he appeared older than he looked now. He was dressed far more formally than usual, in a dark double-breasted suit, more like a caricature of the star witnesses one saw in the tabloids of the thirties. On microfilm, his image appeared as a negative, adding to my sense of disorientation.

Nothing in the story connected to what I knew. None of these assertions—his knowledge of Soviet Communist activities, his involvement with industrial espionage for the Soviets, his association with people who "disappeared" and were presumed assassinated, or the offer by the Soviet Secret Police to train him to be a spy for the Soviet Navy—could possibly relate to *my* father. Yet there it was in the *New York Times*, my father a former spy for the Soviets and now an expert witness against the Soviets. I repressed this implausible new information almost as fast as I read it.

I rolled the microfilm back and forth, but couldn't erase this noxious new fact that my father had testified at the loathsome HUAC. I was appalled. Who was my father? Could he still be the skilled electrician, builder of our house, storyteller, adored friend, dad, husband, ordinary in most ways aside from his puzzling advice and rabid distrust of Communists, or was that a mirage? After all his harangues against Communism, how could he have been part of Soviet espionage? I suspected there were secrets, but never that my father had gained national attention for testifying at HUAC about Soviet espionage and its manipulation of the political activities of the American Communist Party. This was not the man who was now working as the head electrician wiring a new hospital in Queens.

At Little Red, at Camp Hurley, from all my friends and their parents, and even at home I had learned that HUAC had destroyed the lives of innocent citizens and purposefully caused a hysteria that inflamed the Cold War. The mere association of my father, and by connection my family—and me—with HUAC begged for denial. I couldn't accept that the father I knew might be an impostor. Why would the United States Congress think my father had any information that was valuable to our government?

Denial, combined with my sloppiness as a student, caused me to blot out any details in the article or note that the day he testified was in 1939, more than ten years before the McCarthy purges and many years before HUAC stepped up its process of intimidating government and private organizations to adhere to blacklisting. If I had processed this fact I might have cut my denial down to size and pursued this new information directly with my parents, but I didn't. I just sat staring at the stern expression and formal attire of the man who was supposed to be my father. Yet there wasn't any other Robert Pitcoff.

I was drenched in disgrace. I felt like a heavy weight of shame had been permanently placed around my neck. My friends in Outlook would shun me if they learned of my family's connection with HUAC. I looked around the library to make sure no one saw what I was reading. I thought of destroying the spool of film so nobody could ever unearth the article. If any Outlook members learned of my father's connection with HUAC, they might assume I was an FBI informant. My pain and paralysis made me feel like the times I had been punched in my solar plexus by neighborhood gangs. My stomach felt as if it was falling down an endless shaft. It seemed that the library had increased the illumination around my cubicle and raised the heat ten degrees. They were watching me. I had no hope of destroying the microfilm.

"Hi Paul," Diane called out. She appeared from nowhere. Instantly I embraced the microfilm contraption, hoping to hide the screen. The machine bobbed, the light flickered, and the take-up spool landed on the floor, unwinding much of its film. "What's the matter?" She laughed. "You working on something secret?"

"No, I was finished and just couldn't find the switch. I was looking for articles about—" I couldn't finish the sentence.

"This sounds suspicious. You're not one of those plants the FBI uses to watch groups like ours?" Diane chuckled at this absurdity and helped me roll up the film. I had to remind myself the microfilm was too small for her to read without the viewer.

"You kidding? Me? If anyone were a plant it would be Ray or Tina, not me. Never!"

"Take it easy, just kidding. But you need more practice using microfilm. What a laugh. Wait till I tell what I saw."

A few weeks after my entanglement with the microfilm I asked my mother for an explanation. It seemed melodramatic. "We knew that the Soviets would have killed Dad and testifying was the only way to save his life." This sounded like another of her flourishes designed to divert me from the truth. It worked and I didn't ask anything more. Possibly I was still frightened that I would hear more about my father collaborating with the HUAC. Undoubtedly I was in denial, so I tossed this new revelation into my mental wastebasket and returned to the flow of campus life.

28   L+F

SAYS AMERICANS ACT AS OGPU SPIES

Former Amtorg Aide Testifies It Assists Espionage Under Commercial Front

FACTORY SECRETS STOLEN

Dies Witness Declares Two Russians Here Disappeared in Stalin Purge of 1930

TELLS OF OGPU DEALS
Robert C. Pitcoff
Times Wide World

WASHINGTON, Oct. 14 (P)—Robert Pitcoff, a former official of Amtorg, the Soviet trading corporation in the United States, told the House committee investigating un-American activities today that some Americans were members of the OGPU, Russian secret police.

The witness, now a New York electrician but formerly an employe of Amtorg, declared that that agency, ostensibly a commercial organization, "undoubtedly has connections with the Russian Secret Service."

He pictured Amtorg as a beehive of Soviet spies who used the employes as operatives—"one OGPU agent will ask you to obtain some information, another agent will ask you for something else, and we were continually being asked to obtain information."

Through connections with the Communist party, Pitcoff asserted, Amtorg also assisted Soviet trade missions to obtain industrial secrets in American factories.

And he said it was "very possible," although he could not testify positively, that the Soviet agents in this country were paid by Moscow through the Amtorg offices.

Says Two Disappeared

Pitcoff spoke of two Amtorg vice presidents named Ruthenberg and Kossof who, he said, had disappeared in New York under mysterious circumstances.

At the time of the first Russian "pur

termed the activity "practically kidnaping."

Both Ruthenberg and Kossof, he declared, vanished on the days they were to have sailed and Amtorg employes were discouraged from discussing the disappearances.

Pitcoff, who came here from Russia in 1914 and became a citizen in 1930, said he joined the Communist party in 1926 and was active in its trade union work until he quit in 1934. He was employed in the "transportation control" department of Amtorg for four years and obtained a "fairly good knowledge" of the organization's workings, he testified.

He said that Russia sent many trade missions to this country to study American production methods in the aviation, glass, chemistry, oil, paper and "almost every industry" and that much industrial espionage was carried on.

Obtained Entree to Factories

Amtorg arranged for the tours

New York Times article October 15, 1939

© 2019 The New York Times Company | Terms of Service | Privacy | Help | Feedback | TimesMachine Home

"I've been thinking about you and want you to apply to the American Friends Service Committee." Dr. Lee handed me an application. "You'll work abroad doing Peace Corps type of work. Fill it out. I want to make sure you get accepted so let me see it before you send it."

The course of action Dr. Lee counseled in the second half of my sophomore year in 1963 was beyond my range of experiences. None of my friends had traveled abroad. My mother had never been out of the United States except to Canada and my father's travels were ancient history.

The American Friends Service Committee (AFSC) program consisted of helping communities in Europe and Scandinavia. The literature explained that we would be called upon to do physical labor such as planting sea grass, reforesting land, harvesting crops, and turning forests into pastures with homesteaders. The application clearly stated the summer program was for Europe and Scandinavia, but I wrote in Japan for my preference. I still hadn't understood that Europe stood for a specific continent rather than a general term for anything across an ocean. Nevertheless, I was accepted.

Dr. Lee was overjoyed and acted as if he had saved me from academic annihilation. "Nothing you learn in my class will match what you'll get from this experience. You'll never be the same." This observation had a sobering effect, rather than the one he intended. My mother viewed my acceptance as comparable to admission to Harvard, and within hours of the news, she heated up the phone lines with bulletins to family, friends, and I suspect the *New York Times*. My father was pleased that I would do manual labor with people who had to work with their hands.

At the very end of May I spent three days at the AFSC orientation at Pendle Hill, a Quaker retreat in Philadelphia. Two dozen students from around the country came together to learn how to pull weeds and listen to talks about our role in community building in European and Scandinavian countries. When orientation concluded we would sail to Le Havre and travel by train to Paris, where an American Friends representative would see us off to our assignments.

On the second evening at Pendle Hill we assembled to learn of our final assignments. My assignment was announced last. "Paul Pitcoff, you'll be going to KVT, a Finnish aid organization project in Finland." Forebodings ignited in my gut. Finland sounded cold and far off. I couldn't picture where it was on a world map. How would I even get there? Other applicants offered protective advice that only increased my anxiety: "Paul, the mosquitoes are as big as birds." "Tough assignment, Paul. You'll never sleep because the sun doesn't set." "Bad break, you'll be near the Arctic Circle. Get a heavy parka. Watch out for frostbite." I barely held back tears. I didn't want to be eaten by bird-sized mosquitoes, and more importantly, I didn't want to be remembered as someone who got killed simply because he didn't understand the term "Europe."

Early on our fourth morning we were transported to New York harbor and boarded the SS *United States*. More important than heading for the Arctic Circle or embarking on the largest passenger ship in the world was seeing my father, mother, and uncle Howard on the open deck in the middle of a working day, knowing they never interrupted their work. Years later I read *The Man Who Killed the Deer* by Frank Waters, which describes the Pueblo tradition of sending a boy alone at the age of thirteen into the mountains to hunt, kill a deer, and survive. After this initiation the boy became a man. Certainly my bar mitzvah, at thirteen, couldn't compare with the challenge those Pueblo boys faced. I had to wait until I was nineteen to attempt my own initiation rite into adulthood. The unusual family assemblage during working hours added to a sense that I was embarking on an epochal journey. They beamed and repeatedly voiced pride in my mission to help others. After around five minutes, my father's grin turned serious as he pulled me aside. "Let's take a look at your cabin."

We left my uncle and mother and descended about eight decks to the lowest one. We entered my assigned cabin, already occupied by three young men heading home to England. My father graciously asked the men to give us a few moments to say our goodbyes and they obliged.

There was no *New York Times* to fold, signaling a noteworthy comment, but I knew my father had something important to say. I scrunched into a lower bunk, unable to fully sit up. My father stood over me. "I want to give you something before we talk." He handed me a little box containing a red Swiss Army knife. This was beyond his pattern of one gift a year on my birthdays. Breaking his pattern of gift-giving, coupled with the knife's use as a survival tool, made me pay particular attention to what he was about to say. I longed for advice fit for an adult rather than the baffling "don't trust your teachers," or "don't pay more than $75 for a car repair."

"Whatever happens, I want you to promise me something." He had never asked me to promise anything except never to return to Amtorg. He turned somber. His eyes seemed haunted as he looked warily at the cabin door. "You must promise you will not be lured over the border into the Soviet Union."

"Sure. You don't have to worry." I chirped with relief that it was nothing I had any intention of doing. My response was rushed and too casual and didn't prompt the warm reassuring smile I expected.

"Russia is on the Finnish border. If they find you in Russia, you'll never get out." Except for when I went to Amtorg, I had never seen him so pale or so determined that I abide by his wishes. Until this point, my apprehension had focused on getting lost, mosquitoes, frostbite, language incompatibility, and being away from home for a long time. His warning and pallor were so extreme that it made me call forth my well-honed denial tool and brush off his warning as paranoid and irrelevant, since I had no desire of going to Russia.

After steaming to France, I left the other students in Paris and travelled by myself to Stockholm by train. This was my first time away from familiar surroundings, without the possibility of phoning my parents or friends if I was in trouble. I had anticipated that crossing the Atlantic on my own would produce panic when I arrived. Yet oddly, I felt somewhat comforted by the separation from my known world. I had gotten from Paris through Germany, Denmark, and Sweden by myself. This was tangible proof I could make it on my own. By the time I found myself on a ship gliding through the Baltic to Helsinki, my anxieties were partially smothered by a sense that I had a good chance of survival.

I found myself so relaxed I fell asleep on top of my sleeping bag on the upper deck of the ferry to Helsinki until a shadow blocked the rays of sunlight and startled me awake. An older woman loomed over me with such grimness that my first thoughts were that we had hit an iceberg and had to abandon ship. She uttered strange sibilant-sounding words and urgently pointed at my knapsack. I pulled my bag close assuming I was infringing on her space. She bounced her index finger on my American Friends patch and raised her voice in an attempt to force me to understand. We had been told we might meet Europeans welcoming the Friends and were advised to sew AFSC patches onto our knapsacks. This had the opposite effect on the woman, who tried to tear it off.

I was rattled. A young Swedish woman offered assistance. She spoke English and enough Finnish to explain that the older woman wanted me to remove the patch. "She says to tell you we are sailing close to Russia. She says you should know that the Russians don't like Americans and this far north they assume you're spies. She asks if you're a spy." To my friends at Little Red and Camp Hurley, or even with many of my parents' friends, with the exception of my father, the Soviets were seen as heroes, benevolent, or at least benign and misunderstood as potential enemies, yet on this Baltic ferry far away from home, a stranger who lived close to Russia was fearful for my safety. She didn't know my father, yet they were both cautioning me about being so near the Russian border. The threat seemed less abstract than the lectures back home.

I laughed. "Tell her I'm not a spy and I've been warned to stay away from Russia."

The older woman became more agitated and grabbed my arm to compel me to pay attention as she appealed to my Swedish translator. "She says there is no humor. The Russians have, how do you say, taken, no, no, kidnapped people travelling in Finland, who they suspect are spies. She wants you to take off the patch because of the American flag." My translator nodded approvingly at the woman and continued, "I've heard the same stories; it might be a good idea for you to do it." I used my Swiss Army survival knife, for the first time, to remove my American Friends patch.

After we docked I trekked to the Helsinki train station as instructed. In Paris I was given a one-page letter in Finnish, which purportedly explained my purpose and where I was headed, and requested the reader to give me assistance. I presented it to a woman at the ticket booth and watched her expression to see if the instructions made sense or whether I would be stranded in Helsinki. She sprung around the counter and hugged me. From what I could tell she was thanking me for something. She made out a ticket, escorted me to a train, thanked me again, and refused to take money for the ticket.

As the all-night train travelled north through miles of forests and lakes to Kajaani, my confidence took a bit of a dive as I wondered if I would ever find my way back to Manhattan. I questioned whether I should have ever trusted Dr. Lee, the American Friends, my parents, and even myself for not investigating this venture more thoroughly. After the interminable train trip with no sleep, I yielded to my fate and took a bus farther into the wilderness from Kajaani to Kuhmo, a small frontier town a little more than one hundred miles south of the Arctic Circle and near the Soviet border. I showed my letter to someone on the street and was taken to a small restaurant where fifty or so people, almost the entire town, gathered to look me over. The restaurant owner served me an endless meal and wouldn't allow me to pay. Half the gathering insisted on hugging me and taking a group picture, which I later saw in the local newspaper. I was the first American to visit their town, but I considered the possibility that special treatment might have been due to my mother calling ahead to the Finnish government to look after her son!

It was early morning, twenty hours after I left Helsinki. My journey from New York harbor was nearing its end. I held tightly to my seat in a nine-passenger bus driven like a Formula One race car on a gravel road. The driver had the radio booming the Beach Boys singing about surfing, which partially masked the throaty rumble from the marginally muffled engine. He accompanied the singers, but it was clear he didn't understand the words he sang. We drove through endless pine forests with no indication of where we were or any sign of human habitation. Abruptly the driver hit the brakes and the bus skidded to a stop. The trailing dust floated by the bus. The driver retrieved my knapsack and wrote "9 KM" on a pad of paper, hugged me, and pointed toward a dirt path with two slight ruts. The bus bounced away, leaving me feeling utterly helpless with no possibility of rescue.

I was surrounded by dense forests of pines, which offered dark foreboding openings into their midst. I assumed my perspiration was from fear, but after several minutes I realized the air was warm, even though I was close to the Arctic Circle. Puffy clouds decorating an azure sky suggested serenity I didn't feel. As I stood stranded in the wilderness I realized the various cautions had been true. A low-hanging cloud of mosquitoes in the distance noted my touchdown and lumbered toward me. The thumping of my heart obscured the songs of the welcoming birds. Within moments of my having a cardiac event, the mirage of mosquitoes transformed into two curious dark brown cows wandering over to see their first American. They seemed utterly unimpressed.

I gave up anticipating the mosquitoes and worked on solving my dilemma. After walking nine kilometers, I would be marooned. How soon would anyone learn that I had disappeared in a place unknown? Dr. Lee had been crazy to send me on this journey. Before I fully dissolved in worry I resigned myself to the walk. My next concern was how would I know when I had travelled the full nine kilometers?

After walking an hour I had yet to see signs of human habitation except for an occasional cow. One walked alongside of me for a few minutes. I took the lead in our conversation. "Where is everyone?" I spoke slowly and distinctly, but her only response was a curious look and continued chewing. "You must belong to someone?" I said.

"Moo," she replied.

"I'm not sure if this is the right road to where all the students are working."

"Mooo." This time the cow's response seemed extended and I assumed she understood my desperate situation despite the language barrier.

"I'm here to help farmers who are homesteading. Your government gives them land if they can work it for five years. Have you seen any other students around? You know anything about any of this?" The cow stopped chewing for a moment and cocked her head to ponder my ceaseless questions. She looked at me with detachment. The grass hanging from her mouth suggested amusement with my situation, but she offered no answers.

"I'm a bit nervous. I may be here too soon and then no one will be there. Maybe I should go back to the crossroads and wait for another bus to come by tomorrow, or do they only come once a week?" Most likely she had never been exposed to so many questions or my kind of anxiety, but I needed reassurance. She projected an attitude that everything takes care of itself and gave me one last look, grabbed a mouthful of grass, and wandered into a field. "Nice talking with you," I shouted.

I had no sense of where I was other than somewhere in Finland, 4,000 miles from home. For the first time my mother and father had no idea where I was, couldn't find me if they tried, and I couldn't call them for help. Surprisingly, my wave of confidence returned and I felt giddy and anxiety-free about the separation, if not my immediate situation. After two hours I spotted a log cabin. The path leading to it had a four-inch-square sheet of paper nailed to a tree, with the letters KVT, the name of the Finnish organization that organized this service project. I understood how Amundsen felt when he reached the South Pole. An uncontrollable shriek of triumph exploded from my mouth, which shook the forest so much that a dark-haired woman popped out of the woods. She wore overalls and was effortlessly dragging a fifteen-foot log. I gawked at the huge sheath knife hanging on her belt.

"Hello. I'm Hella." She spoke English without difficulty. "Who are you?"

"I'm Paul Pitcoff. Am I glad to find you! I'm from America, the United States. This has been some journey and I'm—"

"You're late." Hella didn't want to hear my story and wouldn't be charmed. "It's almost three o'clock so no point sending you out to do haying today. See that barn?" She didn't wait for my response. "You sleep in the hayloft. It's a log floor so you need to make yourself a mattress from hay. You'll find a bag to stuff it into." She pointed to a small log building. As I walked away she continued, "After you finish you can help Julie and Berta make dinner for everyone."

I was crestfallen and at the same time euphoric. I had arrived safely at my destination. Even if Hella couldn't appreciate my accomplishment, I did, and took a moment to celebrate how far I had travelled beyond the five boroughs of New York City.

Berta came out of a log cabin to give me a more welcoming greeting. She explained that so far there were only two guys— Paavo, the co-leader along with Hella, and George from South Africa. The remaining fourteen students were girls from Finland, Sweden, Norway, Denmark, Germany, and Great Britain. The men had to sleep in the hayloft in the barn of this abandoned farm. A log with a diameter no larger than ten inches rose to the hayloft at a 45-degree angle. A dozen notches were cut into the log, most likely for a small animal to get enough of a grip to climb the steep angle.

"Where're the stairs to the loft?" I asked.

Berta pointed at the log. "You get up there and I'll throw your stuff up." She lifted my pack and sleeping bag as if they were weightless balloons. There was no way I could get up the log, but this was my first public exhibition of my worthiness for frontier living. I crouched like a monkey using my hands as well as feet and made it up halfway before my feet slipped off the log and I landed hard on my crotch and slid down the log, being reminded of the notches on the way down.

"Too slow. Let me show you." Berta held on to my pack and ran up the log as if she were skipping up a slightly gradual walkway. "Now you try." She extended a hand from the opening in the hayloft. After two more failed attempts and to the great relief of my crotch, I learned to balance and run up the log.

———————

The midnight sun lasted for the first few weeks and when it finally set it was only for a few moments. The lack of darkness at night released me from the sensation of time. Exchanging stories with students from other countries, physical labor, and living on the frontier of wilderness produced abundant energy for the eighteen or more waking hours of each day. Our group of nineteen ate breakfast together and in groups of twos or threes we typically walked three to five kilometers to our separate assignments helping eight different homesteading families.

We lived on an abandoned farm that had a one-room log cabin with a small addition that served as a kitchen. Its windows had no glass or screens. It was common for a passing cow to stick her head through a window to check out our meal preparations and add to the conversation. The larger room was sparse, with only a hand-cut wooden table and two long benches. A three-seater outhouse with small, medium, and large holes, stocked with newspapers for dual purposes, was a short stroll from the barn. Finally, an abandoned rickety shack served as the obligatory sauna, essential for every Finnish household.

Each day, except Sundays, we cut hay with a scythe, raked it to begin the drying process, forked it onto drying poles, eventually lifted it into haylofts, and finally salted it to prevent spontaneous combustion. The only departure from our routine was forest clearing for claiming more pasture and haying fields. This required using dynamite to blast away boulders, cutting down trees, pulling out stumps, and burning the debris. I had been warned that Finland would be cold. Hah! It was so warm we worked with our shirts off.

Every three days Hella, our leader, rotated our work assignments to a different farm, and switched our partners. Depending upon the farm assignment, we might walk two to three miles after a communal breakfast at our abandoned farm and return in the evening for our group dinner. Two members of our group would stay back and cook and clean. I was paired with at least one Finnish student to translate and another student from a different country. Swinging a scythe is an art and it took me weeks to cut the grass close to the ground without burying the scythe into the earth. The farmers were forced to stop their own cutting to sharpen my blade, which cut more rocks than grass. On a particularly frustrating day I turned to the farmer I was "assisting" and asked Berta to translate: "Please tell Antti that I'm sorry I'm making more work rather than helping."

Antti focused on my scythe's nicks and sharpened it with a half dozen expert strokes with a sharpening stone. He then leaned my reconditioned scythe against a hay pile far from my reach and motioned for me to follow while Berta continued to cut hay. He pulled me to an area outside his barn. He pointed to my missing biceps and shook his head, and then pointed to my head and smiled. He clamped a fifteen-foot log to a holding clamp and demonstrated how to use a drawknife to strip the bark off, so the log could be used for hay drying. My first try met Antti's approval. He indicated this was my new assignment.

As I was working, Antti took off one of his rubber boots and banged it several times on the worktable. At the same time he shouted several words over and over again. I wasn't sure if he had changed his mind or wanted me to find boots to replace my sneakers. "Khrushchev, Khrushchev," he roared.

I smiled while he pointed east and held his hand up as if he was warding off some force. Then he pointed to me, "Cuba, Castro."

Berta eventually walked over to interpret. "He wants to know if you saw Khrushchev at the UN banging his shoe on the desk and whether you worry about Cuba. He asks how anyone can get work done in Cuba when they have to listen to such long speeches by Castro." I was struck by my new discovery that whether they were farmers in an isolated part of the world or New Yorkers, everyone paid attention to world politics in the nuclear age.

Antti lit a cigarette and poured coffee for the three of us, adding the equivalent of four teaspoons of sugar to each cup. The farmers were missing most of their teeth, which they compensated for by using their Puukko knives to cut anything that would normally have to be chewed. He seemed to be telling Berta a story. Tears formed in Antti's eyes and I resisted asking for a translation as he talked. He wiped his eyes and turned to Berta to translate. "He's telling me a story," she said. "The Russian soldiers killed his brothers, father, and mother during the war. Most of the farmers here have similar stories. He says the Finns never wanted to fight and the government had to get them drunk to do so. That's why our government still doesn't allow much alcohol in Finnish beer now." Berta interrupted herself to clarify something with Antti and I sensed he was waiting to see my reaction.

"I'm sorry. I never knew Finland had to fight the Russians." I touched his large hard hand. He used his other to wipe the wetness from his eyes. While not as fanatical as my father, it seemed that the Finnish farmers had a similar anti-Soviet perspective. My father's bon voyage warning had echoed all the way to Finland. An ocean apart, I now saw more clearly that despite the baffling manner in which he offered advice, it contained an underlying wisdom.

Berta continued, "When drunk, the Finns were good fighters and the Russians had to send in their crack troops. He says the Finns never wanted to be allies with Germany, but we were forced because the Russians invaded us. Countries make war. No one asks us, who have to fight."

Antti took off a dull gray metal ring from his wedding finger and handed it to me to inspect. "Nice ring," I said with enough enthusiasm that it didn't need translation. Antti smiled, but didn't seem pleased.

He continued with Berta and she translated, "He says that after the war the Finns had to pay reparations to Russia. The Finnish government asked everyone to donate their gold wedding rings and any gold jewelry. The government gave them iron wedding rings in exchange."

I stammered and searched for a response, pretending my tears didn't exist. "I never knew any of this. What's the relation with Russia now?" I asked.

"He says the Russians still control much of their lives. The Finnish government is forced to build roads leading up to our borders in remote areas where we don't need them and we aren't allowed to use them within a few kilometers on our own side of the border. This way the Russians can easily invade if they want. There are Finnish radios for us to use to report the first signs of a Russian invasion. He wants to take you to see one of the border towers with the machine guns."

My father's warning turned less opaque. "If we are not allowed I think we'd better not. How close are we to the border here?" I asked.

Antti laughed when he sensed my fear. "Don't worry. We're safe here, about ten kilometers from the border, but he knows a way to get close to the towers without being shot," Berta translated.

My father's cautioning, the warning on the ferry, learning what the Finns had endured because of the Soviets, coupled with a group of us now trekking behind Antti through a dark pine forest with no apparent trail, accelerated my fear level as we closed in on the Soviet border. "Be quiet," Antti ordered. Our group froze and he pointed

toward a short rise in the forest that left off into a clearing. I wanted
to believe that what I saw was merely a movie set, a guard tower
rising from a barbed-wire fence, machine gun barrel, a red flag with
hammer and sickle, and two men dressed in soldier's uniforms
standing to the side of the gun, in the midst of a vast Finnish forest.
Antti cupped his hands over his mouth and began to sing a song at
the soldiers. The barrel of the machine gun panned and my heartbeat sounded like bullets. I peeked out from the scrawny tree I was
using for cover and saw the machine gun aimed in our direction. I
needed no prompting; I pivoted, ran down the hill, and flopped
down behind a huge fallen tree. Antti stopped singing, but held his
ground. The other students, including our co-leader Hella, were
now cowering along with me. We waited for the sound of gunfire.
Instead there was the faint sound of some kind of chant or upbeat
song. We peeked our heads over the log and saw a red flag waving
from the tower and Antti waving back with his white handkerchief.
He shouted something sounding like Russian back to the tower and
then loped down to our defense barrier and laughed, pushing his
finger through the rotting tree to demonstrate its inability to
stop bullets.

Berta translated. "Antti is friends with those soldiers. They
come from a farm no more than thirty kilometers on the other
side." If only my father could be more accepting as these two
citizens on either side of the Soviet/Western border were. I knew
my father to be compassionate for anyone caught up in political
quagmires, and only wished he could bring such understanding into
his political polemics. We headed back through the forest. Hella
explained that Antti was late for milking his cows and we would
have to race back through the forest. Hella could see I wasn't up to
sprinting and asked for a volunteer to keep me company in case a
bear attacked me. Liz, a medical student from England, cheerfully
took on the burden.

If not for the mention of bears, I would have relished this opportunity for time alone with Liz. Over the weeks I had found myself absorbed in watching everything Liz did. She cut and tossed hay with an infectious enthusiasm. She threw more hay than I could, told stories about life in England, and instinctively knew my vulnerabilities and how to tease me out of my hang-ups. But now I saw Liz as a liability. If I confronted a bear, I couldn't just run and abandon her to fend for herself. "Wait, Hella, what happens if I see a bear? Do we run? I can't climb a tree." I was baffled and irritated by our leader's casual interest in my survival.

Hella unbuckled her belt and handed me her ten-inch sheath knife and holster. "Here, you must know how to use a knife. You're from New York City. I saw *West Side Story*. Use this and you'll be OK." While I studied the knife, Hella ran down the trail to catch up with Antti and the other students. I wanted to follow, but Liz held me back.

"Liz, I can't use . . . don't know how to use a knife."

"If we talk loudly bears won't bother us." It was about nine in the evening. The forest was dark except for scattered rays of the midnight sun poking holes through the canopy of trees. "You must have beautiful sunsets and sunrises back in the United States," Liz said.

"You too?"

"Let's go to that lake we passed. The sun is finally setting this week and we can watch it set and rise all within a few minutes." She led the way. In June, the sun stayed in the sky for twenty-four hours. As we moved into July it set for a few minutes each night. While we sat at the edge of a lake, the sun completely departed and then, moments later, began to rise a few yards from where it had vanished. It was as if the sun had had second thoughts about creating darkness and returned to keep the world illuminated. There was nothing to do but embrace and relish the silence of our thoughts.

After a few minutes Liz spoke. "I never believed this could really happen. Seeing this kind of life. Working together with people from so many different parts of the world. We won't forget this as long as we live." Those were my thoughts too. "Tomorrow I've got to help a boy on a farm about twelve kilometers away. He has some kind of growth and there are no doctors up here. It's a long walk and I wish you would come with me."

In spite of being a hypochondriac and scared of all medical interventions, I wouldn't admit that to Liz. "Sure, maybe I can be your nurse." With luck she wouldn't need my assistance.

The next morning Liz and I struggled to follow a scarcely apparent path through the forest to the Kokko farm. The family greeted us with the usual cups of lavishly sugared coffee, served with freshly baked bread. The father brought out Jaakki, whose face had ballooned to the size of a softball on the left side, the skin turning yellow. He made an attempt to be respectful, but his eyes were unfocused. We had no translator, but the family had been told of our purpose and Liz indicated the need for boiling water. She eyed the Puukko knives worn by the mother, father, and an older brother and decided they were too large for her to handle. "It looks like an abscess and if it's not drained an infection could reach the spinal cord or brain so it's serious." She asked me to boil my Swiss Army knife, the one my father gave me before I sailed off to Europe. Her commitment to helping Jaakki, coupled with her buoyant manner, somehow emboldened me to watch as well as help.

Liz cut open Jaakki's abscess and drained the pus. She had me boil some napkins and hold them against his cheek to stop the bleeding. I followed her instructions, surprised that I wasn't queasy. If a ten-year-old didn't flinch during this primitive procedure, I could at least muster the little courage I had. We cleaned up and Liz kissed me. I felt again the heightened connection with someone as we worked together serving purposes beyond ourselves. The combining of social commitment with personal commitment intensified our energy and passion. It recalled my mother falling in love with my father when he was standing on a soapbox, organizing workers. Liz and I fell into a close relationship and the resulting joy awakened my photography urge, reminding me to finally unpack my Nikkormat camera. For the remaining two weeks, when I wasn't enjoying my farm work with Liz, my camera and I used all our spare time soaking up the unusual light of northern Finland.

CHAPTER THIRTEEN

"I HAVE TO LEAVE ON FRIDAY. I don't want to," Liz said. I stood silent, bewildered, and fully unprepared for what I had known was an inescapable parting. "You said that after you leave Finland you'd still have five weeks before your flight back to America. Why don't you stop off in London? My uncle would let us stay at his flat. I could show you around the city."

Unlike the Pueblo boys, I hadn't killed a deer, but I had gotten myself to Suomi (the Finnish word for their country), survived—or rather, thrived—for four weeks living in primitive conditions. Now I was making plans to travel in Europe on my own. It was as if a dam had cracked and a surge of confidence carried me toward becoming a man. "It'll be strange here without you. Of course I want to see you again." I thought about how my mother panicked if anyone showed up suddenly to just say hello. "Would your uncle really let me stay?"

On the morning of August 1, I reached Hook of Holland, and boarded a ferry to make the short crossing of the North Sea to Harwich in Great Britain. When the ferry landed, I would take a train to London to arrive at the time Liz and I had arranged. It had been almost three weeks since we'd seen each other, and I wondered if she would be there or even remember me after resuming her normal life. If I couldn't stay with Liz's uncle I had no backup plan for living on my remaining $102.23 for the next four weeks.

After a stormy crossing I landed in Harwich, where I was directed to a customs line exclusively for Americans and then detained by a threatening British customs official. He asked many questions for more than two hours, but never disclosed the reason for such scrutiny. I assumed it was my nationality that had caused my brief but critical detainment. My politics was keeping me from reuniting with Liz. I missed my scheduled train, the one Liz would meet, and I had no way to contact her. She might assume I'd thought better of meeting again and leave the station after my scheduled train emptied without me.

My train pulled into London at 9:14 p.m. and I jumped to the platform even before the train stopped. The scene I had imagined, Liz waiting with outstretched arms welcoming me to London, dissolved into a different and harsh reality. While the platform emptied I became increasingly despondent. Except for a conductor checking his notebook, there was no one left. I was torn between the emptiness of realizing I would never see Liz again and an apprehensiveness about what I could do alone in Europe for the next three weeks. I hefted my backpack, grabbed my sleeping bag, and drifted up the exit ramp toward the main waiting area.

Where would I stay? In most of the cities I had visited there was a central registry at the main information booth that connected travelling students with families who rented out rooms for a modest cost. I hoped, but doubted there would be one in London. Certainly there was none at Grand Central in New York.

I circled the information booth with a loneliness magnified by being in the midst of people knowing where they were going. I ceased arguing with my body and allowed my backpack to slide off my shoulders and drop to the ground. Someone came from behind and picked it up. "I knew you would get here. Guess you had a rough crossing." I turned and Liz gave me a long hug. After what seemed like hours she pushed me away to look up at the clock. "It's late and we've got to catch the underground before it stops running."

It was six weeks since I had taken the ferry from Stockholm to Helsinki and I felt changed. Finland had been a springboard that bounced me from the hesitancy of adolescence to an embrace of maturity. In many ways my parents had set examples for me in being fickle in adhering to all rules. Risk-taking often produced better results than rule-following. Whether taking on a house to make livable, which no one else would dare, or representing oneself in court against an ambiguous police charge of going through a red light, or not accepting the rules for entering Stuyvesant, my father and mother had prepared me to be comfortable with travelling to and working in a foreign land without knowledge of the rules. I had failed many paper exams, but I hadn't failed this test. I would return home with my rite of passage successfully achieved.

Liz's uncle Tom, and his wife, Isabella, hosted Liz and me in their one-family home on the outskirts of central London. Tom and Isabella gave up their bedroom for Liz and treated me to the only guest room. Everyone shared one bath. I was pampered during our five-day stay. Each morning we were greeted with eggs, sausages, toast, multiple jams, tea, and conversation. Such as, "Why do you all carry guns in the colonies?" Liz's uncle challenged me.

Liz shot back, "Tom, Paul doesn't have a gun. Behave!"

"Maybe not, but he's a Yank and they are a rough, arrogant sort. Could be he's not that sort, but most of them are. That lot think they won the war for us," Tom said.

"Tom, Paul travelled all the way from the States to help Finnish farmers who had nothing but some land to homestead on.

That's not arrogance." Liz's assertiveness rarely smothered her luminous smile.

Oddly, this provocation made me feel as if I was with family. This was like the Pitcoff home, with Liz's resolutely partisan uncle substituting Yanks for Soviets. It was easy to get into the flow. "I've lived in New York my entire life, and aside from the police, I never saw anyone with a gun . . . well, I've seen zip guns."

Her uncle grinned with no warmth. "Exactly my point. Your bobbies carry guns. They use them to shoot people. Our bobbies don't carry guns because we're civilized and don't go around shooting each other. We had enough of you during the war. You should stay in the colonies with your guns."

Tom, like my father, was not going to be swayed in his political beliefs. Isabella tried to lower the heat by asking about our itinerary for the day. Tom cleared the table and laid out a map, kindly showing me where to take a bus to the underground station and how to reach different areas of London. "Take care of my niece. Keep in mind you can stay here as long as you want. You don't seem like much of a Yank." Also like my father, Tom didn't allow politics to permeate his openness to individuals no matter what their beliefs. Our stay with Tom and Isabella allowed us to visit some of the sights of London, see a play, and prepare for meeting Liz's parents, who were waiting for us at their summer cottage.

The family "cottage," which looked more like a castle, was filled with a mob of siblings, aunts, uncles, cousins, and unrelated friends projecting a civility I had never experienced at home. Their British accents made me feel out of place and the need for a necktie. It suddenly struck me that I had been wearing the same two shirts for eight weeks, yet most eyes were focused above my neck, on my hair that hadn't been cut for almost three months. It occurred to me that the customs officials had surveyed a similar sight when I presented my passport after my victory at sea. Liz's father was overly stocky, with a large bushy beard and eyes that penetrated one's soul. Conversation ceased when he talked. I was intimidated.

The second morning after breakfast, we all drove to the family's full-time residence in Surrey. Liz's father, a physician, had to return to work. During the drive the family assured me that "Doc" Forster, as he was known throughout Surrey, was adored and treated as a saint by his patients and the town's residents. Doc Forster listened and solemnly nodded his head in agreement. Liz was expected to carry on the tradition since she was the oldest and Doc had no faith in Liz's younger brother to carry on the tradition.

For three days Liz and I drove to nearby cities and towns, mostly to walk along old Roman walls and visit churches, cathedrals, and see Stonehenge. After dinner on the third night Doc Forster took me into his den to discuss some "serious concerns." He blocked the entire fireplace with his hearty body. The mantelpiece seemed barely up to the task of supporting one of his large arms, which stretched out just under his shotgun. He was costumed to fit the occasion, wearing a tweed hunting jacket with leather elbow patches and most strikingly, a gunstock patch over his right shoulder. He offered me whiskey. I declined, but he poured one for himself.

"I fear my daughter has fallen in love with you." He swallowed his glass of whiskey in one gulp and focused on my reaction. His eyes fastened onto mine. My legs begged me to sit, but fear held me standing. "What exactly are your intentions?" No one had ever asked me about my intentions in such a serious manner. I had no career plans, hadn't thought about where I would live or when to get married or have children. I panicked, thinking how poorly my parents had prepared me for planning my future. I couldn't summon a response and thus waited for prompting. Everywhere I looked there were paintings of classic English hunts featuring dogs and shotguns. I wondered if the skeleton standing by his desk was the remains of someone accidentally or purposely shot.

The only rational explanation for finding myself in this scene was that I was being auditioned for a British B movie. My part was the ugly American coming to steal away an English maiden. There could be no other reason for this ludicrous clichéd exchange. Did he really think I could run off and marry his daughter? Doc fingered the shotgun and his eyes went cold. He had aged in the few minutes we were together. "Liz is going to be a doctor. I let her do anything she wants as long as she works hard at becoming a doctor. No Yank, no boy, is going to stop this," he sputtered. He paused, no doubt to assess how his decree was being received. This was like a parent I had dreamed of, knowing and prescribing exactly what their child should do and be.

"I want Liz to be a doctor too. We've talked about it." My reference to "we" merely elevated his panic.

"I won't permit her to marry a Yank and live amongst a bunch of rebels. I will do anything and everything to stop her from marrying you." I noted the location of the two doors and wondered how fast I could dash to the nearest. Or could I wrestle the shotgun from his hand as he took it off its wall mount?

During the thundering silence I amused myself by thinking this could be an opportune time to suggest that Liz might want to consider converting to Judaism. But I knew this irony would be lost and even if the shotgun wasn't loaded, he might use it to beat me to death. He poured a second glass of whiskey, no longer offering me any. He drained it. He merged toward semiconsciousness. I couldn't deal with what I had gotten myself into. I recognized that my dependence on humor was a defense in accepting that I had no certain intentions and at the moment it seemed potentially fatal. In that moment I realized that my parents' omission of prescriptions throughout my life had created an unambiguous message that if I was to find direction for my path forward it would be without their advice.

"I know my daughter. She's wanted a motor scooter for years and I just bought her one as recognition for finishing her first year at med school. I'll tell her she can't have it if she continues to see you."

My breathing adjusted to normal. Doc had unintentionally revealed he wouldn't blow my head off with his shotgun. Now I could relax and focus even more on my envy of Liz in having such a wise and confident father like hers. I tried to identify with him. "If I were in your shoes I wouldn't want Liz going off with anyone, even if they weren't a Yank."

Liz burst into the male sanctum. "What're you men chatting about? Daddy, you look pale. Paul, it's cool in here and you're sweating. Come with me," she ordered and grabbed my hand. "I have to pick up some groceries. Daddy, tomorrow Paul and I are visiting Geneviève at her family's chateau near Lille. I want Paul to get a feel for the French."

Doc took out his handkerchief and rubbed a smudge off the barrel of his shotgun. "When will you be back? There is no need for the scooter, so I will have it returned," he said. A sense of confusion showed in Liz's face as she momentarily hesitated before leaving the room. At that moment I realized my mistaken judgment and gave my parents a reprieve. Liz's father with all his certainty and desire to control couldn't threaten his daughter out of doing what she wanted. Maybe my parents knew this to be true with me and their absence of advice had been a sign of confidence.

We lived the remaining days of our vacation with much delight, meeting Geneviève and many of her friends. We had become linked in such a short time and under the most unusual circumstances. Finland separated us from our customary environment, stripping away the certainties that had come from familiarity and habit. At this moment, each of us was the only one who fully understood what the other had experienced.

Liz had to return to medical school and I to Luxembourg to catch my flight home. We promised to write and find a way for me to return, although Atlantic crossings were not as commonplace then and not affordable. I ran alongside the train taking her back to Britain. I held her outstretched hand until I ran out of platform, just as I had seen in movies that took place in Europe. I watched the train and her waving arm recede and cried.

I flew home, twelve weeks after I had steamed from New York on the beginning of my personal odyssey. I felt changed. Finland and my trip presented a bundle of opportunities that strengthened me, made my life feel fuller, and made me more hopeful about becoming an adult. I had forged my own way, as my parents had when they struck out on their own. I was thrilled. I still harbored irritation at being shielded from the experiences that shaped my parents' perspectives, but I also realized they had set examples for me, whether crossing the country on our western trip or being part of their dinner parties or observing their close relations with others. I was growing my own life narrative and theirs began to recede in importance. Even if I had not braved nearly as much as the Pueblo boy and minus a deer, I returned home believing my rite of passage had been a success.

———————

Uncharacteristically, my father and mother took the morning off from work and picked me up at the airport after my twenty-three-hour trip across the Atlantic on a DC-6 that had to make two refueling stops, in Iceland and Canada. Our plane changed altitudes to help in de-icing the wings, distressing many passengers. The long flight intensified my feelings of loss and regret in ending this three-month chapter of my life, but paradoxically, I also began to feel elated. I had discovered new features of my identity and was eager to see how they would play out in my life back in the United States.

On our ride back to the city, I detected something different in the interchange with my parents. They remembered every word of the few aerograms I had sent from Finland. There was no annotation or interpretation of my experiences, but rather a sincere interest in learning more from my experiences. I used the good feelings to bring up the Russians. "Dad, I never realized how much control the Soviets have over Finland. I didn't even know the Russians invaded Finland during the war. Now I can see why you didn't want me going over the border." I wouldn't tell him how close I went, for dread that it would unleash that terrible fear or horror of his perpetual secret nightmare.

Releasing his broad smile and watching the road, he patted my knee. "Good. I knew you wouldn't cross the border. If you had, they have our name." Predictably, I didn't ask for further clarification of this non sequitur. I wanted to think that this was just my father's continuing mistrust of the Soviets, mixed with paranoia that they would be singling out the Pitcoff family, but upon reflection I realized I was just back in the mysterious shadow world of my parents.

During my first days home, I could feel that I'd shed my adolescence. I could feel it in the way I walked, and in other subtle ways that allowed me to slow down my anxiety build-ups and face new adventures as well as roadblocks with more confidence. I had less to prove to the world or myself. "Not bad," I thought. My mother hadn't needed to call Finland's prime minister.

My three rolls of slides, taken in Finland and Europe, became the treasured evidence of my odyssey. I studied my photos for hours, reminding myself of the texture of emotions I had felt to fill in the stories I was beginning to frame for future telling. One of my favorites was a double exposure showing both the sunset and the sunrise over the lake where I had sat with Liz. The alliance between the camera and myself was forever fixed, planting the seed for one of my future careers. Although my major was still officially undecided, I thought of photography as my unofficial major, even though there were no photography classes on campus. I enrolled in night classes at an art college an hour's drive away. The classes attracted photographers who wanted to explore the visual elements of humanity and injustice through their work. I was well into the "groovy" sixties, in my own pleasing groove. Back at my college the yearbook editor drafted me to be the photo editor on the basis of my having a camera. My representations of the frivolity and alienation of campus life resulted in one of the first serious reviews of my work: I was hung in effigy by the senior class and my dummy saved at the last minute from incineration by the building and grounds crew.

The following summer was about getting a money-making job. My father casually revealed that Local 3 of the International Brotherhood of Electrical Workers had a summer program for sons of journeymen. He was clearly unprepared for my interest in the prospect, nor did he realize my hankering to learn firsthand what his work must be like, a subject he never disclosed at home. I jumped at the opportunity as well as the sizable salary of a third-year apprentice, twice as much as I could earn from any other job.

A few days later I arrived early at the union shape-up hall, where electricians needing a job showed up to be assigned to a contractor. After submitting my name, I waited through lunch to be given a job. "Paul Pitcoff," the official yawned. "You're assigned to Donglow Electric. Show up Monday at this address, 8:00 a.m." He shoved a scribbled address on a soiled, mimeographed list. "These are the tools you're required to bring."

At home I proudly showed the list to my father. "Dad, what's a Channellock?"

If I read my father correctly, he showed halfhearted approval with a touch of foreboding. "I'll get you the tools. I thought maybe the shape-up would have soured you on the job. I'm surprised you made it through." I gathered my father feared the job would be too rigorous physically and too tough a setting for me.

That next Monday morning I showed up fifteen minutes before eight at a three-story Brooklyn high school built in the 1920s for 4,000 students. I located a small shed with "Donglow Electric" chalked on it. I introduced myself at a volume no louder than the mouse that scurried across the beat-up plywood floor. No one welcomed me. I mimicked the example of the other men, who were changing into their work clothes. My first mistake was hammering a nail into the wall, copying the style of hangers the others used to dangle their street clothes.

"Who the fuck you think you are?" a middle-aged electrician barked. His belly hung over his work belt. He knocked the hammer from my hand. "You here to take jobs away from carpenters? We don't hammer nails, they do." My hammer hit the floor and the head separated from its chintzy handle.

Another electrician joined the rout. "Where'd you get that piece of shit? Probably Sears. Certainly ain't union-made."

This wasn't Little Red, Camp Hurley, or Finland. I hadn't uttered a word other than my name and I was already the target of contempt. As the day progressed each of my tools died dishonorable deaths through self-amputations of critical parts or bending into obscene unusable positions, all noted and mocked by the veteran electricians.

"Where the hell did you get such junk?" the foreman asked as he tossed my broken wire-cutting pliers into a metal discard pail. With a balance of annoyance and pity he lent me his tools. "Use these today, but get proper ones for tomorrow."

Some of the men knew my father, which saved me from running off the job in humiliation. "You Bob Pitcoff's son?" one of them asked. I wearily nodded. "Your dad saved my ass when one of my bosses tried getting me demoted from journeyman. He's stood up for a lot of the guys. You owe it to him not to be a fuck-up," Stan pointed out. "Your tools aren't a good start." Stan was in his late fifties, laconic and yet commanding attention. When the other veteran workers learned I was Robert Pitcoff's son, the mockery ceased. They talked as if he was a legend, standing up for their rights as workers.

When I returned home that evening I confronted my father. "Dad, how could you send me there with such lousy tools?"

"I didn't think you'd last more than a day. No point in wasting the money." He hung out a sheepish grin in apology. "Now that you want to go back, I'll get you the proper tools. But remember it's not a life for you."

Although in good physical shape, thanks to Finland, I came home every day close to being defeated by the toughest physical work in my life. One week we worked in a hellish trench in the middle of a Brooklyn avenue, fitting and hot-tarring large steel pipes that carried new electrical service into the building. In humid ninety-five-plus-degree heat, we stumbled in sand and rocks, our clothes muddied with our sweat. The closed space, the smell, the tar all over us, and the strain of moving and fitting a pipe without slicing someone's finger off stalled our progress almost to a standstill. Tensions rose and exchanges that might have been defused by a joke turned to physical threats.

Standing on the top step of an eight-foot ladder to install fluorescent light fixtures made my stomach pulsate with a level of fear more potent than the Cyclone roller coaster at Coney Island. Running flexible conduit into ceiling crawl spaces that must have exceeded 110 degrees and had not been entered for the past forty-plus years was my least favorite assignment. My electrician's flashlight was thankfully so dim I couldn't make out the skeletons or gangs of rats that surely were around the next corner.

Even with the danger, dirt, fear, and relentless physical labor I looked forward to the different challenges each day, and to the banter with the other electricians. It wasn't a philosophy or political science class, yet we covered many of the same subjects from a worker's point of view. I worked under one of the veteran electricians who had initially given me a hard time. He raved about my mechanic's hands and how quickly I developed the ability to rewire each classroom. The foreman checked my work and told me I was ready to supervise. He assigned a regular first-year apprentice to work under my direction. It was kind of a field promotion without any change in salary or rank, but I took it on with great pride, even knowing it was not adhering to union procedures. At the end of each workday I flicked the switches in the room we had just rewired with new fixtures. When it instantly flooded with light, I felt an immediate and undeniable satisfaction, one I never achieved on such a regular basis in any other career. Rather than being told what life was like for my father, I was experiencing the complexity and challenge of it each day.

Disappointingly, I also experienced my second direct encounter with institutionalized racism, the first being in the Algonquin Provincial Park in Canada. The union had finally succumbed to community pressure and taken in their first workers of color just prior to the summer I worked as an electrician. Their vetting was harsher than for white men. They needed written assurances of character from their local clergy and pillars of their community. They were given the worst assignments of difficult contractors, farthest and most difficult to travel to locations, or the most unpleasant sites to work at. Rumor was it that Donglow Electric had pissed off the union, so the "untrained incompetent summer college students," like myself, and black first-year apprentices were assigned to Donglow. Ironically, we worked harder and produced more for the contractor.

I found myself amidst open racism and in some ways felt a party to it. Caleb, the first-year apprentice assigned to me, received the lowest wage rate, while I was paid at the rate of a third-year apprentice because of the special program for sons of journeymen, even though we began the job the same week and were doing the same work. Together we learned through our mistakes and had fun, which lifted the clouds of prejudice enough for us to enjoy our friendship. I witnessed how Caleb had to be cautious and tolerate the aloofness and resentments of other workers because he was breaking their norms and changing the all-white working environment. At times, it was clear, he was restrained even with me.

As I was pulling new wire through a conduit leading to my classroom, I watched Caleb wiring a fluorescent fixture with careful precision. I thought about when my father began work as an electrician. Like Caleb, he had few opportunities to pursue a career for which he had a passion. He was a Jew and his name often gave it away in professions that excluded Jews. Yet he still found a decent job as an electrician. Caleb had it worse because there was no way to hide the color of his dark brown skin. It was the first thing everyone saw.

"Dad, I don't understand why your union discriminates against Negroes," I said at dinner one night. At camp and at Little Red I had come to learn that unions were the leading organization for protecting the rights of workers. While discrimination was ubiquitous, I had an impression that unions would not support racial discrimination. My father got heated and I regretted having brought up the subject. He spoke with a distinct cadence and carefully pronounced each word, as if he was giving a speech to a group of workers. "No matter where a worker turns, there are corrupt forces that use their labor to advance their own fortunes and power. You know I was a union organizer." I did. I doggedly held on to this fact because I used it to counteract my shame that he had testified at HUAC. "The Communists infiltrated many good unions, but the infection and corruption lasted even after they were purged of Communists. But when unions discriminate against a worker they're just as bad as the capitalists. It's just a different form of enslavement. The union bosses make deals with the contractors for personal advancement. Workers never win."

Speech completed, he softened and relaxed into his chair, his tone changing to one of resignation. "I was prevented from going into radio electronics when I was younger because they were discriminating against Jews then." I sensed a shadow cross my face as I experienced one of the rare times my father expressed lament about his life. My slumping posture told my father to dig into his bountiful resources of optimism and to rekindle hope. "Think of your friend Caleb. He's got a chance to make some good money with a worthwhile skill, a productive career. There'll always be breakthroughs." My father had a confounding way of shading issues, eliminating black or white conclusions.

I longed to feel securely on some side or the other on political issues such as Communism or unions. It would bring me closer to my father if I could be on his side. At twenty, I was more familiar with his contradictions than I was a few years before. He beamed

and his eyes widened when I followed up on a reading recommen-
dation of his, especially if it was about one of his heroes like Eugene
Debs or Clarence Darrow. He referred to Debs as the greatest of
union leaders and Clarence Darrow as the most brilliant of civil
rights lawyers and friend of the ordinary worker. Quoting Darrow,
"Unions have done more for humanity than any other organization
of men," he looked solemn and said Darrow was a giant of a lawyer
and a good human being. He could praise a hero and criticize the
very institutions Darrow fought for?

I think he had met Eugene Debs and he reminded me that Debs
did more to improve the conditions of workers than anyone else. I
wondered if my father had voted for Debs on the Socialist ticket
when he ran for president. Why was my father not convinced that
Communism hadn't tainted Debs? It was puzzling and discouraging
to sense my father's present contempt for unions. Weren't we for
unions? My father's union had made it possible for him to earn a
decent salary and to offer me a summer job with a high enough salary
to offset some of my college expenses. If anyone was getting shafted,
it was the capitalist contractors who had to pay us at a rate of third-
year apprentices when we were untrained, had no experience, and, as
college students, had no aspirations to continue as electricians.

While the union fostered racial prejudice and practices they had
finally allowed Caleb and others to get a toe in the door, and that
would change things for future applicants. Perhaps there was value
in the inconsistencies I experienced through my parents. In a
circuitous way they taught me that certainty about anything
couldn't stick, with the exception of Communism for my father. It
was as if he was carrying a devastating personal grudge that he
couldn't reveal or discard. Must I be ever vigilant in smelling the
toxicity of Communism wherever I looked at an organization? And
smoldering in the wings were our conflicting views over the
Vietnam War, which was turning the Cold War red hot.

CHAPTER FOURTEEN

IN JUNE OF 1965, the war was intensifying. My sense of vulnerability fixated on my inevitable 1A draft status, which would send me to Vietnam. After I graduated as a psychology major in May, photography and the Vietnam War continued to be my competing fixations.

Avoiding the draft, knowing that other young men would be forced to fight for something they might not understand any more than I did, produced a scorching internal conflict. Despite the colonialist policies of our government, didn't I have an obligation to participate along with all the other men who were risking everything in a belief they were doing something for their country? There were days when I knew the right thing to do would be to flee to Canada after I received my induction notice. In the same week there would be days I felt solidarity with other draftees and believed I must stand up to my fate. After work, late into the evenings the internal clash made me feel like I was being pummeled in a tenround prizefight, most frightening since I had never thrown a punch in my life.

The war detonated political clashes with my father that neither of us had the facility to temper. "You don't know, but if the Communists take hold throughout the world we're doomed. You don't want to live in slavery." His blue eyes blazed as if possessed.

"We all want peace, but they can't be trusted. Even Johnson has it right." I felt a shadow cross my face. My heart was palpitating. I trusted his knowledge and wisdom and he was my father. On the other hand, it seemed irrational to believe that we had a better view of how people should live in Vietnam, halfway around the globe and a culture so different from ours. If it was fighting a Hitler who was exterminating millions and invading other countries, I might even volunteer for the Army. "Don't worry, the Army is smart enough not to put you in the infantry and would use your skills in better positions," my father offered. This was even more absurd. Everyone knew the Army wasn't smart and things were growing desperate over there. Forget Communism, this was my life on the line and my father seemed almost oblivious to this.

My mother was typing away on a keynote speech for a social work conference. She feigned total absorption in her work until her son was about to enter the Army. "Bob!" she commanded.

With her he had a more worthy opponent. "Florence, you know what the Communists are capable of. This is not some theoretical armchair discussion."

My mother's interjection cooled me down to room temperature. I could see firsthand his fear of Communism was so extreme it couldn't overcome his desire to keep me safe, aside from his contrived rationale that the Army would find a better job for me than infantry. I forced myself to have empathy rather than explode and reframe his irrational offering as masking his powerlessness to overcome the personal trauma that clouded his normal levelheaded thinking. I said, "I need to meet Ethan at the Art. We're seeing a new Fellini film, *Juliet* of the something." My father returned to his newspaper and my mother her typing, and the cold war at home remained cold.

As I walked down West Fourth Street, past the sprouting hippie stores, I recalled an incident with my father that at the time I had swatted away as being nonsensical. I was in high school and planning for college. "You know," he said, "I could get you a congressional nomination if you wanted to go to West Point." Figuratively I looked all around me to see who he was offering help to, because it couldn't possibly be me.

Eventually words came out of my mouth. "Dad, I can't even march." Surely by then he knew I had no aptitude for military life. But maybe his screwy offer was motivated by a desire to feel he could contribute to the cost of my going to college. I was even more befuddled by how he believed he could get me a congressional nomination. Maybe I wasn't hearing him correctly, but I didn't want to embarrass him by questioning this boast. I was used to these fleeting encounters that amplified my nagging belief that he had another life that I knew nothing about and was too fearful and too unprepared to question.

Now, however, I needed a job. The shadow of the war and my own proclivity toward uncertainty made my increasing independence somewhat dreamlike. Without fully realizing it, photography had become my identity. Harriet, my girlfriend, was a dancer and a supporter of my photography. She enjoyed modeling for me on city fire escapes, dump yards, unfenced rooftops, and in other gritty places. Our dates mostly pivoted around dance concerts or spending hours in my cramped dual-purpose bathroom, which was mostly used for darkroom work. Perhaps the war, romance, and my changeable nature diverted any practical tendency for planning a career or even a path for financial stability. Together we enjoyed the absence of need to be rational that the world or dance and photography seemed to offer. We would build our lives on paths we had no models for.

Without much thought or planning I grabbed the first insignificant job offered me after graduation by the ABC (American Broadcasting Company) Film Services. Most of my tenure there involved bureaucratic clerking, yet it also gave me a start on my education in film. I'd learned about intricate lab methods and a vocabulary that would be of value for my future career as a film-maker. The additional lesson was that I was not suited for a large commercial organization. I needed something better in my life. Camp Hurley had introduced me to the sense of independence and freedom I experienced in the country. Land was cheap and I pur-chased an old barn and some acres up state, thinking we could renovate it on weekends into a home, as I had seen my father build his own homes. I convinced Harriet that we could make an ideal life out of it and suggested marriage as a first step. I could cover the mortgage payments for at least a year from my savings, so I quit ABC.

Neither of us had definite career paths other than ambiguity. Planning the future didn't seem promising in the midst of the upheaval of the sixties and with me facing induction into the Army. Harriet took a job at an advertising agency just to make money. She was equally hazy about her own career or family plans. Our barn offered a focus for my denial over the inevitability of being drafted into the monstrous war. Despite having no hot water, no heat, and no windows that opened, our barn became a haven. Friends appeared almost every weekend to offer hard "unskilled" labor and design ideas. None of us knew what we were doing, which deepened our friendships and teased our fantasies. Although irrational in one sense, the culture of the sixties made it all seem a norm to return to the basics. Harriet and I even contemplated subsistence living, until I had to dig a trench for our garden fence to protect us from the rabbits running off with our lettuce. I knew I was too soft for living off the land.

Away from my fantasy life, I saw a reprieve in NYU, which had begun a graduate film program in their School of Education. That would continue my student exemption from the draft and classes were at night, so I could continue to work. I enrolled and began working freelance in film, starting as a "gofer" and eventually working my way up to doing sound, assistant camera, and camera work on documentary films. This was the way I learned best, like my father telling me to teach myself to drive. I learned by doing, making countless mistakes, and approaching the best of mentors.

Freelancing also meant filling in with other sources of income and acquiring skills I hadn't been prepared for in college. One Christmas, Ken, a striving freelance soundperson/part-time taxi driver, and I sold trees out of a rented U-Haul on upper Broadway. I relied on Mollie's model to please customers and share stories with many happy customers. My father's model of not being afraid to try anything inspired the two of us to place an ad in the *Village Voice* claiming we could do any carpentry or odd jobs. Our first job was removing wallpaper, which we had no idea how to do. Of course we took the job and ran across the street to a hardware store to get instructions and rent a steamer. We continued to rely on the same pattern of accepting jobs before we fully understood how to do them. One of our largest commissions called for replacing a rotted garden fence in the East Village. Another neighborhood hardware store rented us a post hole-digger and gave us the requirements for the distance between posts and what size lumber we would need. I held tightly to the handlebars of the hole-digger as Ken turned on the switch. The behemoth machine was not equipped for burrowing through concrete, but easily flipped me off my feet, turning me into a propeller. Ken unplugged it just before I gained altitude. I estimated a job to build bookcases for a small publishing company. They gave me a copy of their publication, which I unfolded to read on the bus home. The woman sitting next to me began screaming and called me a pervert just as we both laid our eyes on the photos in *Screw* magazine. This impromptu life was a continuing adventure and a buffer from my anxieties over being called to fight in Vietnam and having neither a solid job nor a career plan.

On a plane coming back from doing sound at a concert at the federal prison in Lexington, Kentucky, with the Pacific Gas and Electric band, I compared myself with my father. He had had so many more options closed to him and must have felt vulnerable upon arriving in the United States and having to find some way to sustain himself and improve his life. I remembered my mother telling me how he was completely despondent during the Depression, when he had to apply for welfare. Unlike me he never had anyone to fall back on if he couldn't make it. Both my parents had made it on their own, without anyone to rescue them, in contrast to their proven track record of supporting and rescuing me.

In 1968, President Johnson rescinded graduate school defer-ments. I was now at the height of my depression over the war and on a direct path into the Army. Yet my mother was ever present when it came to emergencies. She heard of a lawyer who specialized in draft cases who worked for Bill Kunstler, the famous civil rights lawyer. She paid the $500 for him to exploit the bureaucratic entanglements related to appeals to keep me from getting killed, wounded, and/or emotionally scarred. She did this while her own stature in the field of social work was gaining national and some international attention and without revealing her concurrent con-cerns for my father's declining health and the racially driven vandalism on their houses on Fire Island.

Throughout my father's life he had developed a wide range of resources to offset his lack of formal education, early immigrant status, discrimination against his religion, and his lack of aptitude for business. He had a healthy and deserved self-confidence in his ability to build houses with his own hands. At times when I was growing up he had dropped stories about how shortly after he returned from the Merchant Marines after the First World War, he bought property on City Island, part of an outer borough of New York City, before subways had extended that far into the Bronx. With his own hands he built a small house, the size of a garage. "After I built the house I found an abandoned boat and a junked automobile engine. I put the two together and motored out into Long Island Sound." He repeated this story a number of times, so I knew this was the point where he would laugh and chuckle as if he was still soaking wet.

Often the story followed some screw-up of his, such as cutting a water pipe without remembering to shut off the main valve, or when the two of us stood up the frame of a wall for a house we were building, nailed it in place, stepped back, and noticed it was upside down. "You should have seen it. The engine ripped out the bottom of the boat and it sank like a stone." I realized how much he respected rather than hid his life's missteps, with the exception of events related to Communism. He was giving me not only license but also encouragement to embrace failure wherever I found it.

He went on to build another house on Long Island at Rocky Point, with my help as a five-year-old. He showed me how to point the drying concrete between the cinder blocks of the foundation. His confidence increased and in the late fifties he and my mother purchased property in Ocean Bay Park, one of several communities on Fire Island. At that time, this long barrier island fifty miles from New York City seemed quite exotic. We had to leave our car on the mainland, take a ferry with all our provisions, and transport our stuff to our building site on a child's little red wagon. (You still do.)

Ocean Bay Park had one general store, only open in the summer months. This was near the beginning of what became a highly popular summer oasis community due to its long stretch of unspoiled white sandy beaches and the absence of vehicular traffic. My parents purchased two ocean-front building lots and my father, with my support as junior helper, built a modest unheated house that overlooked the Atlantic Ocean, all for $3,100. In his character-istic non-prescriptive way he gave me consequential assignments, such as positioning and digging holes for the cedar timbers the house would sit on four or five feet above the sand. He gave me the hole-digger he'd jury-rigged with extensions, a few words of instructions, and sent me to the site. I was on my own in early April, on break from college, sleeping at a family friend's house, but with no one else around. His faith in me had immeasurable effects on my sense of confidence.

Shortly after the house was completed he built a second one on the remaining lot, and rented the first one to offset his source of income during dry periods in his electrical work. While I was working and obsessing about the draft he rented the house to the first African American family ever to rent in Ocean Bay Park and perhaps in any of the neighboring communities. My parents liked renting to a family rather than unrelated groups, which tended to be hard on a house. He told me nothing about the family other than he enjoyed meeting them.

When the family arrived, our second new house, as well as theirs, was tarred. Slurs about "coloreds" were painted on the siding. The police had suspects, but no direct evidence. Years later when he told me about this incident, he exploded from frustration and rage. "Cowards. If they tried it when I was there rather than in the hospital, they'd be the ones leaving the island." He never saw this rental as a political act until it turned sour. Yet it was a continuation of his commitment to racial equality and one that made me proud enough to carry on in my own life and work. He and my mother became friends with the family and a few years later, when they

made an offer to purchase the house, he was the first in the community to sell a house to an African American family.

I was unaware of this incident at the time, as I focused on the
attorney guiding me through a series of legal appeals related to my
draft status that took four years to be officially reviewed and then
denied. But that got me past my twenty-seventh birthday, when I
was too old to be drafted. I had privileged financial and educational
advantages to keep me out of harm's way that drafted combat
soldiers were denied. It was a bit like past wars where rich families
could pay to keep their sons out of the war. My benefit from the
inequality of our society had a personal and tormenting pang in
my head.

While I wasn't present to witness my parents' anxiety and alarm
over the diagnosis of and decisions regarding my father's second,
extensive cancer surgery, I came to the hospital for the day of the
surgery. After his six-hour operation I sat with my father for seven
uninterrupted hours, watching his faint breathing to make sure he
was still alive. He didn't move, except for some spastic painful
grimaces. I realized how much he modeled a life I cherished and I
even longed for the crazy manner in which he gave advice, especially
in this uncertain period of my life. Somehow I could see him devoid
of any tensions around Communism, just his humanity. Though I
was blessed with wonderful mentors he was always my best.

I was fixed to his bedside, holding his lifeless cold hand and
beginning to feel helpless. My mother had to retreat to get some
rest. He opened his eyes and first thing he saw was me. There was
no expression, but he squeezed my hand two or three times with a
degree of strength. He fell back into the drug-induced sleep. I cried
and cried with supreme joy. His hand told me he survived and was
coming back, ready for life. The operation successfully removed the
cancer, but he lost his ability to speak normally, and he now had a

sizable hole in his throat to allow him to breathe. His world was telling stories, debating ideas, and sharing some of his more pleasant memories. Denying him the ability to freely communicate was a serious setback and began a long period of withdrawal and almost halted my father's off-the-cuff, uncommon insights.

———————

In spite of the war I was trying to pull myself up the ladder in documentary filmmaking with a self-confidence I had been building from Camp Hurley through Finland and the electrical work. For six years I had conned my way into getting jobs I had no training for. "You can have the sound job on this film, but only if you know how to do post-sync playback." I had no idea what that even meant, but I assured the producer I was experienced in it. I got the job and rushed to someone who could teach me fast. "You do realize we will be working with 35mm, not 16mm, on this shoot. Have you done assistant camera work with a 35mm Arri?" I hadn't, but assured the producer I was experienced in it. I got the job and found a colleague who had experience with 35mm cameras.

Working in a creative field that had some power for encouraging social reform made me want to work any and all hours of the day and night. I relished the kind of friendships and collegiality fostered by our excitement and discoveries of fresh experimental approaches offered by the new techniques of cinema verité. As a result of the development of portable film and sound equipment, filmmakers could escape the highly scripted and static shooting of conventional documentaries, and film the actual action of the selected subjects with handheld professional cameras. The scripting for such films was done mostly in the editing room after filming. Finally I had found a fit for my disparate interests and passions.

If I had any thought of the future during my first six years after college graduation, it rested more on fantasy than having a plan. My ascent in the world of documentary work surprisingly paid enough to live on and seemed too interesting and enjoyable to think of anything beyond freelancing. My self-assurance grew and for the last two years of my six-year self-education, I raised the money to produce my own film for the School of Social Work at Adelphi University. *The Way It Is* followed a social worker helping a family in crisis on the Lower East Side of New York City. I never expected that this first film would lead to a new career.

My next offer appeared almost like another "gig" rather than the prelude to a long-term career. The dean of the College of Arts and Sciences of Adelphi had approached me at the premiere of my first documentary. The dean needed a filmmaker to teach and then lead a group of eleven college students to make a film about lifestyles in different parts of the United States. He asked if I could teach a film-making course prior to the trip, a first for Adelphi. It was good pay and booked me solid for the month of June, and sounded like fun. Before I could say yes, he suggested we meet. "Don't waste your time coming out to Garden City. We can meet in the city over a drink."

The dean had selected a bar near Penn Station. I halted at the bar's polished entrance, being more familiar with beer-pitcher bars with their sticky floors. I looked like a messenger off the streets, or perhaps a tradesman who couldn't find the service entrance, and felt as if someone would surely stop and question me if I dared to enter this high-end bar. I spotted his large frame and the charming way he turned to others to pitch conversational bouquets and nuggets of information and opinion.

Anxiety pushed itself upon me. This potential job didn't fit me. The idea of standing up in front of a class teaching—even film-making—seemed like a nightmare. I had tried many different schools, private, public, undergraduate suburban college, and even an MFA in film production. None of them made me a better student. For six years I struggled to learn how to make a proper film and had developed a treasure chest of failures along the way that catapulted me into producing a finished and acceptable first documentary, but by no means was I an authority to be looked up to. I remained a work in progress.

The dean turned and noted my presence and motioned me to the empty stool on his left. "I'm drinking Dewar's. Same for you?"

I nodded assent. I lifted myself up onto the stool and placed three manila envelopes on the bar to show I was ready for business. The dean complimented me again on my inaugural documentary film, which he had seen at the premiere hosted by the School of Social Work screened at a theatre at the United Nations. I wondered if the impressive screening theatre had won him over, rather than my rough cinema verité documentary.

"Dean Clemo, I brought an outline of a plan for teaching filmmaking and a bibliography, as well as my film credits so you—"

The dean put his hand over mine to stop me from opening the manila envelopes. "Have another drink first." The bartender poured another Dewar's. "You sure you have four weeks in June to go on the trip? You'll be away from your family a long time, and you won't be living in hotels. The students have no money and could only budget less than two dollars a day for food and lodging." The dean turned to one of his recently acquired friends at the bar. "Paul is taking eleven undergrads across the country to make a film about different lifestyles. Think the plan is they will be living in tents. It'll be the first student-made film at Adelphi. A big thing for us."

I finished my second drink and found myself holding on to the bar top to keep from teetering. This was insane. I had just finished a job as an assistant cameraman on a zany film about the American

Revolution that used a rock band to heighten nationalistic feelings for school children. The money was good, travel was stimulating, the crew was fun, and there was a good chance the producer or other crew members could get me more work if I was just patient. Adelphi's proposal of a four-week film trip would take me out of commission too long. It would be a student film, not mine.

The dean had my third drink placed in front of me before my second was completely finished. "Paul, you're going to do good things for Adelphi. Anyone your age who can produce their own film has something going for him."

In my increasing fog I heard "going" and assumed the dean was talking about having to get going. "I guess you have to catch your train back to Garden City. I should get going too, but don't you want to see my syllabus?" In my mind the word I slurred sounded more like "cymbals," or "silly" something. Inebriated or not, I didn't know what the word truly meant.

I offered the manila envelopes to the dean, because I was in no shape to pull out my teaching plans and present them to him. In his attention-gathering bellow, he suggested I take it easy getting home. "You're hired. Why don't you work on the syllabus after you meet with the students? Just tell me one thing: what do you think students will learn in making a film?"

I slipped off the stool and tried to carefully reseat myself as if I was merely readjusting my posture. I couldn't think of what to do. My career was taking an unexpected turn. I began the third drink. "Dean . . . I have to be . . . honest. I don't know. I'm not . . . a teacher."

"Yes you are. I just hired you. Think this out. Don't worry about the syllabus, don't even answer the question till you meet with the students and find out what they want. If you had answered it, I would have fired you."

The room and lights fluttered. I wasn't sure if I had been there for ten minutes or forty-five, but if I was hearing the dean right I had been hired and almost fired. This opportunity would change my life, if I could just manage to get myself to the door without falling over . . .

The dean looked at his watch. "Better get going. Look, the class meets every Wednesday at 6:00 p.m., so plan on getting to it next week." He pushed back his thinning white hair, rose to his 6' 4" height, and lifted his considerable weight off the stool with the ease of an athlete. A lone woman at the end of the bar was wearing a colorful tie-dyed tailored jean jacket, which gave her the authority of youth. Her gray braid suggested a run on wisdom. She had been listening to this strange hiring meeting and added her parting advice. "You know, none of us dare call him Richard. He just seems like our dean too, even though we've been out of school for decades. He doesn't seem to ever know what he is supposed to do, just does what he thinks is right. It's good luck for you to work for him."

Within a few years, teaching became a joyful collaborative learning process as well as an unexpected acceleration of my film-making skills. Perhaps my erratic upbringing had prepared me to take on the toss-ups of opportunities. I had witnessed my father act as his own defense attorney in the traffic court in Maine and seen my mother rise to full professor without a PhD, providing me with models of filling roles I might not be prepared for.

My experimental program became an official New York State–approved academic department, the Department of Communications. I became the youngest and least academic chair in the university. My career acceleration left me little time to fully appreciate how I was bringing a trace of Camp Hurley to my job, using my enthusiasm for group ventures to guide a program from its inception. I wasn't equipped to be an educator, but found it a mysterious and creative challenge, becoming intoxicated with shaping a course that would make students hungry to learn. My first venture, travelling with students to various unfamiliar places in the United States to make a film comparing lifestyles between disparate groups of citizens, was a grueling and exciting experience, never yet tried at other universities. My students' absence of guile and film experience quickened their desire to learn and be open to new experiences.

I hadn't yet known how to teach so we pursued our learning adventure as collaboration without the weight of predisposition. The resulting film was mediocre in story, but the experience became a touchstone for the possibilities of group creativity and openness to learning. Despite Dean Clemo's unwavering support, many faculty and administrators in the School of Arts and Sciences, in which I found myself, resisted accepting me in their more traditional dominion. Their "suspicions" grew proportionally as my students, a few years later, won an Oscar for their student documentary and my own films won national film festival prizes. My department brought a new kind of attention and heightened reputation to the university as a flood of students signed up as majors in communications.

In the summer of 1977 I was feeling strong about my film work and accomplishments in education. I had been granted tenure and appointed full professor. My wife and son took time for a rare family vacation with my parents in Maine. We had spent most of the day focused around Winton, my seven-year-old son, enjoying a ride on a lobster boat, laughing and telling funny stories, and were now taking a late afternoon break for reading. My father pulled me away from everyone. "Come for a walk with me." His seriousness was a striking contrast with our day. Rarely had it ever been necessary to purposefully separate from my mother, with the exception of our four-hour aborted running-away episode when I was approaching my teen years, and when he took me aside on the SS *United States* to warn me not to enter the Soviet Union.

We walked along a wooden path above the rocky shoreline, defending itself from the Atlantic's slight tempest. My father's minimal ability to vocalize without enormous struggle was mostly drowned out by the wind and thunderous sounds of the sea. We found a bench to sit on and I huddled close to hear his words. He couldn't avoid his usual rhapsodizing about the splendors of nature, the magnificence of the action of waves, and the immensity of oceans. Only much later did I realize that he needed this preamble to move into a disturbing topic. "I'm not going to live much longer, maybe a year, I doubt two."

I took a more careful study of his face and sparkling blue eyes. "Dad, is something wrong? What's wrong?" I couldn't process his disclosure and wasn't sure if he was seriously ill or just being philosophical, as often was his way. "You look fine and still can walk farther than me." This was mostly true, mixed with how I needed to see my father.

He made no notice of my comment while his expression and tone darkened. "The reason I wanted to talk with you is you're going to have your hands full with your mother." This statement rang out above the hundreds of explosive sounds of waves lashing out at the rocks below. While I digested this double-barreled update on what lay ahead for me, he got up and began walking farther down the wooden path. After a few moments I got up and walked doubly fast to catch up with him, feeling like a little boy craving to hear the rest of this unfathomable story. My trusty denial device of humor escaped me. He was being serious. He had always been in tune with his body, better than doctors were, and avoided them except for his major surgeries.

While I panicked at first at the thought of my mother falling apart, I found myself pushing back on his assessment. My mother's susceptibility to panics and finding errant pressures to put her in a "state" had led to much teasing and joking, yet there was solid evidence that she was highly functional and independent: she had built an exceptionally successful career for herself with notable national acclaim; in her own way she had run two homes, the apartment in New York and the house on Fire Island; she had been a strong and consistent supporter for her widowed sister, who raised a son who suffered from life- threatening emotional problems; and she had gotten me into Stuyvesant even though I had failed the test, and kept me out of the Vietnam War through finding the right attorney. Even more, she had supported my father through all his major surgeries and their aftermaths.

I caught up with him. "Mom will be OK and you're not going to leave now anyway. So just keep living and forget this two-year stuff."

He smiled and gave me a warm hug and we turned to walk back to our families. Nothing more was said. I dimly remembered behaviors that I now assembled as motivated by guilt. I had mostly connected them to his hidden political activities, but now I began to wonder if his guilt might be more connected to my mother. We approached a young couple standing by the railing. The young man had closely cropped hair and wore an argyle sweater, the kind no one I knew ever wore. He acted like an awkward twelve-year-old as he assembled his arm around his girlfriend. He was oblivious to the view of the ocean. She used one hand to keep her skirt from flying up in the wind and the other to keep her long dark hair out of her eyes. She looked up into his eyes for a long while and then turned toward the sea, to inhale the salt air and feel the glow of his longing.

As we passed the couple I wondered again, as I had throughout my life, why my parents had gotten married. Their great disparities in age and life goals had seemed at odds with forming a family. I recalled my mother once confessing that her mother didn't approve of him when they first got together. I wondered if my grandmother came to their wedding. It was strange that they never talked about their wedding. Maybe they ran away and eloped.

In April of 1978, I was thirty-five and making the final long-distance preparations for a film about strip mining in Montana. I had a brief visit with my parents in the city. Even though my father, now seventy-nine, was suffering major health challenges, he was still fully active working on his house on Fire Island. I had mostly repressed our conversation in Maine. My mother revealed he was using the Main Public Library in Manhattan to do research, the very same one I had used years before in college. This was new information. "Dad, what're you working on?"

"I'm writing . . . writing a book . . . to . . . explain why the Soviet . . . Union . . . will not survive." Speaking was a painful battle for him after his tracheostomy, but after halting attempts, I understood.

"You really think that? You don't think we're going to have war, do you? What's your theory?"

He turned serious and pulled back as if he had full confidence in his answer. "Bureaucracy." It took several tries before I understood the word, which naturally frustrated our free-flowing conversations.

"He's doing a lot of research and he believes we're headed on the same path here." My mother swept her hand across the view outside the window, indicating our country. "An uncontrollable bureaucracy could undo all of our political accountability. And, by the way, he's planning to join me when I deliver a speech in Toronto at the end of May."

I was pleased that both parents were thoroughly absorbed in their lives and their new apartment just off Bleecker Street, in the heart of Greenwich Village. They seemed interested in my latest film project and were enjoying this visit with my wife and our eight-year-old son. Yet the mention of the Soviet Union from my father revived my embarrassment over his testimony at HUAC. It also reminded me of how little I knew of their secret lives. Rather than push for clarity or resolution, I continued the don't-ask-don't-tell policy our family had honed.

A week later my parents took the train from Fire Island, where my father had been replacing rusted window hinges on his house. On the last leg of their journey, as they were walking home on Bleecker Street, my father had a stroke and died. After my mother phoned from the hospital I drove myself into the city mostly in a daze. I flashed through memories of scenes in my father's life and zoomed in on his beaming smile, when he recognized some achievement of mine. These pleasant remembrances only heightened my shock and pain. My sense of complete alienation thrust me into an automatic mode to confront the immediate aftermath of making arrangements and comforting my mother.

The ritual of informing others, preparations for sitting Shiva, and the funeral arrangements kept my mother and me busy into the night, exchanging concern for each other until my mother took a sleeping pill and offered me one. The afternoon of the next day I sat down at my father's desk, the one he gleefully lugged home from a renovation job when I was ten. The mahogany stain couldn't enhance the flimsy plywood look. My father joked that it wasn't worth the time to cut up for firewood; still it was his sanctuary for important papers and now offered a tenuous link to him. I tugged at the top drawer. A handle came off in my hand, as it always did when he'd given me permission to take one of his three-cent stamps. I banged the drawer with my fist, the way my father had done, and jiggled it open.

I mumbled to myself as I sifted through things in his desk.

There's your green-and-white marbled Sheaffer fountain pen, your prized possession.

I love this picture of you and Mom on a sailboat. You're hanging off a stay with your arm wrapped around her. She's in ecstasy, without a hint of anxiety. Was this when you were in Antigua?

Wow, here's a valentine card she hand-cut into a heart. Such flowery language. She was an unfading romantic and playfully honest: "I promise to do everything for you other than become a good cook or housekeeper." She kept both parts of that promise.

A photo of you on your motorcycle. You were some guy back then. How come I never knew about any of that?

So many papers and bills, too much to go through. I don't want to be here. I want you back.

This looks official. It's your marriage certificate! What a find. It's odd that you and Mom never told me the exact date or even anything about your wedding. Mom claimed your anniversary was late May, around Memorial Day, yet this says June. It says June 1957. FIFTY-SEVEN? How can that be? I was born in 1943.

I leaned away from the desk and considered the puzzling date. Now I understood why my mother asserted it was a cliché to go to Niagara Falls when we were nearing the end of our seminal 1957 cross-country trip. While I thrilled to partnering with Floyd to take a bunch of greenhorns down to the bottom of the Grand Canyon on mules, unbeknownst to me, my parents were living their honeymoon on the rim. For twenty-one years, I hadn't come close to suspecting her clichéd comment had any connection to the actual impetus for that trip. It was a clue, but one I never got. None of their relatives and friends knew of it, or if they did, they never revealed this secret to me.

I checked on my mother in her small office, mindful she was in no shape to explain my discovery. "Paul, I heard you going through

Dad's desk. Sit down. There's something I need to tell you." A Valium and Scotch were helping lighten her pain. "When you go through Dad's desk you may come across a few things you might find unclear." I edged closer to her. "We didn't get married till after you were born." Distracted, she sipped on her drink.

I drew in the silence. One month or even ten months "after" might be one thing, but fourteen years after my birth seemed to warrant a less ambiguous term than "after." How about "we waited for a decade and a half"? Considering the grief we both felt, and too familiar with my parents' practiced talent in concealing their history, I didn't chase for more details. Being labeled with this new identity—bastard—the loss of my father, and concern for my mother killed my appetite to learn more about my identity.

CHAPTER FIFTEEN

MY FATHER'S DEATH PRESSED ME to seek answers to other questions. How could I define myself? Was I an idealist or a pragmatist? Was I a participant or an observer? At times I felt my documentary work was merely a justification for being a paid voyeur. The various individuals central in my documentaries were vitally occupied with improving social justice, while I just darted from one subject to another, finding myself wishing I could take on the roles of each of my different subjects. After one film I found myself daydreaming that I should be aiding undocumented migrant workers; after another film I thought I should be working as a social worker aiding families in crisis, and after another, working as a lawyer preserving environmental viability.

I still hadn't advanced from the role I played of Johnny when I was ten years old, in our class play, *When We Grow Up.* I had to pretend I didn't know what I would be when I grew up and tried many different occupations. Perhaps forever I would be replaying that role. I now felt I should get out from behind the camera and participate rather than witness. I had more status as a full professor than I ever dreamed of or wanted. Yet I felt confined. My Communications Department had grown to the second largest academic department in the College of Arts and Sciences, and I had unwittingly given birth to a swelling bureaucracy, which ironically, as chief administrator, I couldn't fully maneuver myself.

Increasingly I found myself interested in the value of free speech. I had prided myself in creating a safe place for my students to express any idea in their films or discussion, although I encouraged them to thoughtfully defend their positions. The history of how the First Amendment was liberalized by the Supreme Court throughout the twentieth century had made me aware of the value as well as the risks of opening up a class to free expression. I faced the risks in classes with interesting results.

In one section of the senior workshop I assigned students to conduct video interviews with individuals who had a role or experience with the challenges of alternative opinions getting printed or aired in the media, a relatively new initiative in First Amendment law. Julie had taken a previous advanced filmmaking class with me. Her final project was a film about homelessness. I assumed it would be sympathetic, but I was dismayed that the film denounced homeless individuals for degrading her town. The solution proposed by those she chose to interview was to ship the homeless to New York City where they belonged. I felt queasy about having her film shown in our annual film festival, but more so about censoring the hard work she did. Now in the senior workshop she manifested a touch of racism in her ideas of the way society should be arranged that, surprisingly, was not evident in her interaction with workshop students of color. When we presented the video interviews I was impressed that students took the assignment seriously and worked to get interviews with prominent people in the media, such as Bill Moyers, then a highly placed executive at NBC News, and other notable journalists.

Another student, Fabiola, got up to introduce her interview. "I chose to interview someone who has not been given access to the media, and yet has important things to say." Fabiola was one of the more bubbly, enthusiastic students in the workshop. She could make anything happen if she put her mind to it. Her sharp intellect, deep chocolate skin, a lilt in her voice, and her intricate network of braids made everyone pay particular attention. "This is a man who knows about the subject because he is denied access to express his views."

She turned off the lights and switched on the video machine. Reverend Al Sharpton appeared on the TV screen. This was the late 1980s and Sharpton, now an established cable TV news host, was then portrayed in the media as a rogue provocateur. He had recently been criticized for his association with an ugly rape charge, which he had been accused of encouraging, that had been exposed as false. Racists saw him as justification for their attitudes, and many liberals found him offensive.

I noticed Julie straighten up in her seat, and other white students tighten up to the point that the notable silence blanketed the classroom. My first thought was that I would have a race riot in my class and worried how I would cool down what surely was about to erupt in my classroom. As the silence amongst my students intensified, I thought of pulling the plug. My better, more courageous side denied the impulse.

Fabbie, as she was known to everyone, turned on the lights when the tape was finished and asked for any comments. Julie was the first to speak. In her blustery, assured manner she announced, "I've always thought that guy was an asshole. A real asshole . . ." I was about to interrupt her with some platitude about how we must keep our class civil. Even I didn't agree with myself and there would be no stopping Julie anyway. "I have to tell you, and it surprises me, I agree with everything Al Sharpton said."

Such a turnaround from Julie was one of those moments that precipitates change. At home I came to accept and then appreciate the lack of a straight-line narrative. My parents' ability to see many facets of a story made me appreciate the joy of having my own prejudices unraveled. If someone like Julie, whom I had typecast as being irredeemably prejudiced and reactionary, could connect

herself to Reverend Al Sharpton, the poster child for all the prejudices she had previously held, then others too could change their
views.

Incrementally I was becoming more interested in the law, as a
means for addressing inequalities I saw so vividly during many of
my film commissions and also as a means for understanding complex fairness issues. I had worked with legal organizations when I
was producing a film about strip mining and on another film
establishing group homes for adults with cognitive disabilities, and
was impressed with the attorneys' sense of purpose and achievement
in balancing the rights of those marginalized in society. I had a
gnawing feeling that while many of my films had achieved changes
in public policy, there was much more to do. I began to flirt with
the idea of going to law school. Maybe I wasn't the worst student
after all, and I could prove, to myself and the world, that I could do
it and in the process make more of a difference and excite my
students about the importance of the First Amendment and how it
could be used to gain more access for their future work in communications. After all, what haunted me my adult life was HUAC and
McCarthyism, which destroyed the ideals and functionality of the
First Amendment. What a symbolic closing of the circle this might
be for me.

In 1986 I was forty-three years old, and thinking about these
things on an early spring Saturday afternoon, as I drove to
Northport, New York. My purpose was to pick up Winton, my
sixteen-year-old son, who was interviewing George Watt, the
political commissar of the Lincoln Brigade. Winton and I recently
had seen *The Good Fight*, a documentary about American volunteers who formed the Lincoln Brigade in 1937 to join the fight
against fascism in the Spanish Civil War. The volunteers' idealism
was stirring, and the film inspired Winton to choose the subject
for his final research assignment in high school. He discovered

that Mr. Watt lived near us, and was willing to share his experiences.

I held the directions to Watt's house in one hand as I navigated the unfamiliar suburban neighborhood. As I neared his house it occurred to me that Winton might have mentioned the little we both knew about my father's union organizing work as a Communist. My palms moistened on the steering wheel. What would I say if Watt asked about my father? Would I reveal that by the time of the Spanish Civil War my father was no longer a Communist and would soon be a friendly witness for HUAC? I squeezed the steering wheel, and prayed out loud in the empty car, "Winton, please be outside ready to go."

Relief washed over me when I turned onto Watt's street and saw Winton waiting by the front door. I wiped my sweaty hands on my jeans, but my relief lasted only a moment. Instead of jumping into the car he ran over to my side and said, "Dad, George wants to know all about Grandpa. Come in."

Winton led me through a hallway of bookcases to the backyard. Watt dragged over a chair for me, as we stepped outside. He was lean and looked more youthful than his seventy years. He greeted me as if we were comrades. "Winton asks sharp questions. I never expected anyone his age to care about the Lincoln Brigade." My anxiety calmed. "Winton told me about the political group you organized when you were at college. I was impressed that you arranged for Norman Thomas and SDS to speak. Not easy in those days. Winton told me you had to move Malcolm X off campus, because the administration refused to allow him to speak." He and Winton checked for my confirming nod. "You grew up in turbulent times. Vietnam erased nearly everything we fought for." He paused to pour us lemonade.

I shifted in my seat to indicate it was time to get going. "Thanks for taking the time with Winton. We need to go." Watt added ice to our lemonade and began telling Winton a story about a woman who risked her life for him, after he had been shot down over occupied Belgium flying as a gunner for the US Air Force. My thoughts drifted back to my sense of uncertain identity. How could I find my core if I had to conceal the essential facts of my parents' lives and how they came to their beliefs? Throughout my life, the majority of my friends and colleagues considered themselves liberal, and in general we shared similar aspirations for social justice. Responses to discovering I had gone to Little Red were predictable: *You must have been a red diaper baby. How wonderful that your parents were Communists.*

I would avoid exposing my father's HUAC testimony, but felt compelled to refute the red diaper reference. Always with embarrassment, I confessed my father's Republican affiliation. This elicited sympathetic responses: *That must have been dreadful to be betrayed like that. It must have been hard for you to be a liberal and still get along with your father.*

My friends and colleagues were wrong. I was not a liberal, I wasn't a conservative, and not a Communist either. In fact, I felt somewhat self-conscious about not having a definitive label for my political philosophy. I was afflicted with approaches and ideologies that drifted into different categories. If there was any betrayal by my parents, it wasn't about politics. It was about being kept in the dark about my father's political activities, my parents' false marital status, their wacky advice, and for extracting me from Little Red without any logical justification.

Watt was concluding his conversation with Winton. I dreaded what would naturally follow, the topic of my father. I thought about the habitual follow-up question new acquaintances frequently asked, after I confessed to not being a red diaper baby: *"But how could that be? Why would they send you to Little Red, a Communist school?"*

This was a good question and one that had baffled me throughout my life. My attention switched back to Watt. My mounting
distress made me want to bolt. If Watt asked about my father, I
would feel compelled to divulge the HUAC testimony and the FBI
visits. I was torn between loyalty to my father and respect for Watt.
I almost spoke my thoughts out loud. *Dad, why the hell did you turn
so early and why did you have to testify? And why didn't I have the courage
to find out more than you and Mom disclosed?* I willed myself to leave
before the next question was asked.

I got up and Winton reluctantly followed. I was just steps away
from my car. We stopped by the front door to make our goodbyes.
"Nice meeting Winton and you," Watt said. "He told me your father
was a union organizer and also a fellow Communist." George's
manner suggested we were connected by similar beliefs. I was dis-
armed. Misleading a hero of the Lincoln Brigade was not the same as
concealing the information to a liberal colleague or acquaintance.

"I don't know that much but . . . ," I heard the faltering in my
voice as I automatically attempted to obfuscate, ". . . unfortunately . . .
my father turned against the Communists in the thirties. I'm not
sure why. I think it was because he had been born in Russia and felt
especially betrayed by Stalin." I felt trapped in misrepresentations
that weren't of my making. I was concealing the HUAC testimony
and at the same time I was judging my father's actions as "unfortunate," a disloyal act to my father.

George must have heard the shudder in my excuse, because he
wrapped his lanky arm around my shoulder and gave me a hug.
"Your father was smarter than the rest of us. We turned a blind eye
to Soviet brutality in Spain as well as to what was going on in the
Soviet Union under Lenin as well as Stalin. Your father was ahead
of us." This astonishing comment from an unwavering Communist
and Lincoln Brigade hero was the longed-for antidote to my endless
burden of humiliation.

George closed his arm around me again. "Wish I had met your father. He saw the distortion of Communism earlier than most of us. I remained a communist with a small *c.* I bet he and I would have been on the same side now."

No longer could I hold back the infamous betrayal of my father. I felt compelled to reveal all that I knew. "He also testified at HUAC. An article said his testimony was about how the Soviets ran spies in this country. He testified in 1939. My mother said he did it because he was threatened with assassination by the Soviets, but she was kind of an alarmist about things."

"She may have been right." I was stunned by this astounding confirmation. Watt's sense of certainty, given his background, gave gravitas to his validation. "We all now know that in the thirties such assassinations happened. The Soviets got to their targets no matter where they lived. One of the few ways to try to elude their vengeance was to go public. Then, assassination would only corroborate the veracity of what their target revealed."

Watt's acceptance of my father tempered my shame over his testimony, but life had its way of giving me only momentary deliverance. I returned home and became immersed in my present-day life and my interest in my parents' history became sidetracked. I was hurtling to a major career decision, looking for the currents of life to give me direction. My department had grown so large that my job became more managing and less developing, and as I, a twenty-year tenured professor, looked around for role models of forty-year professors, I was shaken by how such long tenure often produced stasis and contented discontent. My twenty years was a miraculous run and I wanted to preserve it before it turned sour. I had lived with uncertainty from childhood so not having a long-term plan at the moment didn't seem mindless. I sat alone in my grand office shedding my last hesitations and signed my resignation letter as professor and chair of the Department of Communications and impulsively went off to law school at age forty-seven.

A year later, I was taking a family law class and brought up the subject with my mother during a particularly pleasant dinner. She had been surprised and I believe excited about my going to law school. Typically, she was thrilled to have a new intellectual area to explore and learn about through my experiences. Her keen curiosity blazed as she prodded me about my experiences of being a student again. "You must admit that family matters can't be resolved by the law?" she baited. Provocation continued to be her lead-in for bracing conversations. Even when my father was undergoing serious surgery, she interrupted our lunch break to ask a group of doctors what they thought was the optimum age for a surgeon. When one unsuspecting doctor took her bait, my mother told him he was wrong and orchestrated a debate among the entire group, which heated to argumentative and continued after she got up to return to the waiting room. In my adult life, some have noted that I too break into commonplace conversations in a challenging manner, not unlike my mother. And neither she nor I labor long with conversational transitions, so I returned her volley.

"Mom, it must have been hard for you to be unmarried all those years. In studying family law, I realize you were in a precarious legal predicament. You didn't have it easy making a career and being a mother. You know, some of the women from my class at Little Red told me you were their first model of a professional woman. Maybe you inspired them."

My mother hesitated, then smiled and cleaned her glasses with a soiled napkin. I thought about how hard she worked to become an international authority in her field. Her books *Mothers at Risk* and *Family Planning: The Role of Social Work* were the wonderfully ironic subjects of her professional work. She became wistful and slightly spun her plate back and forth. Her words were hesitant, and I could sense there was a summing-up of her life as she spoke. "I know I shortchanged you and Dad and now wonder if it was worth it."

It's true that I regretted not having more of her when I was growing up, but as I had learned from my parents, believing that actions had only black or white results was a futile exercise. "You couldn't have found better people for me," I objected. "You 'dumped' me with Grandma at the store." She wriggled her glasses back on, smudged from her cleaning, and smiled at the recollection of her term "dumped." "And there was Bernice, and Murray, and Wyn, and Howard too. And you always came to my rescue when I really needed help." My mother looked as if she was learning this for the first time. "And look at all the mentors I still collect in my life. Nothing could have helped me more than learning what others could teach me." My mother cocked her head and her expression seemed more professional, as if she were processing the psychody- namics of my statement. I didn't want her to escape my appreciation of what she gave as a mother and tried to bring her back to the humor we often mixed with heavy subjects. "I wonder if the princi- pal at Stuyvesant ever got over tangling with you. I just heard from the alumni chair that no student, other than me, ever got into Stuyvesant in the middle of a year."

My mother couldn't accept my praise and looked down at the menu to select a dessert she wouldn't order anyway. I wanted to keep us from getting maudlin. "And you gave me so many stories I continue to retell my friends." Finally, we both broke out in smiles at our mutual recognition of her non-conformities.

CHAPTER SIXTEEN

IN MY LAST YEAR AT LAW SCHOOL, my mother died unexpectedly, just before her seventy-fifth birthday. In addition to my shock and disorientation, her death ended any possible source for revealing my parents' early lives. Months later I remained afloat with ambiguity about my own life and drifted in diverging currents as I passed the New York State Bar and accepted an offer from a law firm to represent children in foster care, whose futures would be determined by family court. I was doing direct services and no longer hiding behind the camera. Yet, to my dismay, I quickly became tormented by the foster care and family court systems. They were illogical and heightened family misery. The law I had come to respect in law school quickly muddied in practice and was too often used as a threat to force parents to "voluntarily" place their children in foster care, as well as a blunt instrument to force the separation of children from their parents.

After only six months I retired from practicing law. A young female lawyer and I left to form a non-profit organization to give teens in foster care self-advocacy skills to prepare for their independence. I trained social workers throughout the country in how to adopt the program and approaches we developed and tested, which we called "Getting Beyond the System." I regretted that my parents hadn't lived long enough to see their son carry forth their idealism in a direct way. I chuckled, knowing that my mother would have needled me, with a touch of approval: "What gives you the qualifications to train social workers?"

At a fundraiser for our program, a young donor praised me. "Mr. Pitcoff, thank you for doing *God's work*."

I had received this comment before and had thought about it. "It's not God's work. I get as much from it, or even more, than the kids."

"Whatever. I wish I was doing this kind of work rather than my job at the bank." She seemed sincere.

"Why don't you?"

"Oh." She looked me over, perhaps assessing the lineage of my suit. "I couldn't live on that kind of salary."

Hearing myself articulate my motivation for my third major career, I realized that it was more truth than idealism. Through the students I had taught, the individuals I had filmed, and the teens in foster care, my professional life had been enriched by close connections with a wide range of people and their inventive lifestyles. The lures were the camaraderie, learning from diverse perspectives, and a sense of working for a collective purpose. Perhaps similar appeals were what attracted my father and so many others into the Communist movement as much as the overarching appeal of Marxism. George Watt had reflected that there was no other time in his life when he felt more hopeful and fulfilled than when he was part of an international movement of people from diverse social, ethnic, and religious backgrounds fighting for and believing in a more just society. It was the fusion of idealism with social connection that pulled people into the movement and was pulling me into helping teenagers in foster care.

I began to feel more prepared to uncover my parents' secrets. I filed a Freedom of Information request with the FBI to begin the process of uncovering my parents' covert lives. Three months later I received a form letter stating that no files related to my father existed. I was nonplussed. Maybe I had made too much of the secrets and they weren't even worth the FBI saving a file.

After a particularly challenging day of conflicts with a foster care agency that wanted to punish a teen by preventing her from continuing in my self-advocacy seminar, I collapsed into my sofa. My quest for calm was interrupted by the intrusive clang of the phone. "Mr. Pitcoff?" an unfamiliar female voice asked. A telemarketer? I primed myself to hang up. "Are you the son of Robert Pitcoff?"

My father had died fifteen years earlier. Was this a lost relative or a scam? My response was tentative. "Could you tell me what this is about?"

"I'm researching for a book about Amtorg, the Russian trading organization. Your father worked there between 1930 and 1934 and I wonder if you could give me some information?"

Why would a researcher be interested in my father? "I don't know anything about his work there. Sorry." I hung up before I heard any clarification or asked for her name. It took time for me to fully accept my rudeness and connect it to my sense of resentment that a stranger could have learned more about my father's activities than me. The insult of being caged in ignorance about my own heritage simmered. I regretted not continuing with the caller. I slumped back into the sofa. I shivered and felt rejected in knowing that my parents had lived their lives without telling their compelling histories to their son, or anyone. The trauma that produced their shame and fear and prompted their cover-ups deprived me not only of knowledge of their political entanglements, but also of sharing the related highs and enjoyments of their life before me.

I sat down and turned pages in my newspaper for no purpose other than to calm down. I needed to convince myself that whatever they closed off from me was driven by a parent's desire to protect their child. I thought about the rare incident just before I departed for Finland when my father might have come close to revealing why I could be in danger if I entered the Soviet Union. But he didn't and I didn't ask. I offered my conscience a rationale for my rudeness to the researcher: I hadn't a single fact to share. If my father had a connection with Amtorg, it had been expunged from my Pitcoff history book.

The call made me feel closer to the experience of many of the teens in foster care. I too was plagued by the loss or the hole in my family history. I too was troubled by how such a void dulled one's sense of identity. My work partner and I had written a book, published by Rutgers University Press, about the lives of teens in foster care. If I could write about the lives of others, why not write about my own life?

I wrote about my interview with Murray for Camp Hurley. The bizarre nature of that meeting caused friends to laugh and it interested them in the extraordinary world of that camp. They wanted to know what it was like growing up around people like my mother and her offbeat friend Murray. My readers' reactions nudged me to enroll in a memoir-writing class. I almost immediately regretted that decision when I found myself amidst aspiring authors vying for the "most victimized life" story. I couldn't and wouldn't compete. Secrets and wacky parental behavior may have seeded my neurosis, but they certainly didn't equal the trauma of separation from one's parents, being moved from one foster home to another, or growing up in a system rather than a caring home. Having heard many harrowing experiences of the teens in my work, I no longer had enough resilience to hear more victimization stories. I dropped the memoir class.

A few months later I tried a different memoir seminar. I chose to write about the FBI visits to my father when I was a kid and the possibility that he had done a little spying for the Soviets. This had the intended effect of gaining attention from the class. The teacher, a prominent writer, bounced back with an assurance that she would get my memoir published if I could document all of my father's activities working for the Soviets. I was seduced by this offer, which accelerated my momentum for seeking out verifiable facts about my parents.

I knew a crime journalist on the *New York Post* and mentioned to him that even though the FBI had visited us, they insisted that no file existed on Robert Pitcoff. The next day the reporter informed me that a friend of his at the FBI had confirmed that a file on my father did in fact exist. That prompted me to file another Freedom of Information request with the FBI and assert that I knew a file on my father existed. I waited.

Meanwhile, I did Google searches on my father, though I didn't expect results. Several hits surprised me. The *New York Times* article and similar ones in newspapers across the country impressed upon me that my father's testimony had been a noteworthy national story. There were other hits, including his full congressional testimony at HUAC. The treasure chest of my father's secrets was cracking open. I was thrilled with the prospect of getting a new glimpse of my father, as close as I could come to sitting down with him and hearing a new story about his life. Pristine printed pages of the testimony skidded onto my printer's tray. I was frightened. I wasn't sure I was up to finding out the truth about his testimony. Warily, I aligned the pages I had ignored for almost a lifetime and filed them in a pristine blue folder.

At my desk, I found myself reluctant to open the blue folder. I had dropped an old stained, sagging, nameless carton next to my desk. I had salvaged it from storage, peeked into it, and discovered it contained papers, folders, journals, letters, and photos from or related to my parents. The disarray made it unappealing to explore and organize, yet I was sure it was a necessary portal into the lives my parents held secret for so long. I found myself giving it a kick. I realized I was frustrated and a bit frightened.

An old memory surfaced from my early teens. I must have been looking for something and came across this very same ordinary carton. Now, sixty years later, I remembered coming across a bound version of the testimony in this container. I recalled holding a large bound volume in my hands labeled *Investigation of Un-American Propaganda Activities in the United States, Hearings before a Special Committee on Un-American Activities, House of Representatives*. The label had little meaning for me then. The book's state of decomposition repelled my teenage curiosity. Unbeknownst to me, that muddle that seemed destined for the trash held key clues to my parents' secret lives.

I paused my memory journey. Would reading the testimony and the surrounding documents when I was a teenager have made any difference in my life? I fingered the carton's flaps, teetering between the affirmative and the negative answer to my own question. There was no answer. I could never know until I reviewed the actual HUAC testimony, accessed the FBI file, and synthesized all the information I could get from books and Google searches.

Prickly regret further delayed my memory exploration. Had I only taken time when I was a teenager to read the contents of that depository of clues, I would have had enough information to come up with questions for my parents then or certainly later while they were still alive. I had squandered the opportunity to pierce their elaborate smoke screen of secrets. I might have offset some of my shame at my father's anti-Soviet rage and his HUAC testimony. I also realized how much hurt I had lived with in knowing my parents had purposely barred me from a momentous part of their lives. I reassured myself that I was too young then to have recognized the importance of potential clues. I was still a few years away from being dazed by learning of my father's HUAC testimony when I was in college. I had been so close, but the mess and disorder in that carton was just too much to overshadow the allure of a stoop-ball game in the park.

My memory excursion ended, I now questioned why I avoided pursuing their secret lives when they were alive. Maybe it was fear all along that I might have discovered truths I couldn't handle. In leaving this carton chock-full of clues, my parents seemingly were not that afraid of my uncovering their political activities. Perhaps I had to face the fact that I had been complicit in keeping the secrets hidden. There is a fine line between what a child asks or fails to ask about their parents' lives and regretfully I'd remained too far away from crossing that line.

At age seventy-two, I finally opened my new blue—not "Red"—folder and read the unspoiled copies of my father's October 14, 1939, HUAC testimony. I tried to remain calm, but even before I completely finished the first of twenty-one single-spaced pages of detailed testimony, I found myself dazed. The "Robert Pitcoff" in the testimony was a radically altered person from the father I knew. It took hours to grasp that the witness testifying was my dad, in spite of the fact that the "Mr. Pitcoff" speaking was identified hundreds of times. The result was emotional exhaustion and a sense of disorientation. Naively, I had expected to discover my father's past life and political philosophy all wrapped up in the testimony. I had built up fantasies that with one reading I would learn that my father was in fact a hero of some sort—or at least come to the unwelcome but definitive conclusion that he had betrayed others. These prospects I had held secret because my foreboding outweighed my hope.

There were times, if I detached myself from the emerging narrative, when I became engaged in a compelling story, history, and mystery. It reminded me of Ma Perkins hiding Soviet escapees on the radio show that Bernice and I listened to with great attentiveness when I was five years old and she stayed with me when my parents were at work. A Soviet agent hiding in the United States shoots one of Ma's protected escapees. Bernice assured me this was only make-believe, but it was the Cold War and even at five I had heard enough about the evil Soviets to be afraid. Yet the testimony, if I could believe it, suggested that Ma Perkins had been less fictional than Bernice was willing to have me believe.

Much of the dry, staccato sequence of questions and answers revealed nothing directly about my father's feelings or motivations. For the most part my father was questioned and likely prepped by an ex-FBI agent, Rhea Whitley, who was known as an expert and dogged examiner hunting out subversives.

Mr. Whitley. Mr. Pitcoff, what is your address?

Mr. Pitcoff. 143 Lincoln Avenue, the Bronx.

Mr. Whitley. What is your business?

Mr. Pitcoff. Electrician.

Mr. Whitley. Are you a citizen of the United States?

Mr. Pitcoff. I am.

The Chairman (Congressman Martin Dies). By naturalization or birth?

Mr. Pitcoff. By naturalization.

The Chairman (Congressman Martin Dies). When were you naturalized?

Mr. Pitcoff. In 1930.

The Chairman (Congressman Martin Dies). What country did you come from?

Mr. Pitcoff. Russia.

Mr. Whitley. When did you join the Communist Party of the United States?

Mr. Pitcoff. In 1926.

It was clear to me that my father had been well prepared, since normally he was prone to more lengthy responses and illustrative and elaborate storytelling. I wondered whether the questions about naturalization and Russia were efforts to intimidate him by amplifying his potential vulnerability to deportation, as well as establishing his identity. My father's syntax seemed obsequious, something I had never experienced with him, even when he was dealing with authority figures. After all, he was the father who took on the judge and police officer Reed in Maine, fighting to disprove the credibly correct allegation that he had indeed run a red light. His sharp cross-examination of Officer Reed might have been an imitation of the aggressiveness of the Dies Committee format and maybe even a kind of payback for what he endured during his preparation and testimony. Yet my father was eternally a humanist. He appreciated anyone's struggles and possibly his public acknowledgment of the professionalism of Officer Reed to the judge might have been inspired by how he had wanted to be treated by HUAC. I now realized that his former experience in the legal arena of HUAC made him believe and act like a real-life Perry Mason who could protect the little man—himself and the hapless driver who followed us through the red light—in a court not friendly to New Yorkers.

As I read on, I felt I was reading poorly written fiction, with my father's name hijacked for a character in a spy novel. I wasn't sure I could even like or trust this impersonator of my father.

Mr. Whitley. By whom were you solicited or recruited in the Party?

Mr. Pitcoff. By a man by the name of Carl Brodsky.

Mr. Whitley. Is he a member of the Communist Party?

Mr. Pitcoff. Yes, sir.

Mr. Whitley. Is he a brother of Joseph Brodsky?

Mr. Pitcoff. Yes, sir.

Mr. Whitley. Joseph Brodsky being an attorney in New York?
Mr. Pitcoff. Yes, sir.

Such deferential *Yes, sir, Yes, sir, Yes, sir* seemed robotic. More alarming was evidence affirming my most shaming apprehension—that my father had ratted on innocents or fellow Communists. Yet there wasn't any value in identifying Brodsky in 1939. I looked him up and he had acknowledged being a Communist as far back as 1919, when he published in *The New York Communist*, edited by the even more famous Communist John Reed. My father's testimony was not exposing a person who concealed being a member of the Communist Party. The anticipated distress of having to absorb that my father had identified others softened, but as I traced Brodsky's background, a new coincidence, one of many more to come, rattled me. "Brodsky" was Mickey's, my first love's, last name. From the moment I learned her name at the communal sink, brushing our teeth, I would never forget it. I never heard her mention any connection or family affiliation with Communism, something that would not be unusual for the times, but I wondered if my mention of her name might have alarmed my father and factored into his prohibiting me from continuing my involvement with her. Most likely not, but all these new facts fed my imagination, which had been starved for information most of my life, so I was bound to make the most tenuous connections, with each new detail hatching multiple new questions.

It took weeks before I was fully prepared to reread and accept that my parents' lives had been on the edge of political threat and uncertainty. Several times my father was questioned about Amtorg Trading Corporation, the official Soviet trading organization within the United States and used by the Soviet Union as an unofficial embassy until diplomatic relations with the United States were established in 1933. It also was at the center of the Soviet Union's spying operations in the United States. Except for the connection with Amtorg, there was nothing in the testimony that I would have ever summoned to describe the father I knew. I now understood that what I took at the time to be irrational rage, when I told my father I had delivered tickets to Amtorg, was more likely an eruption of a life he wanted to forget or hide along with fear that he or even I might be targets for retribution.

> *Mr. Whitley.* In your position with Amtorg, were you able to get inside knowledge of its workings, contacts, and relationships in this country?
>
> *Mr. Pitcoff.* Well, I had fairly good knowledge of the workings of the organization.
>
> *Mr. Whitley.* What was the relationship between the Amtorg and the Communist Party of the United States? Were they close and cooperative?
>
> *Mr. Pitcoff.* I should think very close . . .
>
> *Mr. Whitley.* Why do you appear here as a witness?
>
> *Mr. Pitcoff.* I appear here today because I fear there exists a grave danger that this so-called regimented form of capitalism which is advocated by the Communist Party, and which it has endeavored to have instituted, is bound to gain ground everywhere. The Communist International was and is maintaining a regime in Russia that is endeavoring to spread, and is using all means possible in order to do that.
>
> *Mr. Whitley.* In other words, you feel that there is real danger in this country?
>
> *Mr. Pitcoff.* Yes, sir.

It seems almost impossible that it was my dad, in the national spotlight, who was raising alarm about the Soviet influence in the United States. How could it be conceivable that he and the

Congress believed he was credible in making this dangerous assessment of Soviet intentions? No amount of testimony, FBI files, and
scribbled notes could ever give me the full nature and texture of his
relationship with Soviet Communists or how he could have become
an expert in Soviet tactics. It was much easier to relate this testimony to an actor in a spy novel than to my dad.

> *Mr. Whitley.* Mr. Browder in his testimony stated that the Communist
> Party was just another political party that made its own decisions
> in the light of conditions in this country, according to what the
> political needs of this country are. What was your observation as
> an active member of the Party in that respect?
>
> *Mr. Pitcoff.* If you mean by that the membership of the Communist
> Party makes decisions here in the United States regarding affairs
> in the United States, that is not true, because the political line of
> the Party is handed down from above, and it is decided by the
> Party, or representatives of the Party, in Moscow, together with
> the head of the International who, in reality, is Joseph Stalin.
> Then it is, in turn, brought back to the United States. Sometimes,
> without even the formality of a convention of the Central
> Committee, this Party line is put into effect.

It still didn't seem possible that my father, the one I knew, was
serving as a national expert on the Soviet power over the American
Communist Party, knowing his testimony would be covered in
major newspapers across the country. The father who gave me so
little advice other than "don't trust your teachers"—a touchstone for
wariness of authority—was himself serving as an authority on the
danger to the nation. Outside of Maine, I had never witnessed my
father use such formal syntax and profess such certainty about
anything other than the scourge of Soviet Communism.

The testimony was real, but I distrusted its veracity, except perhaps for the one paragraph that sounded like the father I knew.

Mr. Whitley. Why did you resign from the Party?

Mr. Pitcoff. I was brought to believe that the Communist Party was a workers' party to improve the condition of the working people in this country as well as throughout the world, but during my stay in the Party I became increasingly convinced it was instituting a form of slavery for the working class in Russia and elsewhere, wherever they possibly could, as no other regimented form of capitalism has succeeded in doing. When I learned that what was the real practice of Communist Party was a form of regimented capitalism, and that I had just been regimented in a capitalistic political system of brutal fascism. I said I chose the democratic form of capitalism and resigned from the Communist Party.

The wording still seemed stiff, as if he sees himself as an object: "I was brought to believe," rather than the agent of his beliefs. But I hung on to his steadfast alliance with workers. This, along with his encouragement of my efforts for social reform, gave me hope that I might find additional evidence that he hadn't just resigned from the Communist Party to join forces immediately with the proponents of capitalism.

Over the many months I reread the testimony, I could feel my own denial welling up. I felt like I was in a tug-of-war between my father in the HUAC testimony on one end of the rope and my dad as I knew him on the other end. I felt myself being dragged into a murky underworld as I struggled to assimilate what seemed like implausible information about my father's connection with spying.

The Chairman (Congressman Martin Dies). . . . Did these various commissions get naval secrets or aviation secrets or military secrets?

Mr. Pitcoff. Aviation secrets, yes. There is, or was, a special department in the Amtorg which is called the aviation department, and that department is headed by a military officer of the Soviet Union.

Along with his seditious activities as a Communist operative at Amtorg, the testimony revealed that his legitimate responsibilities included requisitioning cargo space to ship supplies and machinery to Russia as well as organizing the financing of such shipments. He travelled to different port cities to perform his work, and I am sure he took pride in his considerable responsibilities. I became convinced that his motivation for keeping this secret from me, even throughout my adult life, came from an overwhelming erosion of his pride. He himself had been duped. His loss of self-confidence in his own idealism was so disturbing that he wouldn't disclose attaining a high degree of administrative responsibility to his own son. Similarly, his reluctance to talk to me about the respect he gained as a master electrician could have been a result of seeing himself diminished in his status from administrator at Amtorg to a master electrician.

The "HUAC Robert Pitcoff" testified about his involvement in the American Communist Party as a Secretary of the Building Trades Department and as a labor organizer and Manager of the Transportation Control Department at Amtorg Russian Trading Corporation. He characterized Amtorg as "a beehive of Soviet activities," which was picked up in headlines throughout the country. He and other Party employees at Amtorg arranged for Soviet espionage, for the purpose of obtaining manufacturing secrets to advance their industrialization, which were given to Soviet agents working in the United States.

Mr. Pitcoff. . . . Naturally to do that, they must obtain secret pro-
cesses of manufacture and production . . .
The Chairman (Congressman Martin Dies). Do you know whether or
not there are many secret agents or OGPU agents operating in
the United States for the Soviet Union?
Mr. Pitcoff. Yes, sir. In Amtorg it is quite obvious or visible, and even
the work of the agents crisscross in the different organizations.
One secret agent will come to you soliciting you to find certain
information and another will come asking you to acquire other
information for some other agent.

I could no longer be secure in just seeing my father as the
hardworking electrician, buoyant storyteller, family house builder,
and open-ended philosopher while grappling with his sworn
testimony that revealed so much more. Learning for the first time
that my father was recruited by OGPU (Soviet Security and
Political Police, forerunner to the KGB) to function as a secret
agent for the Soviet Navy, and then be planted in the navy of some
unspecified country, was true, yet beyond what I wanted to
believe.

Mr. Pitcoff. I had the experience at one time of being called to a
secret meeting with a member of the Party who had been sitting
on the same committee with me, and who asked me at that time
whether I would be interested to become a secret-service agent
for the Soviet government in the navy of some foreign country.
The Chairman (Congressman Martin Dies). When was this?
Mr. Pitcoff. That was in the summer of 1931.
The Chairman (Congressman Martin Dies). And he asked you if you
would be willing to become a secret-service agent of the Soviet
government in some other country?

Mr. Pitcoff. Yes, and I told him that I didn't think my qualifications warranted such a job, because I was not familiar with it and he said that would be taken care of: that I would be sent to Russia for two years to be trained.

The Chairman (Congressman Martin Dies). Did he tell you that they had a number of secret agents in the United States?

Mr. Pitcoff. Oh yes, and I asked for time to consider it for a while, and after considering it I declined the offer. Then subsequently another member of the Communist Party told me that he was approached by the same man for the same purpose.

The Chairman (Congressman Martin Dies). If you are an American Communist, and are approached by a leading Party official and requested to go into the secret service, or are instructed to do it, and you refuse to do it, what is likely to happen to you?

Mr. Pitcoff. We are not usually instructed. Most Party members accept it willingly if they are chosen. However, if you decline, you are not being trusted anymore with any work of importance in the Party.

Photo of Father testifying, which appeared in
various newspapers throughout the country

It seemed almost impossible that my father could have trans-formed from a covert life to being just a father who occasionally put down his *New York Times* to give me some baffling advice. No wonder he was reluctant to give me definite advice and preferred to encourage and push me to learn from experiences and not authority. I flashed back to the way he played chess with me. He was a skilled student of the game and played for hours with his friends. But if I questioned him about different strategies his response was, "You'll have to learn for yourself." The first three moves of a game were fun. I had three good opening moves. Predictably, when I made my fourth move my hope for winning a game on my own dissolved. "Are you sure you want to move there?" Sure I was sure, but I never said so. It would have been helpful if he just showed me the better move. Instead he asked me more questions. "Think about what I'll do." "Is there a better way you can get an opening around my king?" "What will happen to your rook?" It became clear that if I were to learn the game I would have to develop my own approach. These sweet memories of chess melted. I wondered if his reluctance for prescriptions and absolutes had been connected with his disillusion-ment in the absolutes of Communism.

Even while jostled and squeezed by workers riding home on the subway, I was trying to imagine how the OGPU recruited anyone, especially my father. I searched the faces of women and men, mostly fatigued from a hard day at work, and couldn't imagine any of them being a spy or even having the time to be active in politics. My father rode the same subway home from work every day, and I suppose no one ever imagined him having contacts with the Soviet secret service.

When I arrived home I sat down at my desk and stared at the droopy carton. I fixated on trying to discover counter-evidence that proved my parents had some normalcy to their lives. I cradled what looked like a Valentine's Day card my mother had cut out and pasted with red hearts. It was penned in red on heavy ivory stock and was the only example I ever saw of her deliberate printing, rather than her illegible cursive handwriting. It must have been written when my father was in Antigua.

The times are hard, oh Bob my dear,
I'll have to be grateful for one man, I fear.
But my sweet will have women galore
And I'll be brave and won't get sore.

If I don't cook and scrub for you,
You feel my love can't really be true.
But babe, my love is high and lofty.
I'm really a sophisticate, you want a softy.

You know your politics, you know your history
But I'm to you an eternal mystery.
I love you; I love you, you great big mug.
I warn you I won't go if you get smug.

And so my precious and so my sweet,
I'll flirt a little, but never cheat.
If you love me and tire never,
Damn it, I'll love you for ever and ever.

I fingered the card. It was the only unsoiled paper in the carton, with not even a trace of a cigarette burn. I felt like an illicit voyeur reading my mother's personal love offering, when she was just around twenty. Even at her young age, she knew enough about herself that she wouldn't cook and scrub, and those tasks remained ones she would never bother to master. Reading into her rhyme, I recognize her attraction to the intellectual part of the relationship. In the end it was their shared curiosity for the adventure of learning that kept them together for twenty years before they were married and together forever, even after they were married.

I became more curious about my mother's misleading explanation of why they hadn't married till I was fourteen. "We were all anarchists," she had explained with the sincerest of expressions. They lived as if they were married, and yet my father's divorce decree from his first wife was dated just a month before our family honeymoon trip across the country when I was fourteen. My mother couldn't admit that to me, even when I was an adult, but why choose anarchism as the excuse? As with so many of her diversions, I came to realize they were often sprinkled with half-truths. The act of living together, unmarried, while my father was still legally married was in itself an act of anarchy, especially in those times. And in a sense our family unit was a shared endeavor outside the conventions of law and societal approval. My mother's reference to anarchy was a generalized concept rather than a reference to a political movement. For her it was a reference to a lack of obedience to authority. My father's subversive work at Amtorg to help the Soviet Union was a blatant form of rebellion against the established order, and on the less extreme end of the scale, returning a Klein's department store dress to Macy's or breaking the rules of Stuyvesant could also be seen as anarchistic actions within her meaning of the term.

I speculated on the big hole in between 1934 and the 1939 testimony. While the testimony suggests that my father rejected Communism in 1934, I wondered what my father did to protect himself if he truly feared retaliation from the Soviets. There was no straight line in my quest; patterns and conclusions showed themselves like sunbeams breaking through the haze of gray clouds and just as suddenly disappeared. More often than answers to my life-long questions, a surge of new questions tripped up my progress. For instance, did my father turn immediately from being a Communist to being a Republican?

I recalled my mother's story about my parents' trip to California sometime after my father left the Communist Party in 1934. It had whiffs of Bonnie and Clyde on the lam, as she told it. Finding no work for my father and only part-time waitressing for my mother, they decided to go back East. They bought a beat-up car for twenty dollars that my father rehabilitated for their cross-country return. On their first leg of the return trip, my mother drove the car into the cornerstone of a building on the UCLA campus. Both my father and the front fender were wounded more in pride than body. My mother continued driving until they reached the desert, when my father made her stop to let him out. He vowed to walk the rest of the way unless she promised never to drive again and he started off on foot. She shadowed him, honking and hooting. He ignored her. Finally, my mother gave in and never got behind the wheel again for the rest of her life. Like many of the stories they told, this one combined my parents' typical balance of self-effacing humor and the melancholy of adversity. All three of us laughed out loud, since the hardships of that experience remained in the past.

My mother's explanation for the precipitous move to the West Coast, which was all the more puzzling in light of her near-neurotic attachment to New York City, was the search for work. Yet in the height of the Depression there were fewer jobs in California than back East, where both parents had the advantage of knowing people and my mother could have easily worked in the family store. So other explanations seem more likely: getting out of town to escape the Soviets' retaliation for my father's betrayal or getting away from the US government's demands that my father cooperate in fighting the American Communist Party. He used an alias, Robert Strong, when in the West, which added to my suspicions.

It was hard to grasp how my parents—who behaved as if they were a "normal" middle-class couple struggling for upward mobility—could have led such covert, transgressive lives. That first snapshot of me on the roof of my grandmother's tenement, with my father missing and my mother looking bewildered or shocked, had always unsettled any confidence that my parents had planned for me to join the lives they were creating together. Speculating on the expressions, postures, and missing father in that haunting photograph reminded me how much my desire for family normalcy had been a flickering pipe dream from the very beginning.

Bill Kunstler's remark that activism was "where the girls were" offered a clue to understanding how I came into the world. My mother was young and idealistic and already associating herself with the political left and at the same time coming of age. My father, more mature and already in the thick of political activities, on a soapbox organizing workers in Union Square, had already developed a keen eye for attractive, intellectual women. Their idealistic passion for justice invigorated their love, and their love sweetened the appeal of idealism. Luckily for me, their idealism had borders, and my father wisely and courageously rejected the OGPU offer to become a Soviet spy and thus remain safe in the United States, continuing his relationship with my mother. When I traced backward to my very beginning in life, I chuckled at how it was supercharged by these confluences of romance, idealism, Communism, and ducking mortal threats.

My emotional resistance to accepting that I was an inconvenient accident was crumbling and I dug deeper into my inherited treasure carton with less fear. I could now skip forward from my parents' history, pre-me, to my own appearance in their lives. My parents only vaguely recounted the events connected to how we became a family, and if I wanted to connect the HUAC Robert Pitcoff with my dad, I would have to do my own investigative work. From letters and bills I pieced together a fragmented story. My parents moved to Philadelphia around 1941. Sometime after, my father went to Antigua to work as an electrician for a civilian contractor preparing runways for the US Air Force. While not directly in the war at '43, the base served planes to hunt German U-Boats that operated in the Caribbean. That timeline suggests that I was likely conceived in their trailer home outside of Philadelphia on one of his leaves from Antigua, or possibly on the one trip my mother took to meet him halfway, somewhere in southern Florida.

Neither my father nor my mother were prepared to begin a family. His life was too unsettled at age forty-five. He had every reason to believe he was in danger from the Soviets. Even after ten years with my mother he was still legally married to his first wife, who would not give him a divorce for another sixteen years. My mother desperately wanted to establish herself as an independent professional before considering a family. She didn't feel capable of the responsibility of a child, and having one with a man legally married to another woman couldn't have made it tempting. As I sat on my knees shuffling through correspondence and photos, arranging new evidence on my floor, I chuckled to myself at my newest identity—a "love child" conceived in a trailer.

It is more than odd that my mother would live in Philadelphia, away from her close-knit and supportive family and from her connections in social work. Most likely, Philadelphia was chosen because it was a place where my father could hide from possible retaliation by the New York Soviets until things cooled down. The only reason my mother had to go to Philadelphia was her sweetheart. She took a job as a sales clerk at Wanamaker's Department

Store, certainly not a step forward to a career as a social worker. A few months after she got pregnant, she moved back to New York on her own to have her baby. My father came back to New York sometime after I was born to set up a life with his newborn and newborn's mother.

CHAPTER SEVENTEEN

COMBING THROUGH THE LETTERS, bills, dated photographs, and notes now strewn on my floor drained me. They were as baffling as they were enlightening. I was maddened by the many missing pieces of my parents' lives. I couldn't resist thinking that my parents were kind of impostors. This thought gained momentum as I entered New York University's Tamiment Library and Robert F. Wagner Labor Archive. I was more annoyed than usual in having to be cleared by a security clerk, as if I might not be who I claimed. I knew this was displacement, but a wariness of what awaited me in the library swelled as the little cage of an elevator took me to the fourth floor.

My latest Google search had turned up a new hit for both parents in connection with one of their closest friends, one of my favorites, Tommy. Letters from both parents were reported to be in his collection. This new piece, like every new bit of evidence, seemed to make the unfolding story more complicated, sprouting more doubts and too often leading me further away from the identity of my parents. My yearning to withdraw from this day's mission was so extreme that I tried to pretend I was a hero for executing the simplest deed of requesting the papers of Thomas Stamm. The librarian treated me as if I were just an ordinary researcher. I fooled her. Maybe I too was an accomplished impostor.

I sat down at a long empty table waiting for the library boxes to be delivered from the archives. I waited less than ten minutes, which seemed like years as my mind projected dozens of unrelated childhood memories. My patience had escaped and I worked at concealing my agitation from the few scattered researchers at other tables, who had absolutely no interest in me. I feared my teeming and uncontrolled speculations might produce an emotional meltdown if the boxes weren't brought to me soon. The path back to the elevator would lead past the librarian's desk and my cowardice would become evident, although what was left of my rational mind told me no one was that interested to even notice. I wasn't prepared for any new discovery that would further offset my sense of who my parents were and in turn uproot my own sense of identity. My doubts as to whether I could ever get at the truth grew, and I feared that in the end, all I would gain from my search for their secrets was just more unsubstantiated theories, but no definitive conclusions.

I shook myself into thinking about the many times my family spent with Tommy's family during my first twenty years. His daughter was a few years younger than me. She was a surrogate sister. Tommy was the rare adult who didn't use his age to distance himself from children. On the contrary he was a playmate of the intellectual sort, although I couldn't frame it that way as a child. He worked up a child's curiosity by becoming an enthusiastic explorer of any topic with the most thought-provoking questions and analysis. He and my father played chess for hours and after they finished he would delight in playing another hour with me and offer new and unusual strategies. Any family outing that included Tommy and his family elevated my expectations for the upcoming adventures he would lead us to. He kept conversations brimming with excitement regardless of the time or activity.

Sadly, Tommy and my father had a falling-out over politics. It was after I had left home and the details were never made clear to me. I knew my mother was deeply saddened, but no amount of coaxing could get the two men back together again. That Tommy's "papers" (whatever that really meant) would be in a library made no sense, and I found myself feeling clammy as a librarian approached my table with the boxes. I thought he had worked for the *Encyclopedia Britannica* as a fact checker and had another job as a buyer for a toy company. Neither job warranted any kind of interest for a library.

I checked the well-indexed list and thumbed through the folders of original documents to find the correspondence between Tommy and my parents. I felt reverence as I handled the lined yellow legal-size papers filled with my father's and mother's handwriting. Their correspondence was not the formal testimony voice of my father, nor the redacted transcripts of the FBI interviews. Here were unguarded thoughts that actually had the familiar syntax of my parents, along with typed responses from Tommy. The essence of these well-preserved papers showed the source of my father and Tommy's bitter split after thirty-seven years of a close friendship. Tommy was forever the idealist, convinced Marxism was the only promise for the working class and his lasting hope of bringing down the repressive elements of capitalism. My father, a former Marxist, had become disillusioned with pure idealism, as he wrote on the back of a used envelope I had come across in my carton. He had been wounded by how he had been duped by the Soviets and used every occasion to point out how the Soviet form of Communism had proven Marxist theory unworkable. Although this was the first time I ever saw it so well described in their long and detailed polemics, I knew from when I had learned about their split in the sixties it was not a new dispute in their relationship.

Thus it remained a mystery as to what suddenly triggered their irreparable break-up. Perhaps holding on to their intractable positions for so many years, and the experience of recognizing that their youthful ideals had not come to fruition, disillusioned both men enough to act out and use their friendship as a target.

In their verbal angry back-and-forth volley, I felt nostalgia for a time when their hope for a better social economic order had more fully engaged their lives. Yet the letters were over a half century old and with the perspective of time and political history they seemed almost childlike in the sense of trying to prove who had the better mastery of historical evidence. I was sad in seeing the evidence of how Tommy and my father had allowed dogma to destroy a solid lifetime relationship. My father, in almost all other areas, was willing to display uncertainty and open-mindedness, yet the wound from his previous faith in the promise of Communism had been so traumatic that he tumbled into a single-mindedness, the kind of rage I had witnessed and dreaded when I was young.

My mother, in her supportive, provocative, and ironic manner, tried valiantly to override their political differences, believing their relationships trumped ideologies. She offered to host a dinner party for the two couples to restore their relationship. "If Chairman Mao and Nixon could shake hands, surely Tommy and Bob could," she wrote. Neither gave an inch. My father's third rail of anti-Communism had been touched and he abandoned flexibility. I had an impulse to tear up the evidence of my father's stubbornness about politics, but in my hands were my parents' actual handwriting and reminders of their ceaseless attempts to bring meaning to their lives. Tommy was just as steadfast and even more so, which had the effect of softening my annoyance and faulting of my father.

I noted that the researchers in the library were oblivious to my emotional turbulence. I felt excited as well as nostalgic for touching the very letters my parents had written in this unexpected setting.

Without concern for the content, I savored the emotions for a few moments. Eventually, I became curious as to why Tommy's papers were in the library in the first place. My parents' letters represented the smallest fraction of the journals, letters, and audiotapes in his archive. I opened random folders and was stunned. Apparently my Tommy was the founder and leader of a radical group, the Revolutionary Workers League (RWL), and publisher of *Revolt*, a highly intellectual newsletter advocating radical means of displacing the capitalist system, published in the late thirties through 1940. Article after article demonstrated how the current political order in the world was stacked against labor. It seemed preposterous, since the Tommy I knew was mild-mannered, fun-loving, and the most gentle of men. It was inconceivable that he could have been a revolutionary leader. What had been hidden from me reinforced my sense that he, along with my parents and many of their friends, was an impostor too.

I thought about my other Google searches for my parents' friends. Ray Shorr, whom I knew as a photographer for *Life* magazine, had been an acrobat in the circus. No wonder he could walk into the ocean on his hands. Yet I was never told this wonderful background of the man who always served me "my usual" when mixing drinks for the adults. Their friend Mike, the behind-the– Iron Curtain reporter for the *Herald-Tribune*, who had such vivid knowledge and experiences with Eastern European Communists, was most surely a CIA asset, along with other journalists working behind the Iron Curtain. Joe, the extremely austere and dignified diplomat, by all reports worked high up in the CIA during his posts in Europe, engaging in covert actions to limit the influence of Communism in foreign governments. Perhaps for my parents and all their circle of friends, impostoring was just a way of life.

I left the library with startling surprises. Another adult I thought I knew well had turned out to have a life far different from the one I had observed when I was growing up. These diversions from my goal of uncovering my parents' narrative were becoming too unwieldy. I returned to the central story and reread the HUAC testimony to see if I could make more sense out of my parents' lives.

———————

From the time I was four, my parents took me to grown-up films that were often about everyday people in danger—*Casablanca, High Noon, Key Largo, North by Northwest, DOA,* and others. Some ordinary person gets caught up in an unforeseen and/or grisly event, which calls on them to use their mental and emotional powers to survive. After seeing the movies, I listened in on my parents' lively conversations about the plots and emotional makeup of the characters and assumed they were speculating, that what we saw on the screen was light-years away from their own experiences. It seemed inconceivable that my father had contended with threats of deadly danger all around him. I was wrong. He had been connected with people who were assassinated and others whose families were sent to Siberia in retaliation for political activities. He testified to it.

Mr. Whitley. Do you know anything about Juliet Poyntz's disappearance?

Mr. Pitcoff. I knew Juliet Stuart Poyntz very well. She was a prominent Party member and worked for the Party at large . . .

Mr. Whitley. Did you hear any discussion among Party workers as to what type of activity she was engaged in shortly before she disappeared?

Mr. Pitcoff. Yes, sir. I was told she was an OGPU agent.

Mr. Whitley. You were told by Party workers that she dropped out of active Party work, and had gone into the work of the OGPU?

Mr. Pitcoff. They do not refer in the Party to them as OGPU agents. They refer to them as secret workers.

My mother's offhanded remark that my father testified "to save his life" echoed in my thoughts. What I had taken as hyperbole on her part, or even hysteria, now seemed more rational. The smoke screens they deployed and the limited information they offered me about their past lives, along with my shame over my father's cooperation with HUAC, had made it hard to understand the context in which he testified. Their evasions about their past lives raised barriers I would not, and dared not, enter, like their reliance on speaking Yiddish when they didn't want me to understand. Yet maybe those barriers were erected with my help. When my mother offered useful clues, I was the one who hadn't pursued them.

Obviously HUAC, and its creator and chairman, the infamous Congressman Martin Dies, who built his political career on flushing out Communists, with such courageous accomplishments as outing ten-year-old Shirley Temple and other potent threats to our nation, didn't give a hoot about me. My skepticism about the veracity of anything testified to at HUAC prompted me to research many of its stated facts. My father said that he knew Juliet Poyntz "very well." I read and reread this statement with a smile of recognition, remembering my father's weakness for intellectual and attractive women. Poyntz had been a member of the Daughters of the American Revolution, but then became radicalized. She helped found the American Communist Party and was an officer in the Ladies' Garment Workers' Union, a spy for the OGPU in the United States, and an early feminist who taught at Barnard. In 1936 she was invited to Moscow by Stalin to view firsthand the results of the revolution. When she returned to the United States she reported to friends on the brutal Stalinist purges and her disillusionment with Soviet Communism. Her fatal mistake was announcing to others that she was planning to write a book revealing her new conclusion that Stalinist Communism produced a "blood bath of innocents and dissidents." Shortly after, Poyntz was spotted being forced into a car in the middle of New York City, leaving behind all her possessions and money in a bank account. Years later, the infamous Soviet spy Whittaker Chambers, who later turned against the Soviets, confirmed that Poyntz was decoyed by a Communist friend who led her into an OGPU trap, forced her into a car, and then murdered her to keep her quiet.

My father's friendship with Juliet overlapped with my mother coming into his life, around 1933, and so my mother must also have known of Poyntz's suspicious disappearance, which deepened her trepidation about what could happen to my father as a result of his turning against Soviet Communism.

This journey of discovery of my roots had few of the pleasures seen on *Finding Your Roots*, PBS series. I found myself increasingly wishing that my new career as detective could be replaced with something less emotionally unsettling. If my client would pull out or fire me I wouldn't mind. True, my client was me, and I wondered why he and I wanted to pursue this any longer. To give myself relief from absorbing the testimony I casually grazed through the index of witnesses for this 1939 hearing, not expecting to recognize anyone else, but another big chunk of a secret fell on my head. Joe Kornfedder, alias Joe Zack, had been a good friend of my parents.

I remember Zack as a pleasant, bald, roly-poly man, just an ordinary guy who carried a sense of emptiness in his efforts at being jovial. In fact he had led a radical and dangerous life. Earl Browder, head of the American Communist Party and a former friend of Zack's, colluded with the US State Department to try to get him deported because he was considered "too radical" by both groups. As part of the effort to overthrow "the yoke of capitalist control," Zack encouraged labor to take more radical actions beyond what was advocated by the American Communist Party. This is likely one of the few times the State Department and the American Communist Party ever cooperated.

Zack broke from the Party in 1934 and, like my father, denounced the Soviet Union. His wife and son, living in Moscow, were subsequently arrested and charged with being related to an "enemy of the state." His wife was sentenced to eighteen years in the Gulag and their son was reportedly put into a home; neither was seen nor heard from again. I came across one of those coincidences that made me rethink a past event. In 1921, Zack was a delegate to the Joint Unity Convention, assembled to bring together the various factional Communist organizations in the United States to form the American Communist Party. Some report that Lenin planned the agenda and sent a letter addressing the delegates. The convention was held at the Mount Overlook Hotel, the same abandoned hotel my father and I hiked to, which impelled my mother to call the police to look for us. This produced yet another reversal in interpretations of events in my childhood. At the time, what I thought was my mother's completely irrational reaction, requiring two state troopers and a priest to calm her down, could plausibly be more rationally explained as caused by her emotional association with Zack and all the prominent Communist delegates meeting there.

Like so many of us confronted with reinterpretations of events we assumed had only one rational explanation, I found myself stubbornly resisting. I felt so foolish having believed that the disclosure of secrets would be cathartic and would resolve my identity issues. Instead they aroused more sympathy for my parents and pangs of regret that I hadn't been more sympathetic of the pressures they had in their lives. I recalled such scenes as my mother's pure panic when my father was delayed in getting home and I had to console her as she stood behind the curtains waiting frantically for the first sight of him coming down the block. Now I realized that she had reason to fear that he, herself, and her son could be in danger. Prominent in her mind was the knowledge of Juliet Poyntz's alleged assassination, Joe Zack's wife and son being sent to Siberia as retribution for his betrayal of Soviet Communism, and several of my father's colleagues at Amtorg who permanently disappeared when thought disloyal by the Soviets.

―――――

My post-retirement career as a private investigator, with myself as my sole client, was more taxing than I had anticipated. My assignment: uncovering the covert political and domestic secrets my parents never revealed, just like a whodunit novel, was leading to twists and turns I had never envisioned. The treasure chest of hidden secrets, my fragmented memories, and research didn't fully complete my assignment and questions still remained. Why did they extract me from E.I. at such a pivotal moment in my adolescent life? Especially, why were they resolute in keeping their lives secret from me when in almost every other sphere they were remarkably unguarded, flexible, and inclusive? Even though I knew I might be heading for a dead end or worse, my compulsion to make sense of how their extraordinary experiences shaped their undertaking as parents remained. My challenge was to remain objective and not shape facts to justify my chosen view of my parents. I had to brace myself for discovering startling truths as well as blind alleys.

Far back when I was eleven, I wasn't able to challenge their decision to extract me from Little Red, and then E.I., nor did I believe in their reasoning: finances or exposure to different kids. For over sixty-five years of my life these two convenient rationales never seemed to have the sticking power of plausible truths. There was no major change in their financial situation, and private school was not as relatively expensive as it is now. My father's proposal that a different experience would be beneficial had a bit more credence, given his extreme anti–Soviet Communist view and the

Communist leanings of Little Red. His "Don't trust your teachers" could suggest this motivation for extracting me. Yet in every other way he supported my attendance at Little Red. He never hinted that I not associate with anyone connected with Little Red or any known Communist, for that matter. He enjoyed many of the parents, in spite of the fact that most were Communists or sympathizers. He exhibited the same commitments to advancing racial equality and the rights of workers as we all supported at school. It seems unlikely that he had any animus against E.I., so perhaps the motivation came from outside our family's world, but still from the life that they had hidden from me so diligently.

During the time my parents made the decision to extract me from Little Red, Senator McCarthy had focused his hunt for Communists specifically at Fort Monmouth, where my uncle Howard worked as a civilian nuclear physicist. McCarthy theorized that the best place to uncover "commies" in the Army was at Fort Monmouth in New Jersey. He targeted that facility because of its proximity to left-wingers in the Northeast and its collection of highly educated soldiers and civilians working on atomic bombs. The Army felt compelled to demonstrate its diligence in purging anyone believed to be a Communist, so my uncle was targeted, fired, and blacklisted from ever gaining another government job, which at the time was the only employer of nuclear physicists.

Apparently my father felt that his testifying at HUAC would give him special credibility to vouch for my uncle's loyalty and he sent a letter in support to the Atomic Energy Commission. The Director of Security of the AEC responded in writing that my father's loyalty itself was questionable because he had been a registered member of the American Labor Party in the 1940s. This must have been a sober blow to his self-esteem and a warning that he might not be as trusted by the government as he assumed.

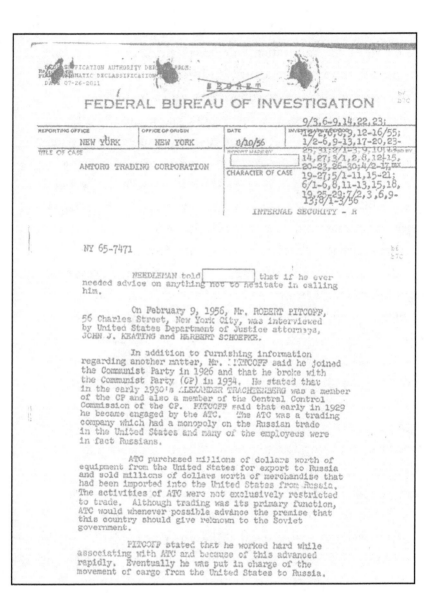

First page of FBI files related to two visits to our home

The FBI files were perhaps the documents I most sought because they represented the only actual contact I experienced with my parents' covert life. Even at eleven I was wary of my mother's explanation that "they just happened to be in the neighborhood." The agents came to our home on March 25, 1954, and then again on February 9, 1956. In their reports, they display either ignorance of my father's 1939 HUAC testimony or purposefully discount it as proving any particular confidence in his loyalty. I felt a familiar sense of distress or shame as I read their requests that my father testify again, now in the McCarthy-era HUAC.

My shame lasted but a minute; he refused their request, using his recent throat cancer operation as an excuse. The agents noted that he spoke in a "hoarse, subdued voice," as if they were suspicious of his excuse. I wondered how my father felt having to justify why he couldn't or wouldn't testify. He revered the FBI and undoubtedly felt important in providing corroboration to their intelligence. At the time my father was an outspoken supporter of Eisenhower and a vigorous antagonist of Communism. Paradoxically, even though I had spent a lifetime trying to deny his cooperation with HUAC, I found myself offended that he wasn't fully respected by the institution he championed. After all, he was my father and doing what he believed in.

The first FBI interview, where there is obvious tension between the government and my father, took place during the period when my parents decided to extract me from Little Red. Maybe I was taken out of E.I. not because my father feared I would be tainted by the Communists, but rather to prove to the government that there was no question about his unwavering loyalty to our country.

Fear of retaliation by the Soviets and broken pride for being duped were likely generators of my father's tortured abhorrence of Soviet Communism and his uncontrollable tirades when the subject came up. His doctrinaire reaction in this one area was a fearful breach of his generally open-mindedness in most other areas. I found myself linking it with Sergeant Raymond Shaw, who, in the film *The Manchurian Candidate*, is brainwashed by the North Koreans to act against his own nature and instincts. It took me most of my life to recognize that his uncontrollable anti-Communist outbursts were tied to the shame and guilt for having been so duped by the Soviets. Unfortunately, this pervasive sense of guilt, even though unacknowledged by him, was an emotion I absorbed and carried forward, tried to ignore, fought, and denied at different stages of my life. Not knowing the source of his fear and sense of humiliation, I contracted the disease in the same mysterious manner we catch a cold, without seeing the particular germs that infect us. My symptoms resulted in attaching the shame to my father's politics and his friendly testimony at HUAC.

Most likely I was too young for this to be explained to me while I lived at home, and perhaps they feared that I might unwittingly reveal things they wanted hidden from the Communists or the FBI. Or maybe they were worried that I might be ostracized if their covert history became public knowledge at my Communist-leaning school and camp. These pressures—which had had such a huge effect on my parents' behavior and philosophy, and in turn on me—I would not have understood when I was eleven.

But it was one thing to hide their life experiences when I was a child and during the McCarthy period, and quite another to keep these secrets from me when I was an adult. That was harder for me to live with. Maybe they didn't trust my capacity to understand my father's mistakes or his assistance to HUAC. Or perhaps they felt too much guilt in having placed me in a path of possible danger. Conceivably, they might have feared I would reject them in some way, but I would have argued that knowing would have made it easier to sympathize with my father's foul, almost brainwashed, anti-Communist rages, and my mother's heightened anxieties over the Soviets' capacity for revenge.

I put down my pen and looked out the window for relief. Below two men wrestled a luxury Sub-Zero refrigerator off a truck and aimed to get it up twelve steps of a stoop. In sweltering heat, they heaved the behemoth, making as much headway down the stairs as up. Stubbornly, at their possible peril, they worked out the leverage angles and exhausted their strength. Maybe my parents were right, and I wouldn't have absorbed the truth so well. After all, I sat in my air-conditioned apartment feeling as if I was suffering because of the secrets my parents withheld from me. In contrast, before my eyes, poorly compensated workmen were experiencing real danger with one misstep. Thinking of shame, I quickly realized that my feeling of distress was what was truly shameful.

CONCLUSION

BREAD CRUMBS. Once again my eyes dart across scattered letters, scribbled-over envelopes, and paper scraps with jotted thoughts—the pieces of a jigsaw puzzle spread across my desk without the finished picture to guide me. My impatience demands I finish this case or journey, even if the full mystery will never be solved. Like the shame and guilt I contracted from my father, my craving to uncover my parents' secrets was a long-festering infection. With luck, I'm now inoculated from those jagged feelings of hurt and frustration. My memories of the events and relationships with my parents remain mostly intact, even if my interpretation of them has shifted. Surprisingly, my original assumption was mostly wrong: my identity hadn't been dependent upon learning their secrets.

Robert and Florence refused to be leashed to their missteps and mistakes and drove their lives forward as if everything was normal. Like many parents, especially those engaged in taking political action in the thirties through the McCarthy era, mine purposely refrained from revealing their activities to their son. Friends and family had suffered reprisals from the Soviets as well as from our own government. Keeping secrets was essential to protect jobs and even lives. Young children could not be expected to take on that responsibility, thus better to keep them in the dark unburdened.

Equally compelling was the desire of Cold War players to protect their daughters and sons from the menace of hopelessness, another reason not to provide details of the political upheavals going on in the world and at home.

As with so many survivors of the global terror of the Second World War, my parents forced themselves to live in the present. Their past was proof that prescriptions for life rarely hold up over time, especially in different historical contexts, so they jettisoned them. After my birth, they reinvented themselves, burying their former political intrigues, and searching for new opportunities around my mother's career and their attempt to build some kind of family unit neither had ever experienced before. But they couldn't fully seal the door on their past, so shame and anxiety seeped through the cracks and attracted my attention.

Withholding couldn't have been comfortable for my parents. Storytelling was one of the most cherished Pitcoff family talents. If there was advice to give it was always wrapped in an anecdote, rather than directly given. Even a simple weather report often had an addendum of some tale connected to a particular storm or heat wave. Spinning yarns and telling reliable stories were the most prized of my parents' talents, one I would work to master and enjoy throughout my own life. I assume, in different ways, the three of us felt wounded from having the most interesting and influential periods of their lives held secret. After years of ponderings and research I have come to believe that my parents wanted their story told, but didn't know how to break through some inner conflict. Thus, they left me only a trail of bread crumbs.

With the fuller story now in front of me, I find I may have deceived myself in the ways my father was duped by the Soviets. Certainly the political machinations and potential threats were strong rationales for my parents to conceal their dramatic, life-shaping experiences, especially when I was young. Yet the conflict that compelled the secretiveness may have had a more complex origin than I had theorized at the beginning of this journey.

In 1942 and '43, Florence Haselkorn and Robert Pitcoff were living unconventional lives, felt threatened, and were focused on my mother's long-held aspiration to have a career. Their accidental pregnancy was not just an issue of bad timing, but a disruption of a stronger career desire for my mother. Moreover, my father was still legally married and fourteen years away from a divorce. Guilt overrode informing a young child that his seemingly married parents were not legally married, until they could reconcile their new and awkwardly formed family situation.

Their guilt in bringing me into their shaky and possibly threatening situation triggered a more personal and perhaps more long-lasting guilt than the one over being duped by the Soviets. And thus with more discipline than they showed for most other endeavors, they kept the fact that they had neither planned for nor wanted the responsibility of a family concealed. Never could they have admitted that a family and a child fell much lower in priority than building my mother's career, resolving the messy marriage my father couldn't get out of, commitment to his first son, and finding suitable work back in the United States. How ironic that I began tripping over these most emotionally threatening secrets when I was as young as three and asked my mother for a sibling, not knowing about my half-brother. Even at that age I felt skeptical of my mother's response: "You were born because Dad and I loved each other very much. We want our love for you to be special and couldn't think of having another child."

Intentionally or unintentionally, this guilt-ridden secret mingled into the secrets around their clandestine political activism leading up to my birth. For them, there was no bright line between the big secrets in their lives: the mistake of working for the Soviets, the threat of physical harm from resigning from the Party, the stigma attached to testifying at HUAC, throwing their lives into disorder in having a child without any idea of how a baby could fit into their complicated lives all merged. If one such secret was revealed, they may have feared it would be like a loose thread, which, when pulled, unravels the entire garment. Then, every secret would come loose, especially the one they thought I would be most upset about: the precipitous origin of my birth. I am sure they suffered a chronic conflict between withholding and revealing, with irresolute and insufficient attempts to break open their past, which regrettably I failed to pursue while they were alive.

As I weigh these new thoughts, I find another of those confusing notes in my father's hand, written on a ripped-off calendar page with shards still hanging around the torn holes. He wrote it nine years before he died. He makes a convincing argument for something he and my mother never did: passing on their narratives.

January 27, 1969

For many months I lived with an urgent desire to put down on paper my experiences, my thinking, some of my convictions, so that whoever may be interested may gain some imperceptible knowledge of what one human being does or neglects to do with his years of his life. In doing this work I am particularly conscious of the questions that future generations of my children, grandchildren, etc. will ask as to what kind of people brought them into the world . . . Long ago I concluded that a human being should not necessarily be notorious to reveal his life's story.

I am now convinced that every human being who can think and write should reveal to his forthcoming generations the origin of his life, his childlike experiences and environment, his adult life, his happiness, his failures, his social relationships, his formal and informal education and every other aspect that had a direct consequence on his or an indirect influence on social life.

I am almost convinced that every human life has in some infinitesimal manner influenced social life and if that life's story is revealed to future generations the mere knowledge that the person was present on earth for a number of years suffered or enjoyed living, worked, gave birth, —

Thursday   JANUARY 1

9.00   New Years Day

10.00 January 27-1969

11.00 For many months I lived with

12.00 an urgent desire to put down on

1.00   paper my experiences, my thinking,

       some of my convictions, so that

2.00   whoever may be interested in reading

       these accounts may gain some

3.00   imperceptible knowledge of what

4.00   one human being does or neglects

       to do with the years of his life.

5.00   In doing this work I am particularly

Conscious of the questions that future

Friday   JANUARY 2

generations that of my children

10.00 grand children etc will ask

       as to what kind of people

11.00 brought them into the world.

12.00 I often ask myself, who

1.00   were my predecessors, where did

       they come from, how did they

2.00   live, what did they look like,

3.00   etc etc etc the questions are

4.00   endless, but there are no answers

       except for my mother father and

5.00   my maternal parents.

       Long ago I have concluded

First page of Father's notes he never followed up on

327

Maddeningly, it ends there. Without carrying through with his intended ambition. Yet the note is evidence that before the end of his life he had the intention to share all the events that shaped his philosophy. How sad for my parents to never have learned that now; when I look at that first snapshot of my grandmother holding me on the roof of her tenement and my mother in the background looking shocked and fearful, I feel sympathy for that young woman and admiration for all her work and adapting she had to do to make a life work well for herself, my father, and me. And I have similar sympathy for my father, missing father in the photograph, who had to leave a secure job in Antigua and face possible retaliation from the Soviets to return to New York to take responsibility for his new family.

It feels comforting to shed the shame and stop using the label "impostors" to describe my parents. I feel more settled, accepting that my parents were just jugglers of their life trials and adventures. Their model enabled me to have a range of diverse careers, friends, and experiences, and avoid the trap of dogmatic thinking. Not fully trusting my teachers or authority has not been a bad way to approach my life. Being enveloped with uncertainty has made me more prepared to take on and adapt to opportunities not fully defined.

Ironies keep tumbling out of this journey. Guilt and their mistakes in their former lives contributed to my parents' unorthodox behavior, which in turn added to my ability and desire to take the blue highways of life, the backstreets and dirt paths. They have offered me more opportunities than the red highways, which may be faster and more lucrative, but leave little time for enjoying the ride.

Perhaps the final irony here is that while I was convinced that my obsession to uncover the secret lives of my parents would hold some dramatic life-changing conclusion about my identity, it didn't work out that way. With more revelations about my parents' lives I feel little change in myself nor do I view my relationship with them dramatically differently other than gaining more understanding of motivations for their behavior. When I re-question myself as to why I entered into this journey, I wonder if what grabbed me the most was the allure of a good mystery, one where I was a leading player.

I picture myself meeting my mother in that same restaurant where she doubted her worthiness as a parent. I tried to console her then, but hadn't yet fully realized how much of my successes could be traced to the environment she and my father provided for me. Late in life I went to a therapist and during an early session, I was bemoaning how my life seemed to have none of the traditional long-term planning for career and life goals. Many of my friends had known what they wanted to do and worked hard at the traditional roads to attain their goals and success. I had been a filmmaker, a professor, an academic administrator, an attorney, and a program developer for teens in foster care. I felt that because I had not been formally trained for these careers, and never had a plan leading to them, that I wasn't good at anything. Even in my sixties, I was still uncertain of what I wanted to do when I grew up. My therapist listened. Her expression and body language telegraphed nothing. For the next stifling long fifteen-second silence, I assumed she was reviewing my emotional disorder. Finally she labeled my syndrome. "You're an opportunist."

I railed. This couldn't be a more repugnant label. "How can you say that? That's not fair. I don't think I'm an opportunist." I felt like defying this accusation by walking out, maybe even slamming the door.

"You don't understand. It's a strength, a positive strength of yours. You take opportunities and make something happen from them. Some people need to have a plan and structure, but you've been able to make a good life by finding opportunities and making something out of them, which you enjoy and which helps others. It's an admirable talent."

If I was back in the conversation with my mother at the restaurant I would have related this insight to her and I know she would have been intrigued. I would have added that this talent for adaptation had its origin with her and my father modeling uncertainty, offering baffling advice, dumping me with unpredictable stimulating people, and making me learn through experience. She and I would have had a good laugh, of that I am certain.

ACKNOWLEDGMENTS

It took a village of mentors and supporters to help me get to a place where I could reflect cogently on my early life and find universality in one's search for meaning from family secrets. My father and mother taught me the value and pleasure of story telling as a means of achieving some understanding of one's life. Mollie Haselkorn, Bernice Lincoln, Wyn Moroz, Murray Ortof, Mickey Brodsky, Howard Haselkorn, Dr. Frank Lee, and George Watt were principals in my story and lifted me till I could fly on my own. My wife, Harriet, my son Winton, and my grandson Noah devoted endless hours to hearing me tell, retell, and read and comment on the stories of my life, and encouraged me to finally make sense out of them as well as what I finally put into print.

I've been blessed with the collaboration of writers in various workshops, who have labored over the text, and added their wisdom in how to make the narrative work best. Sidney Stark, my writing partner, has been a mentor, supporter, and taskmaster through the deepest doubts and highs in writing the book. Walter Bode, my editor, helped me find themes and direction I would never have discovered on my own. Aviva Blumberg, my therapist, showed me how the writing process would help unscramble meanings and find universals in my story that might provide insight as well as entertainment for others.

Dan Janeck devoted hours to finding numerous inaccuracies, misspellings, and nonsensicals. Katie Holeman used her considerable talents to design and put the book into a form that would be pleasurable to hold and read in book or e-book form.

I had a number of close friends and writing workshop colleagues from various walks of life who took the time to read drafts of the full manuscript and offer feedback, including Denise Dailey, Marti Gabriel, Marge Hudson, Scott Hudson, Don Kaplan, Betsy Krebs, Janet Mackin, Kathleen McGraw, Alex Pitt, Claire Reed, Phil Smith, Helena Sokoloff, and many others who I have not mentioned.

ABOUT THE AUTHOR

Paul Pitcoff has had multiple careers in education, film, law, and youth development. He has a Master's in Fine Arts from New York University, and a law degree from Cardozo Law School.

Paul founded the Department of Communications at Adelphi University. Concurrently, Paul produced and directed numerous award-winning documentary films.

After twenty years, Paul left his tenured position at Adelphi to work as an attorney in the area of child welfare. After several years he and Betsy Krebs founded the Youth Advocacy Center, where they developed a program to prepare teens in foster care for independent living. The program was replicated throughout the United States and was offered at universities including Columbia, Harvard, and Hofstra law schools.

In 2006, Rutgers University Press, published Paul and Betsy's book, *Beyond the Foster Care System*, about preparing teens in foster care for independent living.

Paul is currently at work on *Tenure*, a novel set at a university.

Momentum Ink Press

Momentum Ink Press is a private micro-press cooperative advancing the work of writers unavailable through traditional commercial publishers. Each book is carefully reviewed by a collection of authors and designers, ensuring an authentic artistic version of the writer's best work. By selecting and reading a Momentum Ink Press book, you are joining and supporting a community of readers and writers dedicated to giving voice to talented authors purposely avoiding the commercialization of art.

CPSIA information can be obtained
at www.ICGtesting.com
Printed in the USA
LVHW010455120520
655409LV00019B/2530